Palgrave Macmillan Studies in Banking and Financial Institutions
Series Editor: **Professor Philip Molyneux**

The Palgrave Macmillan Studies in Banking and Financial Institutions are international in orientation and include studies of banking within particular countries or regions, and studies of particular themes such as Corporate Banking, Risk Management, Mergers and Acquisitions, etc. The books' focus is on research and practice, and they include up-to-date and innovative studies on contemporary topics in banking that will have global impact and influence.

Titles include:

Yener Altunbaş, Blaise Gadanecz and Alper Kara
SYNDICATED LOANS
A Hybrid of Relationship Lending and Publicly Traded Debt

Yener Altunbaş, Alper Kara and Öslem Olgu
TURKISH BANKING
Banking under Political Instability and Chronic High Inflation

Elena Beccalli
IT AND EUROPEAN BANK PERFORMANCE

Paola Bongini, Stefano Chiarlone and Giovanni Ferri *(editors)*
EMERGING BANKING SYSTEMS

Vittorio Boscia, Alessandro Carretta and Paola Schwizer
CO-OPERATIVE BANKING: INNOVATIONS AND DEVELOPMENTS

Santiago Carbó, Edward P. M. Gardener and Philip Molyneux
FINANCIAL EXCLUSION

Allessandro Carretta, Franco Fiordelisi and Gianluca Mattarocci *(editors)*
NEW DRIVERS OF PERFORMANCE IN A CHANGING FINANCIAL WORLD

Dimitris N. Chorafas
FINANCIAL BOOM AND GLOOM
The Credit and Banking Crisis of 2007–2009 and Beyond

Violaine Cousin
BANKING IN CHINA

Robert L. Carter OBE and Peter Falush
THE BRITISH INSURANCE INDUSTRY SINCE 1900
The Era of Transformation

Franco Fiordelisi and Philip Molyneux
SHAREHOLDER VALUE IN BANKING

Hans Genberg and Cho-Hoi Hui
THE BANKING CENTRE IN HONG KONG
Competition, Efficiency, Performance and Risk

Carlo Gola and Alessandro Roselli
THE UK BANKING SYSTEM AND ITS REGULATORY AND SUPERVISORY FRAMEWORK

Elisabetta Gualandri and Valeria Venturelli *(editors)*
BRIDGING THE EQUITY GAP FOR INNOVATIVE SMEs

Munawar Iqbal and Philip Molyneux
THIRTY YEARS OF ISLAMIC BANKING
History, Performance and Prospects

Sven Janssen
BRITISH AND GERMAN BANKING STRATEGIES

Kimio Kase and Tanguy Jacopin
CEOs AS LEADERS AND STRATEGY DESIGNERS
Explaining the Success of Spanish Banks

M. Mansoor Khan and M. Ishaq Bhatti
DEVELOPMENTS IN ISLAMIC BANKING
The Case of Pakistan

Mario La Torre and Gianfranco A. Vento
MICROFINANCE

Philip Molyneux and Munawar Iqbal
BANKING AND FINANCIAL SYSTEMS IN THE ARAB WORLD

Philip Molyneux and Eleuterio Vallelado *(editors)*
FRONTIERS OF BANKS IN A GLOBAL WORLD

Anastasia Nesvetailova
FRAGILE FINANCE
Debt, Speculation and Crisis in the Age of Global Credit

Dominique Rambure and Alec Nacamuli
PAYMENT SYSTEMS
From the Salt Mines to the Board Room

Catherine Schenk *(editor)*
HONG KONG SAR's MONETARY AND EXCHANGE RATE CHALLENGES
Historical Perspectives

Andrea Schertler
THE VENTURE CAPITAL INDUSTRY IN EUROPE

Alfred Slager
THE INTERNATIONALIZATION OF BANKS

Noël K. Tshiani
BUILDING CREDIBLE CENTRAL BANKS
Policy Lessons for Emerging Economies

Palgrave Macmillan Studies in Banking and Financial Institutions
Series Standing Order ISBN 978-1-4039-4872-4

You can receive future titles in this series as they are published by placing a standing order. Please contact your bookseller or, in case of difficulty, write to us at the address below with your name and address, the title of the series and the ISBN quoted above.

Customer Services Department, Macmillan Distribution Ltd, Houndmills, Basingstoke, Hampshire RG21 6XS, England

The British Insurance Industry Since 1900

The Era of Transformation

Robert L. Carter OBE
*Emeritus Professor of Insurance Studies,
University of Nottingham, UK*

and

Peter Falush
Consultant Economist

palgrave
macmillan

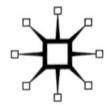

© Robert L. Carter OBE and Peter Falush 2009

All rights reserved. No reproduction, copy or transmission of this publication may be made without written permission.

No portion of this publication may be reproduced, copied or transmitted save with written permission or in accordance with the provisions of the Copyright, Designs and Patents Act 1988, or under the terms of any licence permitting limited copying issued by the Copyright Licensing Agency, Saffron House, 6-10 Kirby Street, London EC1N 8TS.

Any person who does any unauthorized act in relation to this publication may be liable to criminal prosecution and civil claims for damages.

The authors have asserted their rights to be identified as the authors of this work in accordance with the Copyright, Designs and Patents Act 1988.

First published 2009 by
PALGRAVE MACMILLAN

Palgrave Macmillan in the UK is an imprint of Macmillan Publishers Limited, registered in England, company number 785998, of Houndmills, Basingstoke, Hampshire RG21 6XS.

Palgrave Macmillan in the US is a division of St Martin's Press LLC, 175 Fifth Avenue, New York, NY 10010.

Palgrave Macmillan is the global academic imprint of the above companies and has companies and representatives throughout the world.

Palgrave® and Macmillan® are registered trademarks in the United States, the United Kingdom, Europe and other countries.

ISBN-13: 978–0–230–21964–9 hardback
ISBN-10: 0–230–21964–0 hardback

This book is printed on paper suitable for recycling and made from fully managed and sustained forest sources. Logging, pulping and manufacturing processes are expected to conform to the environmental regulations of the country of origin.

A catalogue record for this book is available from the British Library.

A catalog record for this book is available from the Library of Congress.

10 9 8 7 6 5 4 3 2 1
18 17 16 15 14 13 12 11 10 09

Printed and bound in Great Britain by
CPI Antony Rowe, Chippenham and Eastbourne

Contents

Insurance Key Dates and Events — vii
List of Tables and Figures — x
Preface — xiv

Part I First Half of the Century

1 The Industry from the End of the Victorian Era to 1914 — 3
2 Insurance in World War I — 15
3 The Interwar Years — 23
4 Insurance during World War II — 31

Part II Lines of Business

5 From Austerity to Prosperity — 41
6 Life Insurance — 61
7 Commercial Insurances — 82
8 Reinsurance — 108
9 Risk Management — 117
10 Lloyd's of London — 126
11 International Business and Europe — 135

Part III Market Infrastructure

12 Competition and Mergers — 149
13 Trade Associations and Other Bodies — 168
14 Distribution Channels — 177
15 The Regulation of Insurance — 191
16 Retrospect and Prospect — 202

Appendices

1 Principal works on pre-1900 British insurance market — 218
2 Reading list on insurance company investments — 219

3	Life and composite offices amalgamated 1989–2000	220
4	Commercial lines premiums 1995, 2007 (£m)	222
Notes		223
References		225
Index		231

Insurance Key Dates and Events

Date	Event
1901	Industrial Life Offices Association founded
1903	Lloyd's establishes a non-marine market
1904	Lloyd's wrote its first motor policy
1906	San Francisco earthquake; Cuthbert Heath devises excess of loss reinsurance
	Marine Insurance Act 1906
	Workmen's Compensation Act 1906
	Accident Offices Association formed
1907	Employers Liability Insurance Companies Act 1907
1909	Assurance Companies Act 1909
	Workmen's Compensation tariff adopted
1911	Lloyd's Act 1911
	Lloyd's writes first aviation insurance policy
1912	Chartered Insurance Institute receives charter
1914	Insurers and government agree on scheme for marine hull & cargo insurance
1916	British Insurance Association established by leading composite insurers
1918	Russian insurance industry nationalised
1919	Holman Gregory Committee examines employers' liability business. Establishment of the state owned Export Credit Guarantee Department
1923	Industrial Life Assurance Act 1923
	Workmen's Compensation Act 1923
1931	Road Traffic Act 1930 came into force
1933	Assurance Companies (Winding-up) Acts
1939	War Risk Insurance Act 1939 to cover war risks for stocks and raw materials
1946	Assurance Companies Act 1946
1948	The NHS and social security scheme to replace WCA insurance inaugurated
1949	Nationalisation of industrial life insurance proposed
1953	East Coast floods
1957	*British Insurance (Atomic Energy) Committee* constituted
1958	Insurance Companies Act 1958
1960s	Round of mergers of major companies

Continued

Date	Event
1961	*Abbey Life* enters market with direct sales force
1963	Formation of Association of Insurance Managers in Industry & Commerce
1965	Hurrricane Betsy and Los Angeles riots
1966	Collapse of *Fire Auto & Marine Insurance Co.*
1967	Companies Act 1967
	Life offices establish unit trusts
1968	Fire insurance referred to Monopolies Commission
	Motor tariff abandoned
1969	Employers' Liability (Compulsory Insurance) Act 1969
	Employers liability tariff abandoned
1970	Dawson's field hijacking of 4 jet airliners
1971	Collapse of *Vehicle & General*
	Engineering tariff abandoned
	Lloyd's establishes *Lloyd's Life*
1972	Monopolies Commission publishes report on Fire Insurance.
1973	Insurance Companies Amendment Act 1973
	UK joins the EEC
	First Non-Life Insurance Directive
1974	Insurance Companies Act 1974
	Stock market crash
	Health & Safety at Work Act 1974
	Flixborough chemical plant explosion; cost £20m
1975	Policyholders' Protection Act 1975
	Social Security Pensions Act 1975 introduced SERPS
1977	Insurance Brokers (Registration) Act 1977
	Unfair Contract Terms Act, 1977
	Tenerife Airport collision of 2 Beoing 747, killing 538
1978	Lloyd's agree to working party to examine self-regulation
1979	Life Insurance Freedom of Establishment Directive
1980s	UK companies buy American life companies
	Mid-1980s around 200 companies operating in London Market
1982	Insurance Companies Act 1982
	Lloyd's Act 1982
1983	Mortgage Interest Relief at Source introduced
1984	Withdrawal of Life assurance Premium Relief
	Explosion of Union Carbide chemical plant in Bhopal killing 8,000 within two weeks
1985	Entry of *Direct Line*
	Association of British Insurers formed from BIA, AOA, FOC and LOA
	Finance Act 1985 withdrew life assurance premium relief
1986	Financial Services Act 1986
	Securities & Investments Board and self-regulatory organisations set up
	Social Security Act 1986
	United Kingdom Provident Mutual forced to merge

Continued

Date	Event
1987	Introduction of personal pensions
	Hurricane in Southern England, Oct 1987, cost insurers £1.05bn
	Lloyd's Renewal & Reconstruction Plan published
	Consumer Protection Act 1987
	London Market Insurance Network (LIMNET) formed
1988	*Piper Alpha* oil rig in North Sea explodes
1989	*Exxon Valdez* grounds causing extensive oil pollution
1991	Insurance Fraud Bureau launched
1992	IRA bombs in London
	Abbey National acquires *Scottish Mutual*
	Chicago Board of Trade commences trading in U.S. catastrophe futures
	Around 70 companies withdrew from London Market 1988–1992
	Cadbury Committee report on governance
	Lloyd's Reconstruction and Renewal Plan published and *Equitas* formed
	Third Non-life and Life Insurance (Framework) Directives
	Hurricane Andrew – the 2nd largest ever hurricane
1993	Bishopsgate bomb
	Pool Re formed
	General Agreement on Trade in Services agreed
	World Trade Organisation set up
1994	Lloyd's admit corporate members with limited liability
	Northridge Californian earthquake
1995	California Earthquake Authority proposed securitised catastrophe bonds
	Prudential ceases to write new industrial life business
	Kobe earthquake
1996–99	Mergers of top UK composites – *RSA*, and *CUGN*:
2000	*Equitable Life* in financial difficulties
2001	Insurance supervision transferred to the Financial Services Authority
	Independent Insurance becomes insolvent
	9/11 World Trade Centre terrorist disaster
	Lloyd's and London company market bureaux merged
2003	Lloyd's set up Franchise Board
2004	Indian Ocean Tsunami
2005	Hurricanes Rita and Katrina in US
2007	*Berkshire Hathaway* provides £7bn reinsurance cover to *Equitas*
	Lloyd's Reinsurance Co. (China) Ltd opened in Shaghai
	US sub-prime mortgage crisis
2008	AIG rescue at a cost of over $80 bn by US government
	World banking and financial crisis *AIG* rescued by US federal government

Tables and Figures

Tables

1.1	British economic statistics at the turn of the twentieth century	4
1.2	British insurance statistics at the turn of the twentieth century	4
1.3	Life insurance in Britain in 1900	6
1.4	Plate glass companies wound up in the 1960s and 1970s	7
1.5	Motor insurance companies wound up 1898–1923	8
1.6	Companies amalgamated and wound up	13
2.1	Economic background to World War I	16
2.2	Life insurance business (£m)	17
2.3	British life insurance business 1908–20	19
2.4	World War I: British offices' general insurance premiums (£m)	21
3.1	Economic data 1920–38	24
3.2	Life premiums of companies established in the UK during the interwar years	25
3.3	Interwar net non-life premiums 1919–39 Companies established in the UK (£m)	26
4.1	The economic background 1939–45	32
4.2	Life premiums during World War II 1938–50 (£m)	33
4.3	BIA member companies' staff numbers	34
4.4	State-backed property insurance schemes during World War II	36
4.5	Non-life business of companies established in the UK (£m)	37
5.1	Worldwide premiums of UK insurance companies (£m)	42
5.2	UK insurance business of British insurance companies (£m)	43
5.3	UK market motor net premiums (£m)	44
5.4	Companies failing within 10 years of formation, 1967–74	45
5.5	ABI members' UK motor underwriting profit and loss 1960–2000	47
5.6	Motor insurance distribution channels (% of business sold)	48
5.7	Motor insurance price index 1994–2008	49
5.8	UK motor insurance top ten insurers	49
5.9	Household and domestic risks. Gross UK premium income of ABI companies (£m)	50
5.10	UK property gross claims for major perils – domestic insurance (£m)	51

5.11	Home insurance price index 1994–2008	51
5.12	Proportion of households buying buildings and contents cover	52
5.13	Health cash plans	55
5.14	PPI gross premiums (£m)	57
5.15	Gross travel insurance premium (£m)	58
5.16	UK personal lines premium income 1995–2007 (Gross premiums, excluding home foreign and reinsurance)	60
6.1	Growth of UK long-term insurance premiums (£m)	63
6.2	New industrial assurance business	63
6.3	Growth of UK ordinary long-term assurance premiums (£m)	64
6.4	New life business regular and single premiums	65
6.5	Key economic indicators 1972–79	66
6.6	UK life funds acquired by foreign companies 1985–2000	75
6.7	Leading companies' worldwide long-term insurance premiums	76
6.8	ABI member companies' long-term premiums	80
6.9	Overseas net long-term insurance premiums 1996–2006	80
7.1	The UK direct fire insurance market 1968	84
7.2	Net written UK fire premiums	84
7.3	UK motor revenue account (£m)	87
7.4	Performance of leading companies transacting marine insurance 1958–69	89
7.5	Worldwide aviation net premiums (£m)	91
7.6	Companies' premiums for engineering all risks	92
7.7	Worldwide contractors' all risks insurance	97
7.8	The London Market premiums for all lines	103
7.9	London Market net written premiums 2000 split by insurer (£ million)	104
8.1	Business written on the London Market 2000	109
8.2	Breakdown of UK companies' reinsurance net premiums (£m)	110
8.3	Development of UK insurers' worldwide reinsurance net premiums (£m)	112
8.4	Distribution of LIRMA member companies' reinsurance premiums 1996	115
10.1	Lloyd's membership	129
10.2	Lloyd's statistics	130
10.3	Lloyd's gross premiums UK – overseas split (£m)	132
10.4	Territorial split of direct and facultative business 2000	132
10.5	Comparison of Lloyd's – Companies' premium growth 1950–2000 worldwide non-life business	133
10.6	Comparison of distribution of lines of business UK non-life market 2000	134

10.7	Lloyd's underwriting results 1996–2006	134
11.1	UK insurers' global net non-life premium income (£m)	136
11.2	Aggregate American underwriting results of the seven leading British companies, 1962–83	138
11.3	Geographical breakdown of ABI member companies' non-life net general premium income	139
11.4	Geographical percentage breakdown of ABI members' ordinary long-term premium income	139
11.5	British companies acquired by European companies	142
11.6	Foreign share of the UK general insurance market Net premiums written (excluding Lloyd's)	143
12.1	ABI member companies' long-term premium income	155
12.2	Acquisitions of companies by major companies	158
12.3	Mergers of major companies 1959–68	161
12.4	Mergers and acquisitions by major UK insurance companies 1970–84	162
12.5	British companies acquired by European companies	162
12.6	Authorised insurance companies	165
14.1	Percentage sources of new long-term regular premiums	181
14.2	The changing shape of the UK insurance market	190
15.1	Companies failing within 10 years of formation, 1967–74	194
16.1	Net overseas earnings of UK insurance institutions (£m)	210
16.2	Trends in insurance employment: Great Britain insurance employment (000) (end year figures)	210

Figures

3.1	Indices of national income, production and fire premiums	28
5.1	Gross domestic product at factor prices	42
5.2	Numbers of cars licensed 1956–70	44
5.3	Underwriting profitability of homeowners' business 1993–2000	52
5.4	Number of people covered for PMI by corporate or personal payers, 1996–2006	54
6.1	Premiums for new UK individual ordinary life business 1983–2000	65
6.2	Sources of life new regular premiums (1999)	69
6.3	Sources of life new single premiums (1999)	69
6.4	Mutual companies' share of new life business 1996–2006	74
6.5	Foreign-controlled companies' share of UK life new premiums 1996–2006	75
6.6	Regular premiums for individual and personal pensions	77
6.7	Premiums receivable for occupational pensions and group life schemes	79

Tables and Figures xiii

7.1	UK property underwriting results 1993–2006	85
7.2	Commercial vehicles licensed 1945–63	87
7.3	The London insurance market	103
7.4	Premiums paid by insurers and reinsurers resident in the USA for reinsurance purchased from the UK and Bermuda	105
7.5	Sources of UK commercial lines business 2000	106
11.1	Shares of ABI companies' total EU net Non-life insurance premiums 2000	144
11.2	Shares of ABI companies' total EU Ordinary life premiums 2000	145
12.1	Classification of risks	151
12.2	Companies amalgamated 1900–20	157
12.3	Companies amalgamated 1921–45	159
12.4	Companies amalgamated 1946–69	160
12.5	Companies amalgamated 1970–99	163
14.1	Sources of new long-term premiums 2006	182
14.2	Sources of general commercial insurance premiums 2000	183

Preface

This book starts at the beginning of what may be labelled as modern times, that is, at the commencement of the twentieth century. It presents a picture of the dramatic changes undergone since 1900 by the British insurance industry, which had steadily evolved over 300 years to meet the demands from first merchants and property owners for financial security against the occurrence of uncertain loss-producing events. In 1900, when the British Empire was at its strongest, insurance was already a mature industry. It was the most diversified, reputable and fully globalised in the world, despite the emergence of new competitors.

We have aimed to throw light on the changing profile of one of Britain's most successful financial service industries, which has continued to prosper, unlike many British manufacturing industries. The last century has been an era of massive economic, technological and social changes that required the insurance industry to show adaptability, innovation, competitive response, dynamism and a host of other virtues that are prerequisites for growth and development.

The industry's success can be attributed to two factors: (a) the growth of the country's industrial and personal wealth and (b) the entrepreneurial and technical skills of the people involved in the industry. This book aims to highlight the insurance industry's response to the changing times and challenges, from the early years of violence and economic austerity to the post-war years of growing prosperity. We have aimed to provide a backcloth of the economic conditions against which the insurance story was unfolding, supported by as much statistical information about the insurance industry's contribution in a changing social and industrial environment as a relatively short volume can encompass.

Besides its valuable role of providing a mechanism for individuals, firms and other organisations to transfer the risk of uncertain financial losses, the industry performs two other important functions. First, life insurance and pensions business is an important means of long-term savings; the Association of British Insurers estimated that in 1999 29 per cent of personal sector wealth consisted of insurance-administered pensions and life insurance. Secondly, insurance companies are major institutional investors with total worldwide investment holdings in 2007 of £121bn for general insurance and £1,478bn for long-term insurance (ABI, 2008).

We cover the developments in insurance business but not the changes that have occurred in investment practice. This subject would warrant a book in its own right. Moreover, much of the data required to analyse changes in practice simply is not available from companies' published reports and accounts. For example, it was not until the late 1960s that companies began to disclose the market values of their investments.

In regards to investment practice, we must be content to explain here that during the early part of the century companies increasingly moved funds into equities to secure the benefits of capital growth and later as a hedge against inflation. Investment practice was largely determined by prevailing economic, stock market and political considerations. For example, in the mid-1970s pressure was being put on companies to provide funds for small firms, and in 1978, in the wake of the Wilson Committee report, there was a fear of government direction of institutional investment. Inflation was the overwhelming investment consideration in the 1970s, with companies facing the dilemma of choosing between equities (that often were thought to be overpriced) and the attraction of the high rates of interest available on fixed interest securities, which, however, lagged behind inflation.

The alternative to investment in ordinary shares was seen to be property, and in the 1970s most of the leading insurance groups acquired property companies. In response to increasing claims volatility during the next decade, companies moved to increase the liquidity of their general insurance funds. However, companies were constrained in investing in overseas assets to match their foreign liabilities until 1980.

However, for readers interested in the evolution of British insurance companies' investment policies and practices, a reading list is provided in Appendix 2.

Regrettably, too, we were not able to produce an analysis of the comparative performance of insurance companies over the long term because of changes in accounting policies, such as in the calculation of claims and unearned premium reserves (see Chapter 16).

Insurance in Britain was in 1900, and remains primarily, a private sector activity, though it received considerable support from the state for its continued survival and growth during the two World Wars. Since then the government has intervened to make sure that insurance is available for some activities that private insurers would have difficulty in supplying, such as medical malpractice for the NHS, and terrorism insurance. On the other hand, the industry successfully defeated attempts to nationalise industrial life assurance after World War II.

The book documents the wide variety of the types of companies active in the industry, as well as the ever-widening range of its products. During most of the twentieth century, until at least 1985, the majority of British insurance companies' non-life premium income was derived from overseas markets and that of Lloyd's still is. Insurance remains one of Britain's most internationally active industries. While the scope of the book is generally directed at the British scene, the benefits of the industry's overseas activities on the domestic economy are also examined.

xvi *Preface*

We also present a 'warts and all' profile, capturing some of the failed and fraudulent enterprises and the overenthusiastic sales drives which negatively impacted on the image of insurance from time to time.

The industry's fast-changing profile is reflected in the multiplicity of firms and supporting organisations that emerge, merge and are disbanded. The industry's importance is also reflected in the plethora of insurance-related legislation, most of which is set out in Chapter 15.

Finally we would like to acknowledge the generous help we have received from many people and organisations who have kindly shared their time and knowledge. In particular we must thank Neil Crockford and William Sennett for help with the development of risk management, Chris O'Brien for guidance regarding life and pensions, Leslie Lucas with reinsurance and Charles Berry with terrorism. Others to provide advice and information included David Bland, David Raymont, and David Worsfold, while the team of librarians at the CII Library under the lead of Robert Cunnew deserves our special thanks together with Joanna Rose of the Association of British insurers for providing so much of the insurance market data.

As co-authors we have debated and argued over many contentious points, but together we accept full and sole responsibility for any errors or omissions that remain.

ROBERT L. CARTER
PETER FALUSH
January 2009

Part I
First Half of the Century

1
The Industry from the End of the Victorian Era to 1914

The British insurance industry at the beginning of the twentieth century (the end of the Victorian era) was undoubtedly the most developed in the world, looking back on a history dating from the sixteenth century, with immense achievements in both life and general insurance. The successful evolution of this sector was made possible by the combination of Britain's scientific, industrial, commercial and imperial achievements, the building of which commenced well before the Industrial Revolution in the late eighteenth and early nineteenth centuries. This advantage was reinforced after the Napoleonic War by the expansion of Britain's colonial empire, which reached across the world by the start of the twentieth century.

Before the First World War, Britain was the world's largest exporter of capital, with an estimated foreign investment of US$18,000m, approximately £3,700m at the prevailing rate of exchange (Table 1.1). It was also the leading maritime nation, controlling over half of the world's merchant shipping fleets, and was in lead position in per capita exports compared with all other industrial nations at $56 in 1913 (Maddison, 1989, p. 44).

During the pre-1914 war period Britain's economic growth was at a fairly modest rate of 0.7 per cent a year, and the Boer War created many problems. But during the decade before the Great War, industry was at full tilt, with iron and steel output reaching 7.8 m tonnes, a rise of 59 per cent during the preceding decade.

Insurance had been a thriving business for many decades, and by 1900 there were 93 life insurance companies and friendly societies and 435 general insurance companies in operation, creating a highly competitive marketplace (Table 1.2).

The early history of the insurance industry has been extensively recorded by academic historians and others, and a short bibliography is given in Appendix 1. As the object of this study is to survey the evolution of the industry from the beginning of the twentieth century only, a sketch of the earlier periods is offered in later chapters to illuminate the structure of the market.

Table 1.1 British economic statistics at the turn of the twentieth century

Population 1900 (incl. Ireland)	41.50 million
National income	£1,750 million
Exports	£354 million
Imports	£523 million
Bank rate	4.0%
Value of pound sterling	£1 = US$4.87
Standard rate of income tax	8 d. (3.3% in the pound)
Standard gauge railway lines in Britain	18,680 miles
Private motor cars in use (1904)	8,000
Shipping capacity registered	11.51 million tons, 51.5% of world total

Source: Mitchell B.R. & Deane P., Abstract of British historical statistics, CUP, 1971.

Table 1.2 British insurance statistics at the turn of the twentieth century

Ordinary life insurance premiums 1900	£33.1m	Policies in force 1.76m*
Industrial life insurance premiums 1900[1]	£10.1m	Policies in force 17.9m
Fire insurance premiums (FOC) 1904[2]	£21.8m	
Marine insurance premiums[3]	£3.9m	
Lloyd's global premium income 1913	£11.3m	
Lloyd's Names 1899[4]	714	

Notes and sources:
[1] *Insurance Directory & Yearbook, 1902*, p. 15.
[2] Members of the Fire Offices' Committee, including foreign business.
[3] *Bourne's Insurance Directory, 1905*.
[4] D.E.W. Gibb, *Lloyd's of London*, Macmillan, 1957, p. 206.
*including annuity considerations.

1900 to 1914

While Britain was at the height of its imperial power at the beginning of the century, its industrial power was facing competition from the United States and increasingly from Germany and France. With regard to insurance, Lloyd's of London and British insurance companies had grown in both size and diversity of classes of insurance transacted, and had gathered lucrative franchises in international business, particularly in regards to the USA, and Canada and other dominions and colonies.

The tariff companies subscribing to the Fire Offices' Committee's (FOC's) minimum rate agreements dominated fire insurance. A few specialist companies and Lloyd's had commenced writing loss of profits insurance, but the tariff companies initially disapproved of it. There was rapid evolution of insurance business during the closing years of the nineteenth century, which formed the basis of its dynamic growth in later years, including:

(a) the creation of a demand for insurance against four new important classes of risk – Boiler Explosion, Burglary, Motor and Workmen's Compensation;

(b) revolutionary changes in the administration of the business, with women being more widely employed (though Cockerell records that in both the *Prudential* and the *Refuge* in 1883 women clerks were segregated from the men) and the use of typewriters and telephones (*Prudential* had installed both typewriters and calculating machines in 1883 (Cockerell, 1983));
(c) by 1900 the recognition of the economic and social importance of insurance (e.g., Workmen's Compensation insurance) and the failure of companies were creating a mounting demand for the regulation of companies transacting not only life insurance but non-life business too to strengthen the security for policyholders; and
(d) the population of companies was continually changing with companies entering and leaving the market. Forty-two new companies were incorporated in 1905; many of them being plate glass companies, though *Capital*, a company formed in 1906 to write accident business, went into voluntary liquidation in 1910. *The Insurance Directory* lists 83 companies wound up from 1900 to 1910.

The predominance of Britain's maritime fleet ensured that London maintained its leading international market role for marine insurance, and the major companies had continued to expand abroad, mainly through the appointment of local agencies. By the last decade of the nineteenth century, overseas business, written either abroad or at home as 'home foreign' business, accounted for some 60 per cent of the fire insurance premium income. Forty per cent of this was written in the United States, with some brokers having formed links with US brokers. Amongst the individual companies the *Royal Exchange Assurance,* for example, in 1910 wrote in its 'home foreign' account almost twice as much business abroad as at home (Post Magazine, 2000). Some companies recognised that insurance should follow trade, not least because of the FOC's cartel arrangements, which effectively precluded companies from increasing their UK market share by price cutting. So if they wanted to grow fast they had to look abroad, particularly across the Atlantic Ocean (Westall, 2006). There were at least 34 companies writing overseas fire insurance by 1904, generating total premiums of £21.4m. Fire insurance was profitable for most of the time, in 1904 producing a trading surplus of 16 per cent of premiums. The largest fire offices in 1904 were the *Royal* (net premiums £2.8m), the *Liverpool London & Globe* (premiums £2.1m), the *North British & Mercantile* (premiums £1.8m) and the *Commercial Union* (premiums £1.8m).

The 1906 San Francisco earthquake and fire, which devastated an area of seven square miles and killed some 1,000 people, was a massive blow to all insurers operating in America. *London Assurance,* the *Royal* and the *London and Lancashire* each incurred over £1m in claims, and the overall net claims ratio reached 90 per cent, approximately double the 1905 figure. Nevertheless Lloyd's quickly paid its claims and no British company failed, despite the industry incurring an overall loss of £5.7m (equal to 24.3 per cent of premiums), though the three companies named above managed to contain their losses to between 12 and 14 per cent of premium income. All but one of the 25 companies listed in that year paid shareholders a dividend, confirming the financial strength of the fire insurance market. However, the increasing size of factories was having an impact on UK fire losses. There were several fires in 1905 with an insured loss in excess of £25,000.

Life insurance was a fully developed and widely marketed product by 1900 with 45 proprietary offices and 25 mutual insurers that wrote only life and annuity business. The latter had very low commission and expense ratios (as low as 7.2 per cent for *Metropolitan Life*), a fact that they exploited in their advertising. Eighteen proprietary companies wrote both life and fire insurances, including some foreign insurers that had entered the UK market, including *Mutual of New York*, *Canada Life* and *National Mutual of Australasia*.

Ordinary life business sales in Britain were confined to the wealthier classes, paying premiums at quarterly or annual intervals, and the number of endowment policies had overtaken whole-life policies by the early years of the century. Industrial life was a working-class business with premiums being collected weekly from policyholders' homes. The accumulated funds held in 1900 by the life companies – the only segment of the industry by then to have acquired a massive customer base – after the steady expansion of business reached over £246m (see Table 1.3).

Personal accident insurance, which had begun with the railway age, was pioneered by the *Railway Passengers Assurance Co.* in 1849. Although the premium income it generated (£2.1m in 1914 (Supple, 1970, p. 421)) was still small relative to fire premiums of £28.9m, the old-established fire companies, always eager to expand their range of activities, by the turn of the century began to get involved in personal accident insurance. This triggered off several takeovers, including the acquisition of the *Railway Passengers* by the *North British & Mercantile* in 1910.

Table 1.3 Life insurance in Britain in 1900

	Industrial life	Ordinary life
Number of companies	14	85
Premiums £m	8.1	23.1*
Number of policies	17.86m	1.76m
Commission & expense ratio	44.4%	14.0%
Life insurance funds	£20.5m	£246.1m

Note: *including considerations for annuities.

Source: Bourne's Insurance Directory, 1905.

Boiler explosion/engineering

The rapid mechanisation of industrial processes and the use of steam and later electrical power gave birth to a new class of business and the formation of the first specialist steam boiler insurance companies in the mid-1800s.[1] However, it was the Boiler Explosion Acts, 1882 and 1890, and the Factory and Workshops Act, 1891, that had stimulated demand for such insurance and cover for liability arising out of the explosion of boilers and other machinery accidents. Next the Factory and Workshops Act, 1891, required the independent inspection of boilers, providing the existing boiler-explosion companies with a new source of business.

The Factory and Workshop Acts, 1901 to 1920, extended regulation and control to all classes of industrial power, including lifts, hoists and cranes, further expanding the demand for insurance, which was to become known as 'engineering insurance'. It was extended to cover the breakdown of machinery. Besides the existing specialist companies, the old-established fire companies also entered the market, often through the acquisition of specialist companies, such as *Royal's* purchase of *British Engine & Boiler* in 1912 and the *London's* acquisition of *Vulcan Boiler* in 1920.

Plate glass

This class of business too originated in the mid-nineteenth century with the formation of specialist companies to provide the insurance against the breakage of plate glass in shop windows. Generally the companies were small mutual organisations established on a local basis. Raynes records around 40 companies being involved in 1890 (Raynes, 1968, p. 287). Yet again, by the turn of the century the major companies were entering the market and acquiring small specialist companies, yet many small companies survived well into the second half of the century serving a purely local business community; see, for example, Table 1.4.

Burglary

Burglary insurance had been launched successfully by the *Mercantile Accident and General Guarantee Corporation* of Glasgow, which issued policies

Table 1.4 Plate glass companies wound up in the 1960s and 1970s

Date established	Company	Date wound up
1872	Bath & West of England	1963
1881	South of England Mutual	1970
1854	Huddersfield Mutual P.G.	1972
1897	Leicester & District P.G.	1972

to cover the risk in 1889 (Raynes, 1968, p. 287). Over the next few years several specialist companies were formed (such as the *Fine Art* (established in 1890) and the *Goldsmiths and General* (in 1891)), so that by 1900 burglary was a well-established class of business. It provided another important new source of income for both Lloyd's non-marine syndicates and the large old-established fire offices. Some companies pursued organic growth by setting up specialist departments, but others sought to take over a specialist company; *Guardian*, for example, acquired *Goldsmiths & General* in 1901, and *North British & Mercantile* took over *Fine Art* in 1917.

Motor insurance

Motor insurance also had commenced in the closing years of the nineteenth century. The *Scottish Employers' Liability and Accident* offered in 1896 to provide insurance for competitors in the first London to Brighton Emancipation Veteran Car run (Raynes, 1968, p. 304). That event celebrated the enactment of the Locomotives on the Highway Act, which raised the speed limit for 'light locomotives' to 14 mph. Originally the limit had been 2 mph in towns, with a man walking in front carrying a red flag.

Other companies saw the opportunities offered by growing vehicle ownership and Frederick Thoresby devised what was to become a 'comprehensive' policy covering a variety of risks (Post Magazine, 2000). Several companies were writing insurance for motor cars by 1900, including the pioneering *Law Accident Insurance Society* established in 1892, which was acquired by the *London & Lancashire* in 1907, and the *Car & General* founded by Thoresby in 1903 (acquired by the *Royal Exchange Assurance* in 1917). *Lloyd's* wrote its first motor policy in 1904 (Lloyd's, 2008). The business grew rapidly, attracting a number of new specialist companies, such the *Motor Union*, which was established in 1906 and acquired by the *Royal Exchange Assurance* in 1927. Other new companies succumbed to competition and quickly failed (see Table 1.5), stimulating a demand for regulation of the business.

Motor insurance was destined to grow rapidly to become a major source of premium income for insurers both at home and abroad, and the business

Table 1.5 Motor insurance companies wound up 1898–1923

Date established	Date wound up	Company
1896	1898	National Cycle & Motor Car
1899	1909	Birmingham Vehicle Owners
1906	1910	Law Car & General
1920	1923	Bristol Automobile & General
1917	1923	United Motor and General

Source: Post Magazine Insurance Directory.

was extended to provide insurance for commercial vehicles in 1906 and for motorcycles in 1910.

Workmen's compensation

The liability of employers for injuries sustained by employees also lay in the nineteenth century with the Fatal Accidents Act, 1846, the Employers' Liability Act, 1880 and the Workmen's Compensation Act, 1897 (see Raynes, 1968, p. 290f.). Although the latter Act did not make it compulsory for employers to insure, the companies soon recognised the opportunity for developing a new class of business, and the *Employers' Liability Assurance Corporation* was formed in 1881 for that purpose.

The Workmen's Compensation Act, 1906, extended the benefits of the Acts to workmen generally, and included in its scope certain industrial diseases. Therefore, employers realised the need to insure against their potential liabilities to pay benefits and damages in tort, and the foundation was laid for what was to become a major class of insurance generating substantial premiums. It remained so until the National Insurance (Industrial Injuries) Act, 1946, replaced it with a comprehensive social insurance scheme covering industrial injuries, resulting in a large loss of premium income for some companies, leaving them only with insurance against employers' liability. A Committee had been set up by the government in 1907 to consider whether the Post Office should undertake workmen's compensation insurance, but decided against it.

The intention to control increasing competition led 24 companies in 1906 to form the *Accident Offices' Association* to better organise workmen's compensation insurance, through the adoption of a tariff in 1909. Raynes records that in 1920 Lloyd's and 65 companies were transacting workmen's compensation insurance, of which 48 subscribed to the Accident Offices' Association tariff (Raynes, 1968, p. 296). Most employers took advantage of the insurance on offer, but others chose to be members of mutual associations, such as the *Iron Trades Employers' Insurance Association*, or to carry the risk themselves, workers' compensation being for a major industrial corporation mainly a high-frequency, relatively low-value risk.

The Employers' Liability Act, 1880, made masters and employers liable for injuries sustained by employees due to the negligence of a fellow workman. It extended the field for the provision of insurance, which the *Employers' Liability Assurance* was established to write. Total premiums for Workmen's Compensation Act policies were £3 million in 1911 (Raynes, 1968, p. 297). Not only might employees seek compensation for injuries sustained due to accident, but injured members of the public too could claim compensation.

Public liability insurance was introduced in 1906 to provide yet another new class of business for insurers.

Credit insurance

Originated by the great insurance innovator Cuthbert Heath (Gibb, 1957), this class of insurance to protect firms against loss due to the insolvency of debtors had commenced in 1893, a feature being that the policyholder was required to retain part of the risk. In 1901 the *Commercial Union* bought out the *Trade Acceptance Guarantee Syndicate*, which had been formed in 1896 to take over the credit insurance that had been written by the *National Provincial Trustees*. Two years later the *Commercial Union* transferred its credit business to the *Excess*, and the business progressed. However, credit insurance was mainly developed in Western Europe during the interwar years.

Contract guarantee

The first contract guarantee bonds to provide a financial guarantee against the failure of a contractor to perform work in accordance with the contract were issued by the *Federated Employers* in 1904, and another company specialising in the business – the *British General Insurance Company* – was registered in the same year (Raynes, 1968, p. 282). Guarantee business was extended to mortgage guarantee in 1904 with the formation of the *Law Guarantee Trust and Accident Society*.

Reinsurance

Attempts to form reinsurance companies were less successful in Britain than in Europe, and German and Swiss insurers came to dominate the business. The *Reinsurance Company* established in 1867 survived only four years, though the *London Guarantee & Reinsurance Co.*, founded in 1869, survived until the late twentieth century. Three British professional reinsurance companies were successfully established in the early years of the twentieth century – the *Mercantile & General Reinsurance Co.* founded in 1907, the *British & European* founded in 1908 and the *Victory Reinsurance Company* founded in 1919. All survived for many years, and benefited from the enforced withdrawal of the *Munich Re* in 1914 during the war.

Lloyd's recorded that Cuthbert Heath wrote the first Lloyd's reinsurance policy for a British company on American risks, and following the 1906 San Francisco earthquake he devised excess of loss reinsurance (Lloyd's, 2008).

New risks

Personal accident and sickness insurance and fidelity guarantee insurance had both been introduced in the mid-nineteenth century, so that by 1900 many companies had substantial miscellaneous accident insurance accounts. However, technological and commercial innovation was still creating new risks.

Aviation

Marine underwriters were quick to respond to the invention of aircraft: Lloyd's wrote its first aviation policy in 1911; the *White Cross Insurance Association* underwrote aircraft against fire risk much earlier (CII, 1968). It was, however, a high-risk business and many companies pulled out, so that the business was not firmly established until after the First World War, when two specialist aviation insurance companies were established, *Aviation and General* in 1919 (though it was wound up in 1927) and an association of *Eagle Star, Excess* and various Lloyd's underwriters forming the *Aviation Insurance Association*, which was dissolved in 1923 (CII, 1968, p. 149). The *Aviation and General Insurance Co.* was established in 1919, and in 1922 the *British Aviation Insurance*, led by Captain Lamplugh, was formed through the merger of *White Cross* and *Union of Canton*.

Household

In 1908 non-tariff companies led the way in issuing the first household policies covering property risks in addition to fire, but it was not until 1920 that the tariff company *Phoenix* issued its first householder's comprehensive policy.

1906

San Francisco earthquake

1906 was a momentous year for the industry. As noted above, a major earthquake and ensuing fire destroyed much of the City of San Francisco, resulting in very large claims for UK companies that had entered the American market. It cost Lloyd's underwriters £50 million (equivalent to $1 billion today) and the companies paid £10 million net of reinsurance, reputedly wiping out the underwriting profit on American business of the previous 35 years (Cockerell, 1983). Cuthbert Heath instructed his syndicates to pay all claims, which greatly enhanced the reputation of Lloyd's. A few months later there were further earthquakes and fires in Valparaiso and Kingston, Jamaica. Cuthbert Heath then proceeded to devise excess of loss reinsurance to provide insurers with the protection they needed against catastrophe losses like the San Francisco claims.

Insurance contract law

After several years of preparation, Parliament in December 1906 enacted what is arguably the most important piece of legislation controlling the conduct of all classes of insurance business. The Marine Insurance Act, 1906, codified the law relating to marine insurance. It 'reproduced as exactly as possible the existing law relating to marine insurance' (Lay, 1925) and dealt with such key issues as insurable interest, the principle of uberrimae fides (of utmost good faith), disclosure and representation, indemnity, contribution and warranties. It was taken as a model by other nations.

The Act defined the assured's duty of disclosure before the contract is concluded as applying to:

> every material circumstance which is known to the assured, and the assured is deemed to know every circumstance which, in the ordinary course of business, ought to be known by him. If the assured fails to make such disclosure, the insurer may avoid the contract. (s.18(1))

It went on to define a material fact as:

> Every circumstance is material which would influence the judgment of a prudent insurer in fixing the premium, or determining whether he will take the risk. (s.18(2))

That duty applied to all insurance contracts, not only to marine insurance, and the 'prudent insurer' test was heavily weighed in favour of the insurer. It attracted considerable criticism over the years as being too onerous a duty for insurance consumers. In July 2007 the Law Commission published jointly with the Scottish Law Commission a Consultation Paper on insurance contract law inviting comments on provisional proposals to modernise the law (see Chapter 16); Australia had reformed its law, including non-disclosure and warranties in 1984.

Also in 1906, as noted above, the Accident Offices' Association was formed to regulate workmen's compensation insurance, and the first public liability insurance was written.

The process of old-established fire offices acquiring companies to expand the business they wrote to include new classes continued after 1900 (see Table 1.6), with 11 companies being recorded by the Post Magazine as being amalgamated in 1906, notably:

> *Alliance* acquired *Provident Life*
> *General Accident, Fire & Life* acquired *Regent Fire*
> *Guardian* acquired *Westminster & General Life*
> *Royal* acquired *Durham and Yorkshire Fire* and *Northern Accident*
> *Scottish Union & National* acquired *Lancashire & Yorkshire Accident*
> *Sun* acquired *Patriotic Fire and Life*
> *Norwich Union Life* acquired *Scottish Imperial Fire & Life*
> *United Provident* acquired *Popular Life*.

Table 1.6 Companies amalgamated and wound up

Year	Companies amalgamated	Companies wound up
1900–04	43	26
1905	3	4
1906	11	3
1907	13	8
1908	9	7
1909	16	9
1910	14	17
1911	4	14
1912	4	13
1913	7	7
1914	3	12

Source: Post Magazine Insurance Directory.

The takeover of another company was not only the quickest way of acquiring a portfolio of new business but also of restoring their rankings among the largest groups.

Regulation

The Life Assurance Companies Acts, 1870 to 1872, had introduced the British regulation of life companies, controlling the formation (including deposits) and winding-up of companies. The underlying principle was 'freedom with publicity', requiring the provision of annual accounts and returns. Each failure of a non-life insurance company increased the pressure for their regulation too. The Employers' Liability Insurance Companies Act, 1907, required companies transacting that class of business to deposit £20,000 and publish annual returns. Then the government enacted the Assurance Companies Act, 1909, which brought both life assurance and other classes of general insurance (fire, personal accident, employers' liability and bond investment business) under control, requiring (i) deposits, (ii) the separation of life and general funds, (iii) the preparation of annual accounts, balance sheets, reports and the valuation of life funds, and (iv) provisions regarding the amalgamation and winding-up of companies. It still left some classes of insurance, notably marine, unregulated, and so it remained until 1946, and Motor only became regulated by the Road Traffic Act, 1930.

The Lloyd's Act, 1911, legally recognised the writing of non-marine business, including reinsurance, set up the Trust Fund for holding the deposits of Names to meet their underwriting liabilities, and authorised the society to use the Trust Funds to pay claims under policies underwritten by members (Raynes, 1968, p. 322).

New associations

As noted above, the *Accident Offices' Association* was formed in 1906. In 1907 and 1908 it tried unsuccessfully to agree on tariffs for burglary and personal accident insurance (Cockerell, 1983) but, as noted above, in 1909 it did agree on a tariff for workmen's compensation insurance.

The *Industrial Life Offices' Association* was formed in 1901, though the *Prudential*, the leading office, did not then join.

Insurance brokers too were feeling the need for collective action, and in 1906 they formed the *Association of Insurance Brokers and Agents*.

The expanding network of branch offices, creating local markets employing large numbers of employees, led in 1873 to the formation by the managers of tariff companies in Manchester of the first insurance institute. Then in 1881 the *Insurance and Actuarial Society of Glasgow* was established and opened to young people for educational purposes. Institutes were formed in other cities, and in 1897 the existing ten institutes formed the *Federation of Insurance Institutes* to become an examining body in 1908. The *Insurance Institute of Great Britain and Ireland* was constituted in 1908, and the *Chartered Insurance Institute* received its charter in 1912 with powers to award diplomas for part-time study. The *Institute of Actuaries* and the Scottish *Faculty of Actuaries* had been formed in the mid-1800s and were well established in 1900 as the educational bodies for the profession, concentrating on life assurance.

The industry was in a healthy state and operating on an international scale at the outbreak of the First World War, which created problems, including the forbidding of direct trade with the enemy Central Powers and the creation of a demand for insurance against war risks.

2
Insurance in World War I

In the closing years of the nineteenth century the British Empire was near its political peak. However, the emerging Continental superpower of Germany and the dynamic growth of the US, the largest producer of industrial output, were already foreshadowing the decline of Britain from the country's position as the pre-eminent economic power. Nevertheless, through its foreign investment assets, colonial presence and its strength in international finance, Britain's political and commercial self-confidence was at its height.

At this time Britain's financial sector – with its wide-ranging banking and insurance assets, with Lloyd's of London as its outstanding representative – was also pre-eminent, although Continental European competitors were growing impressively.

The outbreak of the war in August 1914 created a massive challenge to Britain's fighting capabilities, to its home and colonial population, and exposed the entire industrial and financial system to its most severe test since the Napoleonic wars more than a hundred years before. The vast expansion of military spending during the next four years enlarged the national debt from less than £700m to close to £6,000m during the war, which was to have far-reaching economic consequences in later years. Partly due to the need to fund war spending, insurance companies' holdings in government debt increased massively. In 1913 only 1 per cent of their investments were in government stocks; by 1920 this ratio had increased to 31.9 per cent (see Table 2.1).

The insurance business had become involved in the war struggle, and we consider the two main branches of the business – life insurance and non-life insurance – in turn.

Life insurance

Life insurance business – the only major branch of the industry with a very large customer base – underwent major changes as a result of the outbreak

Table 2.1 Economic background to World War I

	1914	1918	Cumulative change 1914–1918
Population	46.05m	43.11m	−6.4%
Increase in cost of living	*	15.3%	103.0%
Bank rate	3%–10%**	5%	n.a.
Wage rates	100*	189	89%
National income			
At current prices	£2,209m	£4,372m	97.9%
At constant prices	£2,010m	£1,960m	−2.5%
National Debt	£650m	£5,871m	903%

Note: *1914 = 100, first year of index. Index rise in 1915: 23%.
**range during 1914.
Sources: Butler and Butler (2000), Mitchell and Deane (1971).

of the war. The two main branches (ordinary assurances and industrial assurances) served different segments of Britain's population. Ordinary life assurance was usually purchased by the better-off part of the population, whereas industrial assurances catered for the working classes. The difference between the two classes of life business is best characterised by the fact that the average sum insured in 1914 for new policies for the two groups were £202 and £11.7, respectively. The impact of the war on the two branches was different, largely as a result of the different socio-economic position of their clientele.

For ordinary policies, even before the outbreak of the war, members of the Army and Navy had to pay £5 5s extra premiums, with non-combatants an extra £3 3s. per £100 sum insured. All policies which were in force before the outbreak remained in force without extra premiums. However, new policies written after the outbreak of the war for those in the Army and Navy were charged an extra premium of £7 7s per £100 sum insured, and for non-combatants in the forces the uplift was £5 5s. There was no uniformity among companies, however: some uplifted premiums by as much as £15 15s for combatants, while several insurers did not want to take any of the high-risk business. However, there was no change to the premium rates for the rest of the home population.

Life insurers' reluctance to take on war business is explained by the very high mortality already evident in the first year of the war. Of the 11,819 officers serving in the British Army at the outbreak of the war, 1,404, or 11.9%, had died by July 1915. For infantry the death rate was much higher, at 18.3%. During the first 14 months of the war a total of 6,660 officers and 94,992 of other ranks perished (Smith, 1915, p. 3).

Figures from *Standard Life Assurance* (Butt, 1984, p. 157) indicate the impact of the war on the flow of business. These show that in 1916 the number of new policies written by the company dropped to about half of the pre-war level, and only by 1920 did it return to the levels seen before 1914. The company also put a maximum war risk exposure on single life new policies at £2000.

However, death claims during the war increased steeply, but not to the degree one might expect following the carnage on the Continent. The year with the highest death claims recorded by *Standard Life* was 1915, when the amount paid out on death claims was 30 per cent higher than in 1913. By 1918 the excess of payouts in this regard was only 4 per cent up on the 1913 figure. The average life claims outgo for the five years of the war was only 8.5 per cent up on the previous five years.

The war also permanently damaged or extinguished the business of the company in many of its European markets. After the war *Standard Life* was forced to withdraw from a number of these countries in Scandinavia as well as from Hungary.

The war inevitably created an initial decline in new business. The departure of many of the insurance agents as well as their potential clients made selling far more difficult, and it was not surprising that, from the peak year for the ordinary business of 1913 of 305,000, new policies fell to 203,000 in 1916, the lowest year. However, despite the numerous problems encountered by the market, the premium income of both branches of life business surpassed the pre-war figure by 1918 (see Table 2.2). By the last year of the war the number of new ordinary policies rose to 297,000 – only 3% below the pre-war figure – and by 1919 a new peak was reached at 522,000.

The corresponding figures for the fall in the number of industrial life policies in force were much more severe, with a drop from 8.23m in 1913 to 5.28m in 1917. But industrial companies' premiums advanced during most of the war and by 1920 premiums reached £29.3m, a rise of 63 per cent from 1914 (Johnston and Murphy, 1956, p. 182). New business, however, increased thanks to higher levels of employment and wages during the early years of the war, plus the entry to the labour force of a large number of women.

Insurance managers were complaining about the falling price of government securities as a result of rising interest rates. Even after the war life insurance was threatened by four other negative factors besides soaring mortality. These were, according to a contemporary observer, D. H. Gordon

Table 2.2 Life insurance business[a] (£m)

	Ordinary business		Industrial business	
	Premium income	Life fund	Premium income	Life fund
1914	34.3	390.1	18.0	58.7
1918	38.6	411.0	22.4	74.0

Note: [a] Companies established in GB. Including annuities.
Source: Board of Trade. Mitchell, 1990, p. 691.

Smith (Smith, 1915, p. 4):

- the likelihood of earlier death for those injured;
- the lessened vitality of survivors;
- unprecedented depreciation of securities; and
- higher income tax for a lengthy period.

Gordon Smith also drew attention to the fact that life companies

> were subject to an exceptional disadvantage inasmuch as the protection they had sold could not be increased in price.

While this was true for policies written pre-war, new business rates were increased for those in the armed forces.

Overseas ordinary business, with a peak year of 20,000 new policies in 1912, declined even more steeply than home business, and recovered only slowly by 1919. Industrial life companies did not write overseas business.

Careful post-war research by the actuary Mr H. Brown identified the additional mortality cost of the war to ordinary life business (Hill, 1927, p. 136), which was put at £4m a year for 1914–18. However, including industrial life war claims, the industry's total war-related mortality cost was put at £15.5m. Unfortunately these calculations did not disclose the amount of the average war life claim or how many lives were lost due to the war. Although the study quoted does not quantify the loss of life directly related to World War I, military sources put this at 779,468 for the British Empire, including India, the Dominions and the Colonies. Civilian losses in Britain were slight, estimated at 1,000, mainly due to bombing raids.

Despite these massive losses, the overall judgement on the fortunes of the life insurance industry during the Great War was, perhaps surprisingly, a positive one. In the case of one of the leading companies, *Royal Exchange Assurance*, the company's history declared that the:

> REA came out of the War a much larger and more successful office than it had been at the outset. (Supple, 1970, p. 421)

In addition, the company's net fire premiums increased from £880,000 in 1913 to £1m in 1916 and to £1.79m in 1920. Non-life profits increased from £287,000 in 1916 to £457,000 in 1918. Life premiums advanced from £404,000 in 1915 to £492,000 in 1920 (See Table 2.3).

> An authoritative assessment of the war from the insurance viewpoint, prepared in 1925 by S. G. Warner, one of the authors of the War and Insurance study, also states that life insurancehas come through its trial unshaken and indeed

Table 2.3 British life insurance business 1908–20

	Ordinary business		Industrial business	
	No of policies in force (m)	Sum insured and bonuses (£m)	No of policies in force (m)	Sum insured and bonuses (£m)
1908	2.75	767.6	28.54	285.8
1913	3.18	855.0	37.55	428.7
1920	4.16	1,063.0	49.52	635.7

Source: N. Hill (1927), p. 166.

strengthened. At its worst, the storm only touched profits, never solvency. The attack made its mark on the outworks, but left the citadel unshaken. (Hill, 1927, p. 167)

The above source also added that low unemployment and rapidly rising wages also helped the growth of new life business.

Marine insurance

During the pre-war years there was evidence of far-sighted contingency planning by the Committee of Imperial Defence on marine insurance. The Committee was concerned over how to secure the country's vital sea-borne trade during a war. In May 1913 they appointed an advisory group, the Huth Jackson Committee, to consider

> whether a scheme can be devised to secure that in case of war British steam ships shall not be generally laid up and that overseas commerce shall not be interrupted by reason of inability to cover the war risks of ships and cargoes by insurance.... And also secure that insurance rates shall not be so high as to cause an excessive rise of price. (Gibb, 1957, p. 224)

While the marine insurance market had been accustomed – Lloyd's in particular – for a long time to insure hull and cargo war risks on most marine insurance contracts basis, underwriters became more cautious during the months before war. Some underwriters were still prepared to write war risks on a voyage-to-voyage basis. But there was no appetite for writing either continuous marine hull cover or for many voyages. This could hamper the continuation of trade, vital to keeping Britain's defence and commercial life going. After long negotiations between ship-owners' clubs and insurers (the War Risk Mutual Insurance Associations (WRMIA) representing marine underwriters) and the government, agreement was reached on hull risks. This ensured the continuation of commercial marine underwriting. The agreement was implemented the day after war was declared. A marine insurer active at the time noted that many underwriters '...were willing to underwrite ordinary marine risks at nominal rates in order to attract war risk business' (Dover, 1946). In addition to British shipping risks, insurers also underwrote the vessels of other nations neutral in the war.

A corresponding scheme was also implemented for cargoes on 5 August 1914 under the aegis of the State Cargo Insurance Office. Voyages current when war was declared could be completed under the insurance terms arranged prior to the war, and 80 per cent of the additional war risk premium would be borne by the state and 20 per cent by the ship-owner. Voyages after the outbreak of war were insured by the Association at rates of premium determined by the state, with 80 per cent of the risk reinsured by the state at the same rate. Another condition was that the voyages had to be agreed with the Admiralty as to the routes and the ports used. These arrangements were made by a committee on which the Board of Trade, the Admiralty, ship-owners and the Insurance Association were represented. It was also agreed that all cargoes had the right to be insured by the state scheme. The value of the cargo would be fixed according to normal marine policy conditions. The booking of transactions was carried out by the brokers and insurers that originally handled the account. Effectively the insurance process during the war proceeded as in peace time, with the additional support of 80 per cent reinsurance by the state.

The rates charged during the period of the war by the scheme varied according to experience and ranged between 1 and 5 per cent of hull value. However, while the scheme was in force premiums earned amounted to only 1.17 per cent of the insured amount of hulls. Claims totalled 2.78 per cent insured values, thus calling for a significant government contribution. Of the total underwriting loss of £18.5m, the state bore £14.8m and the WRMIA £3.7m (Hill, 1927, p. 42). The underwriting was carried out jointly by Lloyd's and approved British company underwriters.

However, the scheme was brought to an end before the end of the war, in August 1917, when shipping losses became extraordinarily high following the wave of German submarine attacks.

The war-related casualties of seafarers – numbering about 10,000 in crew deaths – were also partly compensated by the state from 1916, when the ship-owners' pre-existing responsibility under the Workmen's Compensation Act was contributed to by the Admiralty.

For the cargo insurance scheme – which was in force during the entire war, to the autumn of 1918 – insured cargoes carried reached a total value of £2,177m. Total premium income collected was £60m with claims of £65m. The claims represented 3 per cent of the insured value during the war. The overall cost of the state insurance scheme to the nation was a charge of 0.25 per cent of the value of the cargo shipped to Britain, or £5m, astonishingly good value for a nation so dependent on ship-borne trade.

Some companies thrived on the upsurge of marine business. One of these was the *London & Lancashire*, whose marine business increased fivefold between 1914 and 1918. (Clayton, 1971, p. 151)

However, premiums for other lines of non-life business were declining during the war. Personal accident business did not cover war risks, and workmen's compensation premiums shrank at an early stage of the war due to the fact that hundreds of thousands of workers left their employment to join the armed forces. But subsequent inflation of wages – amounting to 89 per cent during the four war years – reversed the decline of this sector. The business of motor insurance, still in its infancy, was also active, however: the AOA managed to form a tariff for the newly devised Third Party Motor insurance in 1914. Observers in the insurance press, however, noted that workers' compensation claims increased due to the unskilled and inexperienced labour force (Post Magazine, 1918, p. 5).

Although there are no comprehensive figures on the number of fatalities that occurred to insurance employees during the war, the extent of the loss of life to those working in insurance can be judged from information published by some companies after the war. The *North British & Mercantile Insurance Co.*, which had 892 male staff in the armed forces, lost 112 lives, or 12.5 per cent, during the war (North British & Mercantile, 1946, p. 4).

The industry also suffered from acute labour shortages, and many of the remaining staff were engaged in training the newly recruited people. Company costs were increased by having to move staff from large cities, which also involved paying billeting allowances and travel expenses.

Nevertheless, despite the enormous upheavals during World War I and a reduction in employment in this sector, insurance business continued to grow, partly due the expansion of the economy and partly due to a massive rise in prices (Table 2.4). From the outbreak of the war to the end of 1918

Table 2.4 World War I: British offices' general insurance premiums[a] (£m)

	1914	1918
Fire[b]	28.9	41.7
Employer's liability[c]	3.7	5.2
Personal accident[c]	2.1	2.2
Miscellaneous (incl. Motor)[c]	10.9	19.2
Lloyd's (1913 data)[d]	11.3	n.a.

Sources: [a] excluding Lloyd's (Clayton, p. 152).
[b] Clayton, 1971, p. 154.
[c] B. Supple, 1970, p. 417.
[d] Gibb, 1957, p. 206.

the all-items cost of living index showed a 103 per cent rise (Mitchell and Deane, 1971, p. 47).

It should be noted that there is no firm information on what proportion of this business was written on UK risks and what came from overseas. The figures for Lloyd's, which wrote the bulk of its business overseas, include £8.9m for marine insurance, and the rest was non-marine business and reinsurance.

War damage caused to inland property during the early phase of the war created a soaring demand for property insurance. The war created an opportunity for Lloyd's to offer for the first time insurance against bomb damage. The entrepreneurial Lloyd's underwriter Sydney Boulton wrote a lot of this (eventually profitable) business, as the tariff offices decided to ignore the risk (Gibb, 1957, p. 227). The State Insurance Office, with the help of approved insurance companies, promoted a voluntary fire insurance policy which provided cover for a sum insured of £25 for a premium of 6d. (£0.025 in decimal value) and property up to £75 could be insured for 1s 6d. with policies sold at Post Offices. From September 1917 the government announced that every individual was granted free insurance for war-related claims up to £500. From February 1917 the government reduced the rates charged for the smaller insurances by half. Despite these reductions, the premiums received during the war amounted to £13.6m, with claims of only £3.0m, although the government was due to pay insurers' commission and expenses.

Business development did not come to a halt during the war, as reported by the Post Magazine Directory, with 1915 recording the registration of 17 new insurance companies.

3
The Interwar Years

Britain and her allies prevailed over their enemies during World War I and managed to preserve the Empire. But the massive price paid for victory in terms of 780,000 lives lost and a mountain of national indebtedness created, described in the previous chapter, transformed the country. It became vastly different in its economic, political and social structure, compared with its pre-war state. It lost significant trade volumes to its dominions and the war also accelerated the process which was already giving manual workers an increasing share in the national income. The historian A.J.P. Taylor pointed out that

> a rich man paid 8% of his income in tax before the war, one third of it after. (Taylor, 1965, p. 176)

During the interwar years of 1920–38 Britain was also heavily burdened with a series of economic and political upheavals. The domestic events included the return of sterling to the Gold Standard at pre-war parity in 1925 followed by the abandonment of the Gold Standard in 1931. The General Strike in 1926 and the international problems created by the Great Crash of 1929 cast their shadow on world trade and generated financial problems worldwide for most of the 1930s, until preparations for the next war altered the level of economic activity. The political events included the creation of the USSR and the rise of fascist regimes in Italy and Germany, as well as the Spanish Civil War during the second half of the 1930s (See Table 3.1).

These events negatively impacted on Britain's prosperity, which for most of the period suffered from falling commodity prices and plummeting wage rates. Money wages dropped by 39 per cent between 1920 and 1933, the year with the lowest figure, and the pre-war recovery restored only 11 per cent of the wage decline by 1938. However, during the same period the real wages of those in full-time employment increased by 16 per cent, thanks to a declining cost of living, thus giving those who were able to escape unemployment a useful increase in real incomes. But, for Britain as a whole, per capita

Table 3.1 Economic data 1920-38

	1920	1938	Cumulative change
Population[1]	46.47m	47.49m	+2.2%
Cost of living[2]	151.4	88.5	−41.5 %
Bank rate[3]	7%	3%	n.a.
National income[4]			
At current prices	£5,664m	£4,671m	−17.5%
At 1900 prices	£2,079m	£2,725m	+31.1%
National debt	£7,434m	£6,993m	−6%
Real wage of fully employed worker[5]	102	118	+16%

Notes: [1] Annual Abstract of Statistics.
[2] Mitchell and Deane, 1971, p. 344.
[3] Mitchell and Deane, p. 459.
[4] Mitchell and Deane, p. 368.
[5] Mitchell and Deane, 1924=100, p. 345.

national income at current prices for the interwar years actually declined by a massive 24 per cent, even after the slow rise in real incomes after 1930.

Regulatory drive

The interwar years also saw a marked increase in regulatory activity in several branches of insurance. In the non-life segment there were government investigations relating to the Workmen's Compensation insurance, which was regarded as excessively profitable for insurers. The 15.2 per cent average profit from 1911 to 1918 prompted a parliamentary enquiry, headed by Sir Holman Gregory, which considered:

> whether it would be desirable to establish a system of accident insurance under the control and supervision of the State. (Clayton, 1971, p. 163)

While the report's recommendations included the supervision of premium rates, the restriction of insurance company profits and closer supervision of insurance companies by a government department, these were not included in the Workmen's Compensation Act, 1923. The Act did not make Workmen's Compensation insurance compulsory but a voluntary agreement was reached with the Accident Offices' Association to operate the class at a 60 per cent claims ratio (Clayton, 1971, p. 164).

Action was also taken to compensate miners whose employers became insolvent and thus were deprived of compensation. The Workmen's Compensation (Coal Mines) Act 1934 provided compensation, with fatal accident victims entitled to a compensation of £1,500.

The 1909 Assurance Companies Act was ineffective in preventing large insurance insolvencies because it largely relied on solvency deposits and did not give enough power to the Board of Trade. This provoked the enactment of two new laws (the Assurance Companies (Winding-up) Acts, 1933 and 1935), which increased regulatory powers for the Board of Trade.

Life insurance

Hard times seem to have benefited the saving and life insurance business during the interwar period, as evidenced from the remarks of a post-war observer:

> The growth rates of both premiums and sums insured were higher in the inter-war period than they had been in the more settled and confident years of before 1914. (Murphy and Johnston, p. 74)

Comparing the pre-war and post-war periods (1886–1913 and 1922–37 respectively), the growth rate of premium income increased from 3.4 to 4.4 per cent p.a. (Murphy and Johnston, p. 9), while that of the sums assured increased from 2.8 to 4.3 per cent p.a. (Table 3.2). However, the ordinary life figures contain business written overseas, including in the US, for which there is no available split.

Overseas life business did not then play a significant role: of the 462,000 ordinary life policies written by British companies in 1928, 93 per cent were written in the UK (Post Magazine, 1935–6, p. 563). However, there was already a noticeable presence in the UK of foreign life company operations, which in the same year wrote 26,600 policies in the UK.

Marine

Marine insurance remained a very active and crowded market, with Lloyd's as well as 93 companies writing this account, but most of them suffered from steeply fluctuating premium income after the post-war years of prosperity. The largest account in 1923 was written by the Liverpool-based *London &*

Table 3.2 Life premiums of companies established in the UK during the interwar years

	Ordinary premiums £m[a]	Industrial premiums £m
1919	43.5	25.4
1930	75.5	43.8
1938	102.1	58.0

Note: [a] including annuity considerations.
Source: Mitchell B. R., 1990, p. 691.

Table 3.3 Interwar net non-life premiums 1919–39 Companies established in the UK (£m)

	Motor	Misc accident	Employer's liability	Fire	Marine	Personal accident
1919	n.a.	23.7	6.3	49.5	33.7	2.6
1922	n.a.	34.0	5.7	55.0	15.2	3.1
1925	n.a.	44.5	5.7	60.6	14.6	3.3
1929	n.a.	56.3	5.8	58.4	13.8	4.0
1930	n.a.	55.8	5.8	55.1	13.4	4.0
1931	32.5	22.7*	5.4	51.9	12.0	3.7
1932	31.8	21.6	5.0	50.8	11.4	3.7
1935	33.3	24.2	5.8	48.8	10.1	4.0
1938	37.9	n.a.	7.1	49.5	12.8	4.6
1939	36.6	n.a.	6.9	49.6	14.8	4.5

Note: *Motor insurance premiums included in misc. accident class until 1930 are separated from 1931.
Source: Various issues of *Post Magazine Almanac* and Board of Trade.

Lancashire with premiums of £1.2m, less than half the £2.7m achieved in 1920. This period also led to the winding-up of 14 marine insurers between 1919 and 1930, according to various issues of the *Post Magazine Insurance Directory*.

After a booming marine insurance performance during the immediate post-war period with premiums peaking at £41.7m in 1920, the demand for shipping dropped rapidly. Subsequent years of the 1920s were characterised by falling international trade and growing competition in the insurance market. These pressures reduced marine premium income to a third of its post-war peak by 1930, and by 1933 to £9.9m, which was less than a quarter of the peak year. Even after the trough year with £9.9m premiums, recovery was modest until 1939. These figures exclude business written by Lloyd's, which, though principally a marine insurer, did not disclose a class breakdown until after World War II. However, the Joint Hull Agreement injected some discipline in terms of eliminating the differences in the terms of the cover offered between Lloyd's and the company market. The recovery of the market had to wait for over a decade, for the pre-war economic revival in industrial output and international trade (see Table 3.3).

Motor

The other significant change in the non-life market in the period was the introduction of compulsory third party motor insurance in 1931, as required by the Road Traffic Act, 1930. Britain was late in introducing this legislation, as similar laws were already in force in several Continental markets.

It was not favoured by UK insurers, who feared that it would lead to more claims on worse risks from drivers who did not want to purchase insurance voluntarily.

The 1930s also saw the general introduction of new underwriting and risk selection methods, with the use of no-claims bonuses and differential premium rates applied to different geographical areas and engine sizes. But underwriters were already complaining about the rapid rise in vehicle theft and the difficulty of making a profit. However, the existence of the private car tariff as part of the AOA rate-making arrangement from 1914 and the introduction of the commercial vehicle tariff from 1915 created a measure of stability, with the tariff offices, which controlled around two-thirds of business, acting as price leaders (Clayton, 1971, p. 152).

The number of vehicles on Britain's roads soared during the 1920s (from 362,000 in 1920 to 1.56m in 1930) but the 1930s produced a slower rate of expansion. By 1938, which was the pre-war peak, the total reached 2.64m, with 1.98m being private cars. The number of motorcycles in use also grew, increasing by 250 per cent between 1920 and 1930, which was the peak year with a total of 733,000. But many of the motorcyclists did not have insurance cover: it was estimated that only one-third of them purchased insurance. However, motorcycle numbers dropped sharply even before the war, while private car use continued to grow.

No separate motor insurance premium statistics were published before 1931, as data for this class was not separated from other accident business. In 1931 motor premiums were £32.5m and other accident lines £22.7m. It is remarkable, however, that during seven years between 1932 and 1938 motor premium income increased by only 19.2 per cent, while the number of vehicles on the road soared by 36.7 per cent. The slow premium growth was due to the competitive impact of non-tariff companies. There were 142 companies listed in the *Post Magazine Almanac* in 1929 and this number was very little changed by 1938, with 139 still contesting the market. The largest company writing motor insurance was *General Accident*, the leading non-tariff office.

The increased vehicle ownership adversely impacted on road casualties, with the 1.3m vehicles on the road in 1934 causing 7,343 road deaths. This reflected the largely inexperienced car drivers and road users – with no driving test required until 1943. In later years accident prevention measures and propaganda by government sources as well as by the insurance industry brought the death rate down significantly. By 1963 the number of cars on the road reached 7.3m and road deaths were 6,922.

Fire

Post-war fire insurance premium income advanced steadily from the end of World War I to 1929, with a cumulative increase of 23 per cent from 1919 to 1926, the year of the General Strike. In subsequent years there was a slow contraction in the company market to a pre-war low of £48.8m in 1935. These figures comprise worldwide fire business because no regional separation of the figures was available until well after World War II. Competition from non-tariff offices remained keen, and Lloyd's, also outside the FOC, 'became a formidable competitor', according to contemporary observation in the *Post Magazine Almanac* of 1936. But from time to time very large losses hit the market hard, such as the £1,125,000 tobacco warehouse fire claims in London in 1923. Perhaps learning from the costly event of the 1906 San Francisco Earthquake, British insurers' payout for the 1923 massive Tokyo earthquake and fire was small, arising mostly from shipping losses at the local port, because earthquake damage was excluded from fire policies.

British insurers continued to be very active in both Canada and the USA. This was very profitable business, with typical loss ratios of 45 per cent of premiums, expense ratios of 26 per cent and commission of 20 per cent, leaving underwriting profits of 9 per cent (Figure 3.1). In 1935 only seven out of the 64 companies active in the US writing fire and marine reported an underwriting loss, and profitability was kept up even during the depression years in both fire and motor business (Post Magazine Almanac 1935–6, p. 559).

There are no separate statistics on the proportion of fire premiums written outside the home market, but, in view of the substantial presence of companies such as *Commercial Union, Royal Exchange Assurance* and *Royal Insurance* in North America as well as in Asia and Africa, it must be assumed that foreign premiums accounted for a substantial share. In the case of *Royal Exchange Assurance* the proportion of overseas business of the fire and accident account was as high as 66 per cent in 1931 (Supple, 1970, p. 472).

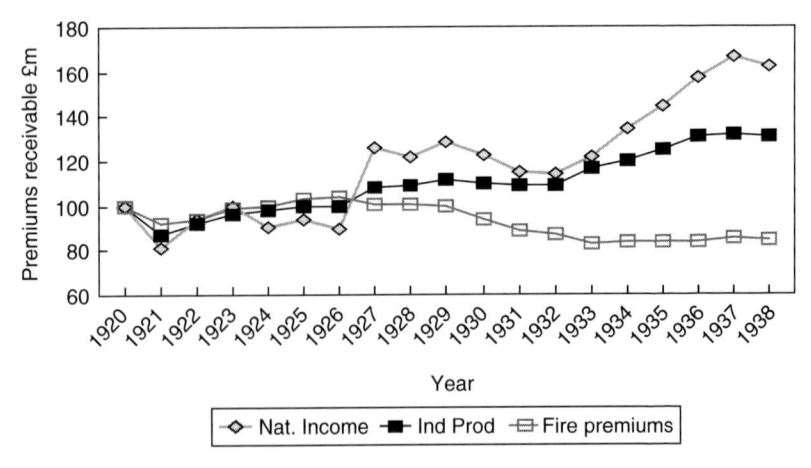

Figure 3.1 Indices of national income, production and fire premiums

Of the liability classes, employer's liability expanded during the post-war boom period but rapidly declined when unemployment soared by the mid-1920s. The peak year for this class was 1920, with £8.9m net premiums, but by the end of the decade the figure was down to £5.8m (see Table 3.3). It remained a very competitive market, with 87 companies vying for business.

Personal accident – with as many as 76 companies active – fared better, with premiums expanding from £2.6m in 1918 to £4.0m by 1929 (see Table 3.3).

The interwar period also saw a new social and legal phenomenon: the emergence of claims consciousness and litigation to pursue claims in courts to extract maximum damages. A senior manager of the *Royal Exchange Assurance* remarked in 1939 that:

> the publicity given to the large awards by the courts is intensifying a claims consciousness on part of the public, which if developed still further may eventually create a new social problem. (Supple, 1970, p. 432)

This explains to some extent why this period saw the rise in the sale of personal liability insurance.

An important new state-owned player also appeared on the insurance scene after the war. The government established the *Export Credits Guarantee Department* (*ECGD*) in 1919 to encourage exports. It specialised in providing long-term credit insurance for export sales, which proved too risky for the private sector operator, the *Trade Indemnity Corporation* (*TIC*). Much of *ECGD*'s cover was granted on exports to politically risky countries, which private sector insurers were not prepared to accept. This was effectively an entry of the state into political risk insurance, for the support of domestic economic activity. By the 1930s the *ECGD* was willing to guarantee some of the exports shipped to Russia, which in earlier years were regarded as politically unacceptable (Haufler, 1997, p. 76). With the outbreak of the Spanish Civil War credit insurers, including *ECGD* and *TIC*, suffered heavy losses from land war risk (Haufler, p. 80). This experience eventually led to an agreement initiated by the chairman of Lloyd's, Neville Dixey, with the major British companies to implement a near total ban on land war risk insurance, although marine war risks remained insurable.

Product variety

The 1930s demonstrate the innovative nature of the British insurance market, manifested by the large variety of different specialist insurance products on offer. The support for this view is provided by the 1935–6 *Post Magazine Directory and Yearbook*, which listed 74 different classes of life and general insurance policies on offer. It would be tedious to list all of them here, as they included the usual fire, marine, life and personal accident classes. However, some of the more unusual, exotic covers are listed below:

Furriers' indemnity
Accountants' indemnity
Dentists' indemnity
Contingency
Foot & Mouth
Swine fever
Key
Libel
Petrol pump installation
Loans on personal security
Golfers' indemnity
Wireless
Women's accident and all sickness.

Some of these new policies (such as wireless, which was becoming widely purchased by households, and petrol pump installations) reflect the changing social and industrial mix of the British scene. The most popular products were offered by large numbers of insurers in 1935, such as Plate glass (130 companies listed) followed by Motor vehicle (129 companies) and Inclusive Householders insurance (115 companies).

4
Insurance during World War II

The 1930s were stressful for Britain's economic and political events. In addition to the Great Crash, major bankruptcies, soaring unemployment, the rise of Nazism in Germany, the Spanish Civil War and Italian adventures in Africa created a climate of economic stress and political turbulence and a feeling of apprehension about a coming war.

By the mid-1930s there was economic recovery, partly due to rearmament and partly due to a steep climb in capital investment. However, unemployment was still 10.7 per cent in 1937 across Britain, with higher figures in Scotland (15.2 per cent) and Wales (24.3 per cent). The country still relied most heavily on coal for its energy, producing 227m tonnes in 1938, although due to labour shortages this declined to 187.2m tonnes by 1945 (Table 4.1).

Life insurance

The reactions to life business were not dissimilar to those taken during World War I, with the adjustments to this branch being largely devised by insurance companies themselves. Both segments of the life insurance industry responded remarkably well to the massive challenges of the war. No-one could have foreseen the extent of the loss of life, which for combatants turned out to be significantly lower than during World War I. During World War II the loss of life in the armed forces and merchant navy casualties totalled 340,000 (including 35,000 in the merchant navy) against 779,468 in World War I. Armed forces personnel wounded reached 282,000. However, civilian deaths in World War I were only around 1,000, but in World War II the intensive bombing raids claimed 76,000 lives in Britain. In addition over 86,000 people were injured in these raids, according to the Ministry of Home Security (Post Magazine 1945–6), and more than 250,000 homes were destroyed. The worst year was 1940, with air raid deaths reaching 23,776.

Table 4.1 The economic background 1939-45

	1939	1945
Population	47.76m	49.18m
Civilian employment	17.4m	16.4m
Armed forces[1]	385,000	5,090,000
Yield on war loan 3.5%	2.94-3.76%	2.77%-3.02%
National debt	£7,130m	£21,167m
Net national income at current prices[3]	£5,037m	£8,340m
Retail price increase	8%	Cumulative increase 1939-45 54.5%
Rise in weekly wage rates	30%[2]	Cumulative rise in earnings 1938-45 80%
Vehicle Licences current	3.16m	2.56m

Notes:
[1] Including overseas personnel.
[2] Increase in earnings from 1938 to July 1940.
[3] Mitchell and Deane, *Abstract of historical statistics*, 1971, p. 368.
Sources: *Statistical Digest of the War*, CSO, 1951.

A flavour of the times may be gleaned from the 1940 summary of the year in the Insurance Directory, which wrote that its volume's appearance was

> several months late, but for that we make no apology. Our premises, offices, works, plant and machinery together with the whole of the standing matter of this year book were completely destroyed by enemy action. Paper restrictions have necessitated some contraction in its features... we are proud that our publication record is still unbroken. (*Post Magazine*, 1945-46, p. 329)

There were initial setbacks in the early years of the war, when ordinary life business declined somewhat. But the industrial life account performed remarkably well: by the final year of the war premium income on this account was 38 per cent up from the last pre-war year and the number of polices in force continued to rise, reaching 81.2m in 1943 (Clayton, 1971, p. 178).

For ordinary life the corresponding premium growth figure was a more modest 15 per cent. Here the number of new policies written fell by 45 per cent between 1938 and 1940 and did not pass the pre-war total until 1946. The explanation lies in war uncertainties regarding personal incomes, higher taxes and higher premium rates due to lower interest rates.

The success of the government's policy in keeping interest rates well below the level seen during World War I was detrimental to insurers' profits as well as to policyholder bonuses on with profits contracts. The fall in interest

Table 4.2 Life premiums during World War II 1938–50 (£m)

	1938	1944	1950
Ordinary life[a]	102.1	109.5	203.9
Industrial life	71.8	93.5	127.6
Total	173.9	203.0	331.5

Note: [a] Including annuities, Johnston and Murphy, p. 74.
Source: Clayton G., British insurance, 1971, p. 192.

rates from 4.2 per cent in 1938 to 3.6 per cent in 1945 was the principal reason for this outcome, which resulted in the subsequent reduction of with profits bonuses from 2.3 per cent to 1.0 per cent on ordinary policies and from 1.6 per cent to 0.8 per cent on industrial branch policies (Table 4.2). Insurance companies' investment income also suffered due to government bonds' yields dropping as insurers purchased some £600m of these bonds during the war.

Once the war began some life companies offered premiums at old (pre-war) premium rates with restricted cover (e.g. the amount payable was restricted to the premium paid or the surrender value, whichever was the higher) (Clayton, 1971, p. 193). The majority of insurers, however, raised premium rates covering full war risks reflecting the implied higher mortality. On policies already in force some companies applied new conditions to reflect the cost of soaring claims. *UK Provident*, for example, paid half the original sum insured plus the accumulated bonus, if the death was war-related.

The problems of maintaining premium collections on ordinary life policies during the absence of policyholders and insurance agents were manifold. Preparations for war involved moving out staff and equipment from London to the provinces, generating large population movements. An example was Southampton, the population of which dropped from 170,000 to 80,000 during the early years of the war. As a result of these difficulties the flow of ordinary premiums dropped by 7 per cent in 1941, but by 1946 it was 32 per cent higher than the pre-war figure. (Johnston and Murphy, 1956, p. 75).

These difficulties for life business – where personal collection of premiums was the main practice – were alleviated by the agreement that the missed premiums could be recovered from the surrender/maturity value of the policy. To give legal backing to this practice the Emergency Protection from Forfeiture Act, 1940, was enacted. Industrial life policies were also dealt with if application was made to the insurer stating that the non-payment of premium was due to the effects of war. Another item contributing to increased operating costs was that some insurers continued to pay all members of staff on National Service the difference between their salaries and service pay.

Table 4.3 BIA member companies' staff numbers

	Staff numbers in June 1942	Pre-war staff numbers
Male	15,418	29,310
Female	2,700	15,103
Total	18,118	44,413

Source: BIA archives MS 21943, Guildhall Library.

Evidence of these staff shortage pressures can be gleaned from a memo by the BIA in June 1942. In a reply to a government request, on the number of additional staff that could be made available for national service, the BIA revealed that 60 per cent of the pre-war staff had already left the industry for either national service or other work. The data shown in Table 4.3 is from 118 BIA member companies in the general insurance and composite company staff, but there were no figures available for the life insurance sector.

Another aspect of the war is revealed by a historical review of the *Prudential Assurance*, which states that, of the 12,000 members of their staff who joined the armed forces, 613, or 5.1 per cent, died during the war (Hosking, 1947, p. 125). During the war the company attempted to replace army personnel with 15,000 temporary staff, the majority of them being women.

Marine insurance

War risks were initially excluded by marine underwriters at Lloyd's and by tariff companies, and soon after the outbreak of the war a war exclusion clause was inserted by all British companies in every non-marine policy insuring property on land. During 1939, when international tensions increased the war risk of shipping and cargoes rose substantially, the British government was keen that trade should not be interrupted. By early 1939 the Board of Trade was authorised to reinsure 'King's enemy risks' on ships, cargoes by sea and air, as was the case in the World War I. This led to the continuation of commercial insurance activity at normal rates, with the government reinsuring the war risk.

Disciplined marine underwriting resulted in increased premium rates, which reflected the additional hazards associated with the war. The competition on rates between companies was controlled by the arrangement whereby all rates were determined by the 'Three Leading Underwriters Agreement'. The rate was set by the three specialist underwriters – including endorsement by Lloyd's – and was accepted by the whole market. These practices ensured that by the end of the war the market was, according to an underwriter active in this market, 'financially stronger today than in 1939 and...more than adequate to take care of the effects of the war' (Dover, 1946, p. 37).

At the outbreak of the war the War Risk Insurance Office was opened, which split marine risks into two groups. The first group was marine risks arising from voyages to and from Britain and the second on voyages between overseas countries. For the first group of risks underwriters were allowed to quote rates higher than the government's published rate, but if there was no private insurer prepared to underwrite it the government accepted the risk. This was a wise arrangement, as it secured the government against competition by rate cutting and still made it possible for an insured that objected to covering its risks with the British government to insure on the open market. Risks for the second group were underwritten at the insurer's chosen rate.

Fire insurance

Fire business remained the largest line throughout the war. The years leading up to the war still produced profits for fire business, thanks to the discipline enforced by the Fire Offices Committee. No home–overseas premium split was available, although much business came from overseas markets, according to *Post Magazine*. The market was very crowded and competitive, with 165 companies writing some business, in addition to Lloyd's.

During the period leading up to the war the government was under pressure to devise an insurance scheme which would indemnify its citizens against war damage (Sharp, 1986, p. 15). The example of the World War I scheme for insurance against damage by aircraft and bombardment was cited and at one stage a similar scheme was considered by the government (Gibb, 1957, p. 231). However, in view of the massive threat of nationwide bombing raids by the Luftwaffe this was not regarded as a feasible exercise in the traditional insurance sense. These anticipations led Lloyd's to initiate an agreement with the major tariff offices that all policies should exclude war risks on land. All British marine and property underwriters also confined land war risks on cargo to 48 hours after discharge of the cargo, but property in Canada and the US was excluded from this agreement. This turned out to be a sound decision, as the property damage during the war turned out to be in excess of three thousand million pounds (Sharp, 1986, p. 15) in Britain alone.

However, an alternative scheme was implemented by the government, and the Board of Trade, in order to protect manufacturers and stockholders from bankruptcy if their commodity and raw material supplies could not be insured. At the outbreak of the war the government became a primary supplier in property insurance. The enactment of the War Risk Insurance Acts of 1939 and 1941 stipulated that private insurance for industrial stocks and raw materials was prohibited and all traders had to take out compulsory cover with the Board of Trade. This was put into effect by two statutes (War Damage Act of 1941 and 1943) which insured all commodities, raw

Table 4.4 State-backed property insurance schemes during World War II

	No. of policies	Premiums collected (£m)	No. of claims	Claims received (£m)
Commodity	9.5m	203	138,000	117
Business	4.1m	77	228,000	90
Private chattels	3.9m	16	2,410,000	86
Total	17.5m	296	2,776,000	293

materials, equipment and private chattels. All insurers, including Lloyd's, acted as agents for the government. They were responsible for the routine work of issuing policies, indexing, banking, etc., as well as for settling claims. The magnitude of this task can be seen from Table 4.4.

Insurers were assisted by the fact that the business scheme was compulsory for firms where the insurable value of property (plant and machinery, but excluding buildings) was over £1,000, with a heavy fine for non-compliance. On private chattel risks, the insurance of which was not compulsory, every householder was entitled to compensation of up to £200, with an additional £100 if he had a wife and £25 for each child under the age of 16. It is notable, however, that of the 13m UK households only 3.9m made use of this scheme, with the rest reckoning that their chances of destruction were too low. However, it was the chattels segment of the scheme that showed the largest number of claims and a sizeable underwriting loss.

Although overall claims received by the state schemes were marginally below premium income, the government was also responsible for paying insurers' out of pocket expenses as well as the running costs of the scheme, put at some £9m (Gibb, 1957, p. 231).

Insurers also made great efforts to prevent fires by advising policyholders on sprinklers and fire-resisting structures. The wartime practice of fire-watching parties also helped, and it is thanks to these practices that, despite the enemy bombing waves, the cost of fire damage increased by only 42 per cent to £12.5m in the peak year of 1940 from the pre-war figure of £8.8m.

In a separate scheme to insure some of the government-owned commodities, insurers charged low rates and divided premiums among participating companies. These arrangements '...demonstrate the ability of offices to subordinate normal healthy competition when it did not coincide with the national interest' (Mason, 1946, p. 200).

Building insurances, not covered by the above schemes, were dealt with by the Inland Revenue. Underwriters again acted as agents but the insured did not pay property insurance premiums. The money was collected instead as an extra 2 s in the pound (that is, 10 per cent) charge on personal income tax by the Inland Revenue. As Table 4.5 shows, there was a continuing rise in premium income in some non-life classes during the war, but most of

Table 4.5 Non-life business of companies established in the UK (£m)

	1938	1944	1948
Accident	4.6	4.7	8.6
Fire	49.5	65.1	127.6
Motor	37.9	26.4	70.4
Marine	12.8	26.3	50.5
Misc. accident (incl. employer's liability)	34.1	48.2	73.9
Total	138.9	170.7	331.3

Source: Board of Trade, *Annual Abstract of Statistics*, Clayton, 1971, p. 194.

the rise was due to inflationary pressures – with consumer prices rising by 54 per cent from 1939 to 1945 – as well as the increased economic activity and output of goods during the war.

It should be noted that the figures in non-life business include some overseas income, although no definite information is available on its size or geographical distribution.

Motor business was well provided with 107 companies writing this line, yet premiums declined steeply by 50 per cent from 1938 to 1943, by which time only a total of 1.54m vehicles were on the road, less than half of the pre-war figure. However, by August 1945 the total rose to 2.56m.

An additional problem for underwriters was a more demanding claims climate. A new angle was that 'a car owner can claim against his own chauffeur should the former sustain injuries as a result of the latter's negligence' (*Post Magazine*, 1939–40, p. 11).

Workmen's compensation premium income, however, expanded during the war, stimulated by higher wages and an increased labour force. Claims experience improved as the war spirit induced workers to return to work as soon as possible.

Marine insurance premiums increased the fastest during the war, mostly on account of the worldwide increase in shipping movements and higher cargo and boat values, as British insurers remained prime providers of war risk cover worldwide. The income in this class also increased materially thanks to the growth of business in the major overseas markets such as Australia, Canada and the US. These figures again exclude Lloyd's business.

A major interruption for insurers during the war was the loss of access to Continental European business, as well as to some of the Asian countries, when these fell under enemy occupation. However, in several lines of business increased activity in friendly markets such as Australia, Canada, New Zealand and the US more than compensated for the losses elsewhere, especially during the later years of the war.

Part II
Lines of Business

5
From Austerity to Prosperity

This chapter describes the development of the personal lines sector of the non-life business of the British insurance market. At the time of writing personal lines insurances represented about 65 per cent of gross non-life insurance premiums (excluding MAT and reinsurance) written in the UK by companies.

While Britain emerged from World War II victorious in May 1945, it owed vast sums to the United States for war materials supplied under Lend Lease, its industry was geared to war needs and much of its pre-war trade was lost, with food and clothing still rationed. There was an urgent need for industry to change over to peacetime production and regain its lost overseas markets, a task not helped by industrial unrest. Nevertheless, national income rose in real terms (see Figure 5.1) so that by the late 1950s the mass of the population had achieved a higher standard of living, enabling them to purchase a wider range of goods and services that stimulated the demand for insurance. By 1957 Prime Minister Harold Macmillan claimed, with justification, that: 'You've never had it so good.'

An increasing proportion of the working force was becoming engaged in better paid non-manual work, with the proportion of non-manual workers rising from 32.5 per cent in 1951 to 37.7 per cent in 1961. Economic growth, which advanced by 50 per cent between 1960 and 1970, produced rising incomes and enabled many lower-income households for the first time to purchase a house and a car, so that the number of cars licensed rose rapidly and the number of owner-occupied dwellings was also increasing (from 6.4m in 1960 to 9.0m in 1971). This new-found wealth increased the demand for personal insurances, notably household, mortgage protection, and car insurances.

The overall development of British insurance companies' non-life premiums may be summarised with two tables. Table 5.1 shows the worldwide premium development of British insurance companies from 1949 to 1967 (no separate figures are available for certain classes or a split between overseas and the home market). This was a period of dynamic

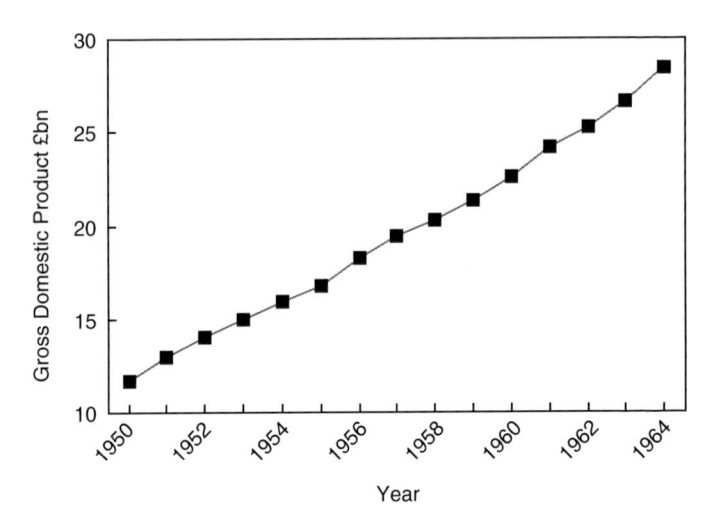

Figure 5.1 Gross domestic product at factor prices
Source: British Historical Statistics, 1990, p. 611.

Table 5.1 Worldwide premiums of UK insurance companies (£m)

	Fire	Accident	Marine aviation and transport	Total
1949	147	171	53	371
1960	300	560	85	945
1967	465	1020	140	1625
Incr. 1949–67	216%	496%	164%	484%

Source: ABI, *Key Statistics 1950–85*, table 1.

growth reflecting reconstruction at home as well as the regaining of numerous overseas markets, although it coincided with the nationalisation and domestication of insurance in post-colonial and other countries. The overall worldwide growth of premiums amounted to 484 per cent over an 18 year period. The fastest advance was achieved by the accident class, notably motor insurance.

Different headings and the separation of domestic and overseas businessshown in Table 5.2 takes the story from 1969 to 1985, with fire and accident business growing fastest during this period.

The rest of this chapter outlines the major components of the personal lines elements of the UK market.

Table 5.2 UK insurance business of British insurance companies* (£m)

	Fire and accident	Motor	Marine and aviation	Total
1969	383	213	97	693
1975	1010	628	221	1859
1980	2411	1564	320	4295
1985	4651	2200	938	7798
Incr. 1969–85	1,114%	903%	867%	1,025%

Note: *members of the British Insurance Association (BIA).
Source: ABI, Key Statistics, table 2.

Motor insurance

Premium growth

Motor insurance, unregulated as a separate class until 1930, grew dynamically. Following the failure of some companies writing motor insurance, the Road Traffic Act, 1930, made:

(a) companies writing motor insurance subject to regulation under the Assurance Companies Act, 1909, including the requirement to deposit £15,000 with the Accountant-General;
(b) it compulsory for the user of a motor vehicle on a road to insure against liability for injury to third parties.

The end of World War II found 2.5m licensed motor vehicles on the roads of Great Britain, a drop from the pre-war total of 3.1m in 1938. 1.5m of these were private cars, the rest goods and public transport vehicles. The total jumped to 4m by 1951, after petrol rationing had ended in May 1950. The motor insurance premium income of British companies, after a pre-war peak of global motor premiums of £37.9m, dropped to a low of £24.6m in 1943, to recover to £33.8m by 1945. The post-war recovery hoisted worldwide motor premiums to £102.7m by 1950 (there were no separate figures for the UK market until 1960). Between 1945 and 1955 the number of vehicles increased from 3.1m to 5.77m. There were as many as 109 companies writing motor insurance, many writing small regional accounts, and the vast majority were profitable. Typical claims ratios were 50 to 60 per cent with combined commission and expense ratios at 30 to 35 per cent. The largest of these companies in 1950 was *General Accident Fire & Life*, with a worldwide motor premium income of £17.4m and claims and expense ratios of 59.3 and 34.0 per cent respectively. Ranking second and third places in premium terms were *Zurich Insurance* at £8.66m and *Commercial Union* with £8.44m (see Figure 5.2).

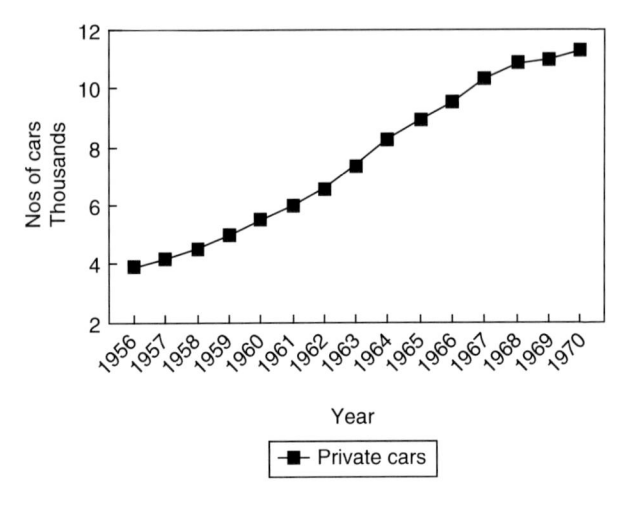

Figure 5.2 Numbers of cars licensed 1956–70
Source: Mitchell B.R., British Historical Statistics, 1990, p. 558.

Table 5.3 UK market* motor net premiums (£m)

	£m	Average annual premium growth rate (%)
1970	216	6.2
1980	1,561	21.9
1990	4,847	12.0
2000	7,648	4.7
2005	8,720	2.7

Source: ABI (*insurance companies annual business, excluding Lloyd's).

By 1960 insurance companies' and Lloyd's domestic motor premium income reached £118m and £15m respectively.

The growing use of motor vehicles, coupled with a regime of compulsory third-party motor insurance, created a fertile business climate for motor insurance, with the fastest premium growth rate experienced during the 1970s and 1980s, as Table 5.3 shows.

In addition to the company market, Lloyd's UK motor business in 1980 amounted to £237m, equivalent to 15 per cent of the company market, which was significantly higher than a decade before.

Underwriting performance and new competition

While individual insurers often complained of heavy motor underwriting losses, there was no published information on aggregate profitability until 1967, when the BIA published data on the global motor insurance market underwriting results. After a 'marginal loss' in 1967, losses rose to £9.6m (−1.6 per cent of premiums) in 1968 and soared further to £39.7m (−6.4 per cent) in 1969, with the bulk of this deficit coming from the highly competitive UK account.

Keen competition in the late 1960s and early 1970s brought the failure in quick succession of almost 20, mainly motor insurance, companies, some only recently formed, in some cases by dubious characters (see Table 5.4).

The failure in 1966 of *Fire Auto & Marine* and the arrest and conviction of its founder Dr Emil Savundra left around 280,000 motorists without insurance cover (see Chapter 12). Those failures persuaded the government that it needed to strengthen the regulation of insurance companies with the passage of Part II of the Companies Act, 1967. However, the tariff companies were constrained in responding to competition by the inflexibility of the motor tariff, which the Accident Offices' Association, under pressure from the ten leading tariff companies, abandoned on 31 December 1968.

The persistence of losses from 1969, together with little evidence that the industry had a viable plan to escape from the adverse trend, prompted Professor George Clayton, one of the industry's most acute observers, in 1971 to 'consider possible remedies for the decline in the fortunes of non-life business' (Clayton, 1971, p. 353). He blamed insurers for being victims of their own previous success in earlier periods, which contributed to London's historic reputation as a financial centre. This according to Clayton 'tended to breed complacency and conservatism'. He suggested that insurers had been 'ill-equipped to respond to challenges quickly enough administratively and psychologically' in the rapidly changing commercial scene. In motor business the pooling of companies' loss statistics by the Motor Risks Statistical

Table 5.4 Companies failing within 10 years of formation, 1967–74

Company	Year established	Year wound up
Bastion	1965	1974
Craven	1966	1968
Fire Auto & Marine	1963	1966
London & Home Counties	1966	1967
London & Midland	1966	1967
London & Wessex	1966	1967
Metropolitan General	1963	1971
Metropolitan & Northern Counties	1965	1967
Midland, Northern & Scottish	1961	1970
South Yorkshire	1964	1967
Translife	1966	1967
Transport Indemnity	1964	1971

Source: *Insurance Directory*, list of companies wound up.

Bureau, formed by the BIA in 1965 to foster sounder underwriting, was a preliminary step, but the data had not been adequately analysed and used in underwriting. *The Economist* commented in 1970 that 'results were disastrous not because marketing is a nonsense nor because price competition is bad but because underwriting was all wrong' (*The Economist*, 1970, p. xii).

Clayton also commented that British insurers had markedly higher administrative expenses than their US counterparts, as confirmed in a comparative study by stockbrokers (Plymen and Pullan, 1968, p. 12), who showed that UK composites' expense ratios were up to five percentage points higher during the 1960s than those of their US counterparts. However, one action that was designed to yield benefits in motor claims control was the establishment of the Motor Repair Research Centre in Thatcham in 1967 to work with vehicle manufacturers and repair specialists to control motor vehicle repair costs.

The industry faced a new crisis in 1971 when a BIA member company, the large, rapidly growing *Vehicle and General Insurance Company*, collapsed, leaving other companies to protect its million policyholders. The government acted promptly to further strengthen regulation by enacting the Insurance Companies Amendment Act, 1973 (see chapter 12).

The 1990s were another torrid decade for UK motor insurers. Only in two years were they able to achieve a small underwriting profit. Clearly the worst feature of the account was the persistently high claims ratio (the cost of claims as a percentage of premiums) which averaged 85 per cent for the 1990s. Only in two years out of ten did the claims ratio fall below 72 per cent.

By the 1980s the direct writers began their conquest of the domestic motor account, pioneered by *Direct Line*, which managed to achieve an operating ratio of 92 per cent, against the market average of 114 per cent for 1989–91. The company also achieved a 38 per cent growth, compared with the overall market premium growth of 8 per cent.

For eight years (1993–2000) commercial motor business averaged an underwriting loss of 11.7 per cent and personal motor a slightly lower average loss of 9.3 per cent, with the average claim for non-comprehensive private car policies increasing by 170 per cent (ABI, 2001, Table 58).

However, claims frequency – the percentage of policies filing a claim during the year – dropped during the 1990s, from 22.6 per cent to 18 per cent for comprehensive policies and even more steeply for non-comprehensive from 13.7 per cent to 8.9 per cent. Motor theft claims costs varied a great deal, but by 2000 they came down from the 1993 peak of £733m to £492m.

For much of the post-war period motor insurers, located in a rapidly growing market, grappled with two challenges: first, how to control claims escalation and secondly, how to run motor insurance with some 100 companies competing for market share, using different and quickly changing distribution channels and marketing strategies.

Table 5.5 ABI members' UK motor underwriting profit and loss 1960–2000

Period	No. of years in underwriting profit	No of years in underwriting loss	Average underwriting result for period
1960–1980	10	10	−2.0%
1981–1989	0	8	−7.2%
1990–2000	2	9	−12.0%
1960–2000	12	27	−5.9%

Source: ABI.

Some companies relaxed their efforts to lower their target claims ratios in pursuit of the investment income and gains to be made on their technical reserves, which could be worth as much as 10 per cent of premiums. However, the accounting implications were not reflected in most motor insurers' presentation of their results: only *Guardian Royal Exchange* and the *Royal* published in the motor insurance revenue account an 'insurance result' which included part of the investment earnings.

It is evident that a large number of companies writing UK motor business were not able to generate viable or profitable business in aggregate during the last four decades of the twentieth century, despite the considerable input of marketing, management and technological innovation exerted by them. As Table 5.5 shows, the results worsened during the latter part of the period.

It must be concluded that British motorists received good value for money by having not paid the full economic cost of motor insurance. Thus we must also assume that motor had been both reliant on investment income and partly subsidised from other lines of business. It is doubtful whether these trends can be continued in future years.

Distribution

1980–2000 was characterised by the struggle to switch distribution channels for motor insurance, involving massive experimentation and innovation. It resulted in the loss of market share for independent intermediaries (brokers) as well as insurance company-employed branch and other staff, and produced the ascendancy of direct distribution methods, which also included retailers, and affinity groups. There was a fluctuating trend, but Table 5.6, covering the early years of the twenty-first century, indicates the movements between the different trading channels.

Perhaps surprisingly, the bancassurance success of banks in the selling of life insurance products was, unlike in some European markets, not widely repeated with motor insurance in the UK (though HBOS was an exception with its *Esure* subsidiary). The multitude of outlets from which motor insurance could be purchased (including supermarkets, the AA, Saga, and the

Table 5.6 Motor insurance distribution channels (% of business sold)

	2001	2005
National brokers	16	14
Chain/telebrokers	17	9
Other brokers/intermediaries	17	13
Total independent intermediaries	50	36
Company agents:		
Company staff	6	2
Other co. agents	4	2
Total agents	10	4
Direct	33	46
Utilities, retailers and affinity groups	6	13
Banks, building societies	<1	1
TOTAL	100	100

Source: ABI.

Post Office), together with the different methods of sale including telephone or internet outlets, created a savagely competitive environment.

Switching between insurers

The drive for market share was evidenced in the increasing switching by policyholders from one insurer to another, which has been found to be highest in the UK and rising over time, both in motor and homeowners' policies (Pitney Bowes, 2008).

This rise was materially accelerated by the increasing popularity of internet-based comparison sites, the aggregators; of which 30 were known in 2007 (aggregators are discussed further in Chapter 14).

The pressure for switching insurers was also stimulated by the rapid rise in motor premiums, for both comprehensive and third party covers. Between 1994 and 2008 the average cost of third party cover increased nearly three times faster than the rate of inflation, while the cost of comprehensive cover more than doubled (see Table 5.7).

The drastic realignment of the market as a result of the competitive pressures can be seen by comparing the Top 10 companies in 1982 and 2004 listed in Table 5.8. The only company that had not been purchased or merged during those years was *Co-operative Insurance*.

Advertising spending by insurers on motor insurance surged. Data collected by Key Note in 2006 showed that motor insurers spent £95m on all media during the year, with five companies spending over £10m each (*Privilege* with £13.8m in the lead, followed by *Direct Line, AA, Norwich Union Direct* and *Churchill*) (Key Note, 2006, p. 44).

Table 5.7 Motor insurance price index 1994–2008

	1994	2008	% change over period
Comprehensive cover	£328.05	£681.93	107.9
Third party cover	£372.15	£838.50	125.3
CPI inflation	n.a.	n.a.	45.5

Source: AA British Insurance Premium Index, Jan. 2008 (changes calculated during the July 1994 to Jan. 2008 period).

Table 5.8 UK motor insurance top ten insurers

1982		2004	
General Accident	1	RBS	1
GRE	2	Aviva/NU	2
NU	3	Zurich FS	3
Royal	4	Fortis	4
CU	5	RSA	5
Eagle Star	6	Co-operative	6
Phoenix	7	Liverpool Victoria	7
Co-operative	8	HBOS (Esure)	8
Prudential	9	Allianz Cornhill	9
Cornhill	10	Saga Insurance Co.	10

Sources: 1982 – R. Carter and A. Godden, *The British Insurance Industry, A Statistical Review, 1983/84 Edition* (Brentford: Kluwer Publishing, 1983), 2004 – Association of British Insurers.

The motor market developed into a very complex and multifaceted business, with over 100 companies active, which are now stretched further by the ostensibly separate schemes run by retailers and affinity groups, although the insurance risk is carried by an authorised insurer. The market is further fragmented by specialist insurers for goods vehicles, bus and coach operators, company fleets, self-drive hire, taxis, uninsured loss recovery insurers, vintage cars, among others. In each of these specialisations there are several competitors, offering a generally sharp competitive climate.

It is difficult to assess what impact the aggregators – the internet sites offering information on premium rates and conditions that were remunerated by the number of hits the insurer achieves on these sites – will make. They may accelerate switching on renewal in all personal lines.

Household insurance

Insurance against fire risks was available for several hundred years for householders, but mostly purchased by the rich. Insurance against theft and burglary and all-risk policies, covering household valuables, became widely purchased from the 1920s. Over the years the risk coverage of insurance policies varied significantly. Property insurance policies had not covered flood damage until after the 1953 East Coast floods, when it began to be offered at an extra premium. Later, after the abandonment of the household tariff, the companies extended cover free of charge to include subsidence on domestic properties, a move that soon proved disastrously costly due to an unprecedented run of hot, dry summers producing massive claims. Insurers also began to offer cover for contents on a replacement basis and against accidental damage too.

Growth of business

No published premium data for the insurance of householders' property spending was available until the 1980s. A discussion paper prepared by the Office of Fair Trading in 1984 indicated that householder building and contents premiums amounted to around a third of insurance companies' fire and accident (non-motor) business (OFT, 1984, p. 20). That would place householders' premium income in 1980 at around £770m. By the twenty-first century the insurance of homes and their contents became the second largest source of UK premium income after motor. In 2007 gross premiums amounted to £6,480m (Table 5.9), an increase of 46 per cent in premiums over a ten year period.

Although no premium figures are collected for buildings and contents insurances separately, trade estimates indicate that the insurance of structures accounts for two-thirds of total premium income. Market analysts estimated that the number of buildings with insurance cover reached 15.2m in 1995, a rise of 8 per cent from 1990, and the corresponding figures for contents cover were 17.9m and 5 per cent (Mintel Financial, 1997, p. 30). Owner occupation increased throughout the second half of the twentieth century, with the proportion living in owner-occupied housing reaching 50 per cent by 1971 and 70 per cent by 2000 and the proportion in rented properties correspondingly falling. Premium income from building structures insurance increased faster than for contents insurance, given the rise in owner occupation and the rapid increase in house prices. The principal categories of claims (Table 5.10) showed wide fluctuation from year to year, although the drop in burglaries in the later years helped to reduce claims from this source, and subsidence costs have also been reduced substantially.

Table 5.9 Household and domestic risks. Gross UK premium income of ABI companies (£m)

1995	2000	2001	2002	2003	2004	2005	2007
4,511	4,494	4,858	4,979	5,597	5,790	6,073	6,480

Source: ABI (excluding Lloyd's and Home foreign).

Table 5.10 UK property gross claims for major perils – domestic insurance (£m)

Year	Theft	Fire	Weather	Domestic subsidence
1990	364	224	1565	506
2000	542	333	860	350
2007	454	458	1847	202

Source: ABI, 2001, p. 57.

Table 5.11 Home insurance price index 1994–2008

	1994	2008	% change
Buildings	£199.62	£208.51	4.5
Contents	£120.88	£128.57	6.6
Inflation	n.a.	n.a.	45.5

Source: AA British Insurance Premium Index, Jan. 2008. (Changes calculated during July 1994–April 2008 period).

Underwriting performance

In contrast to motor insurance premiums, the average cost of insuring home buildings and contents increased very slowly during the period, as shown in Table 5.11, partly due to the competitive nature of the market but also due to improving claims experience because of the increasing use of home security equipment and declining burglary rates.

Profitability and claims ratios and so profitability in household insurance were fluctuating, with claims ratios increasing from 55.9 per cent in 1953 to 65.2 per cent in 2000. As shown in Figure 5.3, underwriting results slipped into the red towards the end of this period (ABI Statistical Yearbook 2001, p. 56).

In response to a rapid rise in claims, insurers began to make increasing efforts to control claims costs more tightly. Despite the industry's efforts to explain that their actions were aimed at keeping down premium rates, such actions displeased many clients. The insurance industry's efforts during 2007–08 to strengthen future flood defence efforts and maintain insurability were also part of the long-term claims control drive.

Policy types

There was no general compulsion to purchase either buildings or contents cover, apart from mortgage lenders stipulating that properties be insured during the currency of the mortgage.

For contents cover during the 1970s most policies offered 'new for old' replacement policies as well as accidental damage, and a growing proportion of companies also adopted an index-linking system for premiums for

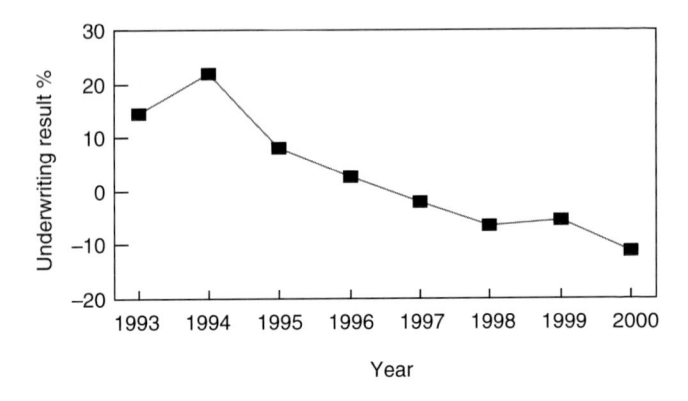

Figure 5.3 Underwriting profitability of homeowners' business 1993–2000
Source: ABI, 2001.

Table 5.12 Proportion of households buying buildings and contents cover

Year	% buying structure cover	% buying contents cover
1990	61.7	74.7
1995	61.1	74.1
1999	61.3	74.6

Source: Family Expenditure Survey, ABI, 2001.

the contents sum insured. This was reflected in the steep rise in average premiums paid during 1978–81, when claims for structures increased by an average 115 per cent compared with 106 per cent for contents claims costs. The all-items retail price index during this period rose by only 46 per cent.

Policy terms and conditions varied significantly between companies. Large differences were offered in policy excess, cover for cycles or freezer contents and other items such as under-insurance, exemptions and exclusions, etc. As a result 30 to 40 per cent of policyholders 'had no idea' of many details of their policy conditions according to the OFT's research (OFT, 1984, p. 30).

Penetration

Many householders did not purchase contents cover. The OFT found that in 1984 79 per cent of householders had a home contents policy but 18 per cent of the sample had neither contents nor buildings cover (OFT, 1982). According to the Policy Studies Institute (Policy Studies Institute, 1998, p. 20), those ratios were little changed in 1998 from those during the 1980s. Around a quarter of households still did not insure contents. Another survey of low-income consumers by the ABI (ABI, 2007b, p. 14) found that over a third of very low-income families had no cover at all (Table 5.12).

Accident and health

Private health insurance began in the nineteenth century with friendly societies and local sickness clubs, operating on a non-profit basis and which largely were absorbed into the National Health Service. The worldwide total of net premium income of UK insurers for accident and health insurance was £6,585m in 2006, two-thirds of which (£4,385m) was written on UK risks. Of the UK total, 74 per cent was health insurance and the remaining 26 per cent was accident business.

Private medical insurance (PMI)

Growth of business

Private health insurance, or private medical insurance (PMI), was purchased either by individuals or by employers as an employee benefit, to provide payment for treatment or hospital charges, doctors' and operating theatre fees, nursing costs and other treatment expenses. Another method of private health provision was a hospital cash plan to pay to the policyholder a fixed daily sum for time spent in hospital. After a modest rate of growth during the immediate post-war years, by 1980 PMI represented 5.8 per cent of home market total net non-life premiums. Rapid expansion during the next two decades raised its share to 13.7 per cent by 2006.

The two largest PMI insurers shortly after the end of World War II were the *Western Provident* (formed in 1939) and *British United Provident Association* (founded 1947). They began to grow rapidly after mergers with numerous smaller provident associations. After 1950, as the benefits of private health care in lieu of dependence upon the cash-constrained NHS were perceived, PMI became more appealing to individuals and employers. PMI premiums amounted to only £1.8m in 1955.

The post-war growth of this business was strongly influenced by both political and economic forces. After a pedestrian rate of growth during the 1960s, there was a spurt of expansion during the 1980s, thanks to the opening countrywide of private hospitals and a change in consumer tastes for a fashionable consumer product in the political climate of the time (Laing and Buisson, 2003, p. 44).

The success of the Labour government after 1997 in reducing NHS waiting lists and providing better patient choice in hospital reduced the incentive to buy PMI. Both company-paid schemes and individually purchased policies declined in popularity, with personal payment numbers dropping more steeply (see Figure 5.4). The total insured population declined by 11 per cent from close to 6.6m in the peak year of 2001 to 5.88m by 2006 (see Figure 5.4). At this level PMI penetration was 10.2 per cent of the UK population.

Increased premium rates pushed up PMI premium income despite the decline in the number of people covered. During 1996–2006

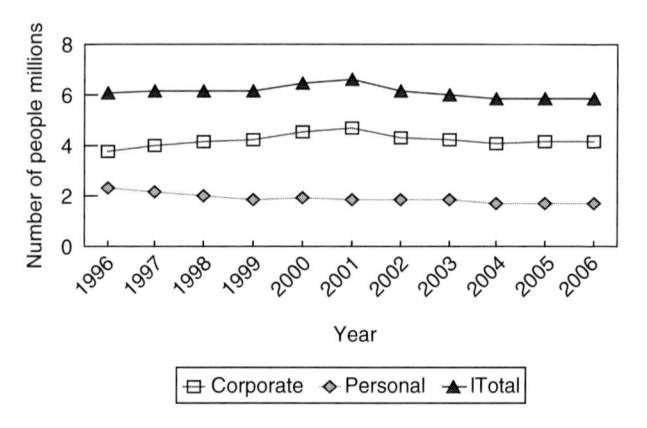

Figure 5.4 Number of people covered for PMI by corporate or personal payers, 1996–2006

Source: ABI (from 2002 figures exclude persons insured with Third Party Administration schemes).

corporate-financed premiums increased by 90 per cent while personally financed premiums rose by 62 per cent; during the same period the average annual cost for an individual subscriber rose from £373 in 1989 to £1,053 in 2000 (Laing and Buisson, 2002, p. 29).

After fluctuation during the 1970s and 1980s, by the early part of the twenty-first century the majority of the persons covered were members of company and other third party administrator schemes. During the five years to 2004, around 50 per cent of premiums came from scheme providers, buying cover for about two-thirds of the people insured.

Market analysts observed that PMI became a largely saturated market for individuals by the first decade of the twenty-first century. During 1990–2002 the proportion of the working population covered by PMI and non-insured schemes varied between 11 and 12 per cent of the population, of which the company-organised schemes accounted for 9 per cent (Laing & Buisson, 2001, p. 31).

After waves of consolidation the PMI market became highly concentrated, with *BUPA* remaining the dominant market leader with around 40 per cent share in 2005. In the second place was *AXA PPP* with 20.9 per cent and third *Norwich Union* with 8.0 per cent. The top five companies controlled 77.8 per cent of this sector.

Complaints

PMI, together with other products in the health range, including critical illness, came to the attention of the Office of Fair Trading during the 1990s because of complaints that some insurers were not offering sufficiently clear information in their policy wording or in the sales process. The industry faced the threat of coming under statutory regulation unless improvements were made (see Chapter 15). In response insurers and brokers made significant changes in product transparency and selling practices, assisted by an ABI Statement of Best Practice in 2006, which required the full explanation of exclusions and moratorium underwriting covering the exclusion of pre-existing conditions. The changes implemented clearly worked, as the number of complaints to the Financial Ombudsman Service declined steeply and in 2007 amounted to only 369, a fraction of the figure for earlier years (FOS, 2008, p. 23).

Hospital cash plans

Described alternatively as Health Cash Plans, the antecedents of this insurance line also go back to the nineteenth century Saturday Funds. It was estimated that these policies insured nearly 7 million lives in 2000 (Laing and Buisson, 2003, p. 37). The figures shown in Table 5.13 refer to contributors, but the number of persons covered is about twice the number shown, as policies often cover more than one person. Cash plans with premiums of £346m in 2000 were 186 per cent higher than in 1990. The claims ratio was usually in the 70 to 74 per cent range, leaving a surplus after marketing costs. The market leaders in the not-for-profit segment are *HSA Healthcare* and *Westfield* while in the commercial sector *RSA* is the largest insurer.

Accident insurances

Accident insurance figures are combined with the Accident and Health total. Personal Accident insurance policies undertake to pay either following injuries sustained in an accident and in some cases sickness too, a capital sum in respect of death, loss of eyes or limbs or permanent total disablement, or an income for a limited period for disablement. The

Table 5.13 Health cash plans

	No of contributors (m)	Contributory income (£m)
1950	3.50	2.0
1970	3.55	5.3
1980	3.10	23.1
1990	2.93	99.0
1995	2.91	234
2000	3.04	346
2005	2.81	440

Source: Laing and Buisson, 2007, p. 60.

business expanded slowly so that in 2006 it accounted for 26 per cent of total accident and health business against 40 per cent ten years before. There were many small friendly societies and collecting societies included in the 554 companies authorised to write accident business in 2000 (ABI, 2001, p. 76).

Income protection

Also described as Permanent Health Insurance, PHI policies pay a proportion of pre-disability income, typically 50–60 per cent, if the insured is unable to continue to work due to accident or sickness. However, as PHI benefits were tax-free, the insured often had little financial incentive to return to work and this drove up claims as well as premium rates. Consequently most policies were limited to a maximum benefit term of five years or less. According to ABI statistics, during the second half of the 1990s the number of new policies sold fluctuated between 117,000 and 152,000 a year, with premium income in the £51m–£57m range. Some of these policies were arranged by employers for their workforce – estimated to cover 1.67m persons in 2000, with an additional 1.37m individuals buying this type of policy for themselves. This left the majority of the working population without cover for income protection.

During the early 1990s PHI attracted many complaints (see Chapter 15).

Personal Accident

This cover could also be acquired either as an individual policy or as group scheme insurance. PA was a rider in many wider policies, such as motor or travel policies, and is seldom purchased as a stand-alone cover. Group personal accident schemes are frequently purchased by commercial firms for their employees, as an employee benefit, or by affinity groups, or sports organisations, such as cycling or flying clubs.

Dental insurance

This was a relatively new insurance product in the UK that was not available while dental treatment with NHS dentists was generally used by the majority of UK residents. After 1992, when NHS fees for dentists were cut and the national scheme lost 1,800 dentists, private dental insurance was introduced. The market leader was *Denplan*, a member of the *AXA Group*, with an 80 per cent market share. The estimated number of people covered was around 1.1m, with premiums around £235m a year in 2000 (A. Couchman, 2001, p. 32). In addition to individual dental covers, there were corporate schemes for employees, which some employers offered as an employee benefit. Some of the health cash policies also included dental care payments, usually up to an annual limit.

Payment Protection Insurance

Payment Protection Insurance (PPI), also referred to as creditor insurance or loan protection, is the largest pecuniary loss product used by the personal sector, being purchased mostly when consumers arrange unsecured lending deals (such as personal loans or when purchasing expensive items) with credit providers but also when a housing loan is secured on the property.

Creditor insurance policies were first introduced in 1972. The consumer credit boom during the 1990s pushed up premium income substantially to 2003, since when it has remained stable at around £2.2bn (see Table 5.14).

The OFT indicated that between 6.5m and 7.5m new policies are taken out each year and the number of live policies stood at around 20 million in 2005 (OFT, 2006, p. 62). It also estimated that total premium income was estimated to be £5.5bn in 2005 as compared with the £2,260m shown by the ABI in Table 5.14.

Complaints

There was growing concern about some aspects of PPI business since the mid-1990s, it becoming evident that it was not suitable for many borrowers. In response to consumer complaints the ABI outlined a statement of practice in October 1995 to cover PPI policies dealing with the construction of creditor policies as well as claims practices.

After continuing press and consumer criticism as well as attention from the Office of Fair Trading, the Financial Ombudsman Service, the FSA, and the Competition Commission (CC), it became evident that 'credit customers, appear to be overcharged by over £1.4bn a year with a return on equity of 499%' (CC, 2008, p. 27). One of the distributors made the point that 'the pricing of creditor insurance invariably acts as a cross-subsidy, enabling lower lending rates' (CC, 2008, p. 33). The CC report also found that the distributors' average margin was 68 per cent of gross written premiums. Insurers, however, came out without censure from the process, with the OFT quoting claims ratios for insuring unsecured loans of 22 per cent (OFT, 2006, p. 37).

Investigations and examination by the supervisory bodies of the participants' practicestook several years. The OFT expressed the view that this was 'a good regulatory example of the joint regulatory strategy working

Table 5.14 PPI gross premiums (£m)

1995	1969	1997	1998	1999	2000	2001	2002	2003	2004	2005	2006	2007
1,139	1,046	1,132	1,438	1,676	1,792	1,751	1,969	2,266	2,321	2,260	2,249	2,227

Source: ABI.

in practice. The consumer protection issues discovered are primarily for the FSA to act upon; therefore we have not addressed them in this report' (OFT, 2006, p. 29).

Further details on the regulatory dimension of mis-selling of PPI are set out in Chapter 15 on Regulation.

Travel insurance

Foreign travel was the main driver in the growth of travel insurance. ABTA, the travel agents' trade body, estimated that package holiday trips from the UK grew from 5m to 18.7m between 1979 and 2006, and the corresponding figures for total overseas departures were 15.4m and 68.5m. There was also a persistent rise in the number of companies offering travel policies, reflected in the *Post Magazine Insurance Directory*, which listed 76 in 2006, an increase of ten since 2001.

Figures collected by the ABI recorded that 21m travel policies were sold in 2006, 54 per cent of which were annual travel policies. Thus it was evident that, despite an abundant number of suppliers, a significant proportion of travellers were not induced by their travel agents to purchase insurance (Table 5.15).

The average claims ratio for travel insurance for 2004–06 was 55 per cent, with the majority of travel claims generated by cancellations and medical treatment.

There are two main types of cover. Travel policies may be 'bundled' with the rest of the travel arrangements made by the travel agent or airlines. According to the FSA, 23 per cent of travel policies are sold by travel agents, alongside holiday arrangements. However, these sales were not regulated in the same way as standalone travel policies. Alternatively, travellers purchase policies individually, having the options of buying a policy for one trip, or an annual policy covering several trips or a multi-trip cover.

The growing demand for travel insurance, besides leading to a rise in the number of suppliers, was also injecting strong price competition. Market research surveys found that the premium charged for a European trip dropped by 14.9 per cent between 2002 and 2007, with a corresponding decline for a US trip of 12.2 per cent (Key Note, 2007, p. 69).

The huge variety of even single trip covers can be judged from the fact that market research found 357 different types of policies on offer by a large

Table 5.15 Gross travel insurance premium (£m)

1996	1998	2000	2002	2004	2006
441	498	341	388	423	551

Source: ABI.

number of intermediaries. Lack of consumer loyalty by buyers led to vigorous advertising efforts by the market leaders. Other promotional methods include cross-selling, which with *Direct Line* involved offering free travel insurance to those who take out a home insurance product.

Complaints

In this intensely competitive atmosphere there were problems relating to the interpretation of policy conditions, which led to disputes regarding claims that generated increasing consumer dissatisfaction and complaints (see Chapter 15 for details) of the regulatory aspects of mis-selling of travel insurances, including the conclusions of the Treasury Select Committee that '... there is increasing concern from consumer groups and sections of the industry that the market is not working as well as it could' (House of Commons, 2007).

Pet insurance

The insurance of domestic pets developed from the older business of livestock insurance. The nature of pet insurance meant that it was to be taken out for the life of the pet. The policy normally paid for vet's fees or hospital treatment and boarding costs, advertising for lost animals, reward for finding, and third party liability, etc.

About 50 per cent of the 26.8m households in the UK have at least one pet and it is estimated that 18 to 22 per cent of pet-owning households buy insurance. The more popular uptake of pet insurance goes back to the 1960s, but its expansion as a mass product can be dated from the 1980s, with the sustained increase in discretionary spending. This was another insurance product that benefited from the growth in prosperity producing increased market penetration. The earliest figure located for pet market premium income related to 1995 at £75m with 959,000 policyholders (Defaqto, 1999, p. 38). While premiums fluctuated, the highest figure was reached in 2007 at £442m according to ABI statistics. Market leader in this class was *Allianz Cornhill* with 46 per cent share, followed by *UK Insurance* (13 per cent) and *RSA* (10 per cent) (Post Magazine, 15 Feb 2007).

Numerous smaller insurers and affinity groups also offer pet insurance, including the animal charity RSPCA (underwritten by *AXA*). The number of insurers offering these covers has been increasing; in the Insurance Directory there were 17 companies listed under this heading in 1999, and by 2007 their number had increased to 28.

Personal lines overview

Table 5.16 presents information on UK non-life personal lines for 1995–2007 collected by the ABI for the company market. It should be noted that the figures exclude Lloyd's, which writes a significant UK motor account,

Table 5.16 UK personal lines premium income 1995–2007 (Gross premiums, excluding home foreign and reinsurance)

Class	1995 £m	2007 £m	% increase
Private car			
Comprehensive	3,516	8,045	128.8
Non-comprehensive	1,030	1,128	9.5
Motorcycle	86	135	57.0
Accident and health	2,201	4,248	93.0
Creditor	1,139	2,227	95.9
Mortgage indemnity	128	42	−67.0
Pet	n.a.	442	n.a.
Travel	459	583	27.0
Household and domestic risks	4,591	6,480	41.1
Extended warranty	836	501	−40.0
Legal expenses	75	541	621.3
Total personal lines	14,031	24,648	75.7

although in other lines their share is not thought to be large. Overall, personal lines slightly increased their share of the domestic market, from 65 to 65.5 per cent over the period shown. The rapid expansion of comprehensive private car insurance, which has been the largest line since the 1950s, continues, with only a minority of vehicle users purchasing third party cover only.

6
Life Insurance

Life assurance falls into the two main branches of industrial life and ordinary life, and in this chapter we shall examine their respective performance during the second half of the twentieth century. Ordinary life includes pensions business. Total ordinary life premiums amounted to £203.9m in 1950; by 1964 they had reached £501m, of which overseas business accounted for 13.9 per cent of the total ordinary life premiums, and they grew substantially thereafter to reach 18 per cent by 2006.

Industrial life

Industrial life business premium income of £143m .in 1953 was almost two-fifths higher than pre-war, the business being transacted by either:

(a) a registered friendly society known as a collecting society; or
(b) an insurance company.

Collectively they were known as the 'offices', of which from the outset *Prudential* was the largest, a position it continued to retain until it ceased to write new business in January 1995. The number of companies transacting Industrial Life business remained fairly steady at around 90 until the mid-1980s, but the number of societies declined from 183 in 1924 to 107 in 1954 (Johnston and Murphy, 1956), mostly through mergers and acquisitions.

Almost from the outset the business attracted criticism particularly regarding its high expense ratio[1], the relatively poor returns for policyholders, and high lapse ratios that in the early 1950s averaged around one-fifth of new policy sales. One observer noted that the expense ratio moved 'from a level of only 40% in the early years to a peak of 47% in 1991' (Sutherland, 1994, p. 95). The steep rise in the expense ratio was exacerbated by the decline in the volume of business, leading to the loss of economies of scale.

Sydney Webb's report in the *New Statesman* in 1915 made several criticisms of the business, including its excessive expense ratios, which ultimately prompted the government to enact the Industrial Assurance Act, 1923, which provided that:

1. the Chief Registrar of Friendly Societies became the Industrial Assurance Commissioner, who was given certain statutory powers, including the right to receive annual returns from the offices;
2. industrial assurance became a separate class of business under the Assurance Companies Act, 1909, requiring a separate fund and revenue account; and
3. the conditions were specified under which surrender values and free paid-up policies were granted.

Sydney Webb had proposed the nationalisation of the business, a proposal that a conference of the National Amalgamated Union of Life Assurance Workers endorsed in 1926. However, the Labour Party could not obtain the general support of the unions (Wilson and Levy, 1937).

Industrial life business continued to grow during the 1920s and 1930s at around 3–4 per cent per annum, and by 1945 accounted for over 40 per cent of total UK life premiums, but fell thereafter to only 3 per cent in 1993 (ABI, 1993, Table 61). In the post-war years 1946–53 the companies and societies combined achieved an annual average growth of premiums of 4.4 per cent (Johnston and Murphy, 1956).

The government in 1948 enacted the Industrial Assurance and Friendly Societies Act, which gave offices the power to issue to persons policies for a payment of up to £30 on the death of a parent, step-parent or grandparent of the insured, but it did not limit the amount where an insurable interest could be shown to exist.

The nationalisation debate was reopened in 1949. Although nationalisation of the whole insurance industry was rejected by the TUC, it proposed the takeover of the 14 industrial–ordinary life offices. But in the face of fierce opposition from the industry, not least by the *Co-operative Insurance Society*, the plans for nationalisation and mutualisation eventually were quietly dropped.

The business continued to grow over the next 30 years, though more slowly than ordinary life, which benefited from the introduction of new products. The criticism of its expense ratios continued, and unfavourable comparisons were made of its returns with those under ordinary life policies and other forms of saving. Offices responded in various ways. Weekly doorstep collections became increasingly uneconomic and the offices sought to reduce administrative costs by moving from weekly to monthly collections of premiums. Also, with family incomes rising and with more holding bank accounts, agents were employed to sell ordinary life rather than industrial life policies where appropriate, and advancing technology also was used to cut administration costs. Nevertheless, it was a losing battle, as shown in Table 6.1. Surrender values of ordinary life policies written by the industrial life offices were apparently higher than those of the ordinary life offices (Derby, 1975).

Table 6.1 Growth of UK life insurance premiums (£m)

	ABI member companies' long-term premiums		
Year	Industrial life	Ordinary life	Total
1965	252	542	794
1970	312	746	1,058
1975	450	1,415	1,865
1980	884	5,480	6,364
1985	1,198	7,160	8,358
1990	1,371	12,858	14,229
1995	1,217	20,784	22,001
2000	754	38,770	39,524
2005	303	36,008	36,311
2006	247	41,503	41,750

Note: Ordinary life includes only life policies.
Sources: Life Offices Association. British Insurance Association.

Table 6.2 New industrial assurance business

Year	Number of policies (000s)	Yearly premiums (£m)
1983	3,553	236
1985	3,351	232
1987	2,844	241
1990	2,051	232
1995	671	92
1998	328	50
2000	95	17
2006	0	0

Source: Association of British Insurers.

In 1991 *Prudential* withdrew from general insurance apart from personal insurances marketed through its direct 'Home Service' sales force. Then in 1995 it closed all Home Service business, ceasing to write new industrial life business. Other companies followed its lead, and the number of collecting societies fell from 30 in 1990 to 14 in 1999 (ABI, 2001, Table 123), so that premium income rapidly declined (see Table 6.2). What had been a major class of business at the beginning of the twentieth century had almost ceased to exist by 2000. While no new policies were issued, there remained 4.1m policies in force still paying premiums in 2000.

Ordinary life insurance

Life insurance in the form of with-profits endowments had already become established as a form of investment for the middle classes well before 1939,

Table 6.3 Growth of UK ordinary long-term insurance premiums (£m)

Year	Premiums	Year	Premiums
1946	135	1983	9,980
1960	312	1990	32,196
1965	462	1995	46,082
1970	616	2000	127,754
1975	1,060	2006	144,803

Note: Includes all types of long-term insurance, including annuities and pensions.
Sources: Life Offices Association. British Insurance Association.

and sums assured under with-profits policies overtook without-profits in the early 1950s. Rising real incomes after 1950 enabled many families to purchase with mortgages their own houses, and life insurers developed a new type of insurance – mortgage protection policies, which in the event of the policyholder's premature death would repay the outstanding mortgage. With-profits endowment policies were used extensively for the same purpose. Building societies acted as agents in the sales of both mortgage and household insurances. Ordinary life business in the UK began to grow rapidly from the mid-1970s (see Table 6.3), with premiums in 1985 being over 20 times higher than in 1970.

New competition

The 1960s heralded the appearance of new competition for life offices and the development of new forms of life policies, with the entry to the market of companies marketing their products through tied direct sales forces, and the advent of linked-life policies stimulated by:

1. Restrictions on the direct sale of unit trusts leading to some unit trust management companies, including in 1961 *M & G* (which was acquired by *Prudential* in 1999) and *Save & Prosper*, to package unit trust units as life policies, which avoided the restriction on the sale of unit trusts.
2. Rising dissatisfaction with the returns under maturing life policies failing to match the investment gains on funds, whereas under unit-linked contracts the investment risk was passed to the policyholder, for whom the return was directly related to the performance of the underlying units, which was particularly attractive during a buoyant stock market. The with-profits life offices had responded with the declaration of occasional special bonuses that recognised realised capital appreciation, and of terminal bonuses (Carter, 1969), which unlike reversionary bonuses could be changed each year in the light of prevailing investment and competitive conditions. *Guardian, Norwich Union* and *Prudential* went further to

meet the new competition in 1967 and 1968 by establishing their own unit trusts (Carter, 1968a and 1969), and *Phoenix* acquired a 25 per cent interest in *Ebor Securities*. The attraction of unit-linked contracts for life insurers was that not only did the insurer carry no investment risk but such contracts needed less backing by solvency capital.

Unit-linked business was a success worldwide. However, in 1972 and 1974, stock market uncertainty provided a boost for sales of traditional endowment policies; and in following years as stock markets fluctuated so did sales of unit-linked policies. Table 6.4 and Figure 6.1 show new business performance over the last two decades of the century; unfortunately no data is available for earlier years. Between 1997 and 2000 unit-linked business

Table 6.4 New life business regular and single premiums

Year	Yearly premiums Non-linked	Yearly premiums Linked	Single premiums Non-linked	Single premiums Linked
1983	834	290	196	1,415
1987	964	525	92	5,268
1990	993	710	1,788	2,696
1993	866	644	3,443	6,588
1997	895	472	8,441	5,438
2000	798	416	15,397	9,221

Note: Linked premiums consist mainly of single premiums.
Source: Association of British Insurers (1983, Tables 62 and 63; 2001, Tables 12 and 13).

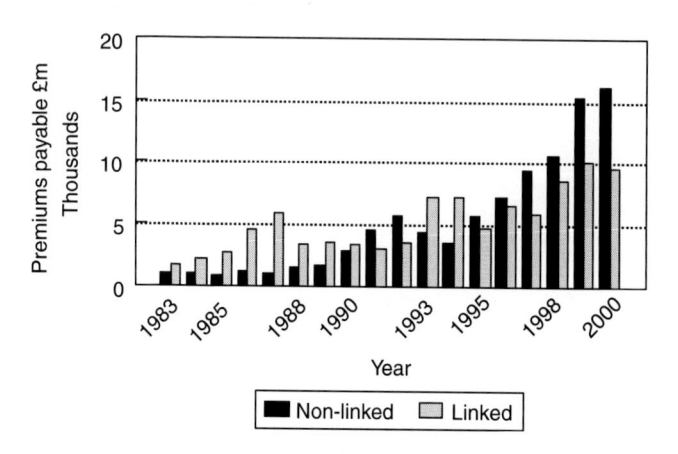

Figure 6.1 Premiums for new UK individual ordinary life business 1983–2000
Source: Association of British Insurers (1983, Tables 62 and 63; 2001, Tables 12 and 13).

grew much more rapidly than traditional business in Western Europe (Swiss Re, 2003). The entry to the market of a new insurer, *Abbey Life*, in 1961 using a direct sales force to sell unit-linked policies that enjoyed the tax advantages of conventional life policies was a major change for the market. Other new companies, including *Hambro Life*, using the same methods followed, and eventually established life offices and composites had to follow suit, in some cases establishing their own unit trusts and direct sales forces.

Life assurance had moved from protection to a savings product. For example, in 1968 *Commercial Union* introduced Guaranteed Investment Bonds, and an 'Equity Builder' product that provided an endowment allowing switching between benefits geared to an investment trust and an orthodox with-profit arrangement (Carter, 1969). Life offices in the 1970s were diversifying into new fields, including the acquisition of property companies, *Abbey Life* having launched a property bond, and later a managed fund.

The economy and tax concessions

Life business was badly affected by two economic crises in the 1970s:

1. The 1972 oil crisis produced a rapid rise in inflation (see Table 6.5) and rising interest rates. The chairman of *Prudential* in his 1972 annual report questioned the ability of with-profits policies to provide a hedge against inflation despite the introduction of terminal bonuses.
2. In the 1974 stock market crash equity prices fell by around a half, which hit life offices that since 1945 had moved more of their funds into equities, but fortunately 1975 brought a strong recovery in stock prices that strengthened solvency margins (see Table 6.5). Falling equity and property prices in 1974 also made unit-linked policies less attractive.

Table 6.5 Key economic indicators 1972–79

Year	Annual % change in retail price index	End of year bank rate	F.T. Actuaries 500 ordinary share index
1972	7.1	9.0	217.0
1973	9.2	13.0	150.0
1974	16.0	11.5	68.4
1975	24.2	11.25	165.1
1976	16.5	14.25	163.4
1977	15.8	7.0	231.1
1978	8.3	12.5	240.2
1979	13.4	17.0	246.3

Source: Mitchell, 1990, p. 225.

During the 1970s life assurance was being used increasingly as a tax-efficient form of savings, especially by the use of unit-linked contracts, which were being aggressively marketed by the new direct selling companies. Particularly it was being used as a means of mitigating Estate Duty, a practice that had first been encouraged by the Married Women's Property Act, 1882, but which the government sought in various Finance Acts to curb.

The government had for a hundred years encouraged saving through life assurance by granting to policyholders tax relief on premiums. Undoubtedly it had been an important selling point in competing against other forms of saving and a major stimulant to the growth of the life companies. The tax regime for life insurance began to change for the worse in the 1970s. The 1974 Budget made income bonds less attractive, though in 1983 Mortgage Interest Relief at Source (MIRAS) helped to increase substantially the mortgage-related regular premium business of most companies (Carter and Godden, 1985, p. 106). However, the rate of relief was reduced successively from 1988 until it was finally withdrawn by the Finance Act, 1999, though the life offices continued to benefit from the booming housing market.

Besides MIRAS the 1984 Budget made a more radical change. In an attempt to put all forms of saving on a level footing, the Finance Act, 1985, withdrew life assurance premium relief (LAPR) on all new 'qualifying policies' taken out after March 1984, so depriving life assurance of a long-standing tax advantage in competing for new business, and in 1988 LAPR was halved for existing qualifying policies.

The industry's performance over the remainder of the century was heavily influenced by legislation and economic conditions.

Lloyd's decided to enter the market for long-term assurances in 1971 with the formation of *Lloyd's Life*, but then sold it in 1985 to the *Royal*, though in 1994 there were still nine Lloyd's syndicates writing life insurance, which generated gross premiums of £46m in 2007. Since 1950 there had been a steady entry of new offices to the market, the numbers of new entrants peaking in the 1960s and 1970s, so that the number of companies writing life business rose from just over 100 in 1950 to over 250 in 1975 (Franklin and Woodhead, 1980). However, they found that UK market concentration ratios for the largest companies had changed little between 1960 and 1975. The following 30 years were fairly turbulent for UK life business, being affected by various exogenous factors. Bancassurance emerged as a force in the market; the *Association of British Insurers* estimated that in 1999 bancassurers had an 11.9 per cent share of the UK long-term insurance new regular premiums, a 9.4 per cent share of new regular premiums, and an 8.7 per cent share of new single premiums (ABI, 2001, Table 39).

As noted above, the introduction of MIRAS in 1983 led to a consequent increase in the demand for mortgage-related with-profits endowments, which in the late 1990s gave rise to complaints of mis-selling after bonuses were lower than expected so that policy maturity values would be less than needed to pay off the mortgage.

The spread of AIDS in the 1980s was a matter of major concern, leading Zurich Life, for example, to double term assurance rates for males. However, AIDS has proved to be less of a problem to UK life offices than was once thought.

The 1980s brought new products to the market. Critical illness and universal life (a form of flexible whole life insurance) policies were imported from abroad. Critical illness cover could be purchased either as a stand-alone product or as an extension to ordinary long-term policies. It proved popular, with the number of new stand-alone policies rising from 64,000 in 1995 to 113,000 in 1999, generating new regular premiums of £52m and £47m respectively (ABI, 2001, Table 34). Another innovation was long-term care insurance. The exclusions and definitions for both critical illness and long-term care insurances eventually attracted criticism, reducing demand, and the Association of British Insurers had to intervene by issuing guides for both insurers and the public.

Distribution

The key issue for life insurers of the 1980s was distribution. The Financial Services Act, 1986, polarised those persons who advise on or deal in 'investment' business into either independent intermediaries or tied representatives of just one company. It provoked insurers into attempting to secure their channels of distribution. Some had already established direct sales forces and others did the same, despite apparently supporting independent intermediaries by being members of the Campaign for Independent Financial Advisers (CAMIFA). There was a scramble to gain competitive advantage in competing for the expanding mortgage-related business by appointing building societies as tied agents (though some building societies chose independent financial adviser status, but along with some banks (notably Barclays) some later chose the multi-tie route). Prudential, Royal and General Accident went further by buying estate agency chains in 1988. In response to the increasing competition and regulatory burden, the Burns–Anderson Independent Network was formed in 1989 to provide services for independent intermediaries. Insurers also looked to gain access to bank customers, leading to the growth of 'bancassurance', which in 2006 accounted for almost a quarter of total sales of life products (Swiss Re, 2007), though its share of non-life insurance had reached only 16 per cent by 2007 (ABI, 2008). Nevertheless, independent financial advisers were quite successful in defending their market share, being better equipped to advise customers on the more complex long-term insurance products, such as individual pensions (57.8 per cent) and group regular business (67.7 per cent) (see Figures 6.2 and 6.3). As can be seen from Figures 6.2

Life Insurance 69

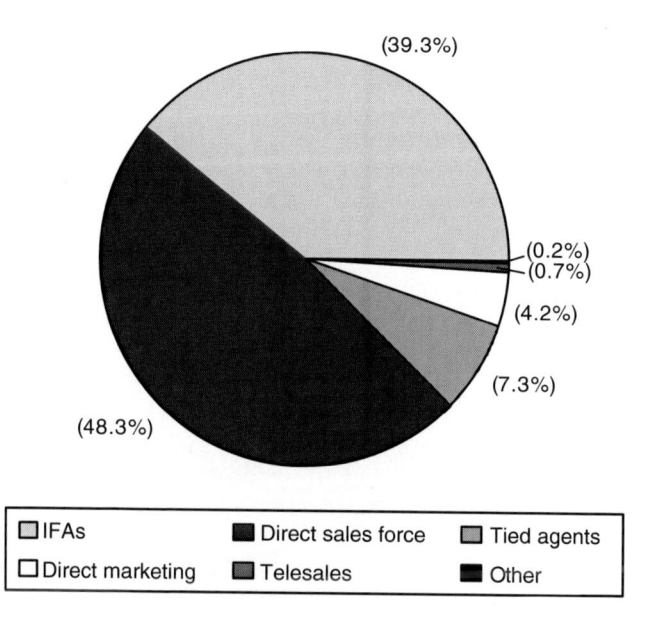

(39.3%)
(0.2%)
(0.7%)
(4.2%)
(7.3%)
(48.3%)

- ☐ IFAs
- ■ Direct sales force
- ☐ Tied agents
- ☐ Direct marketing
- ■ Telesales
- ■ Other

Figure 6.2 Sources of life new regular premiums (1999)
Source: Association of British Insurers, *Insurance Statistics Yearbook 1990–2000*, Table 37.

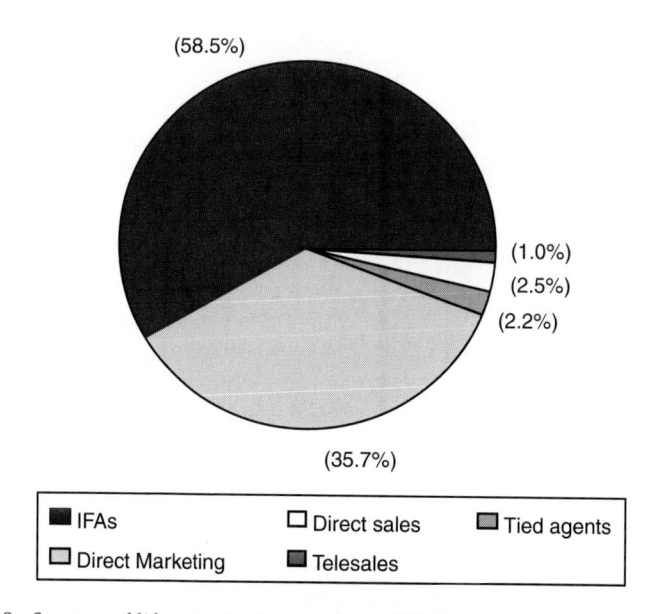

(58.5%)
(1.0%)
(2.5%)
(2.2%)
(35.7%)

- ■ IFAs
- ☐ Direct sales
- ☐ Tied agents
- ☐ Direct Marketing
- ■ Telesales

Figure 6.3 Sources of life new single premiums (1999)
Source: Association of British Insurers, *Insurance Statistics Yearbook 1990–2000*, Table 37.

and 6.3, direct sales forces were a major source of new business by the end of the century.

The industry was surprised in 1986 when the old-established mutual life office, the *United Kingdom Provident Institution*, needed to merge its business with the *Friends Provident*. Then in December 2000 another mutual office, *Equitable Life*, ran into financial difficulties, having guaranteed annuity options that became more onerous because of falling interest rates and improving mortality, forcing it to close for new business.

Bancassurance, defined as 'the joint effort of banks and insurers to provide insurance services to the bank's customer base' (Swiss Re, 2003), was one of the products of the 1990s financial services revolution, though in Britain bank managers had traditionally held insurance agencies. However, Barclays Bank had established *Barclays Life* in 1965 and Lloyds had established *Black Horse Life* (formerly *Beehive Life*) in 1973. The demutualisation of life offices gave banks and building societies an opportunity to acquire a life insurer, beginning with the acquisition of *Scottish Mutual* by *Abbey National plc* in 1992. Life offices too were seeking to diversify into a wider range of financial services. The *Commercial Union*, for example, in 1972 acquired *Mercantile Credit*; in 1974 the *Norwich General Trust*, which had been established by *Norwich Union*, bought the *Anglo-Portuguese Bank*, and in 1986 the *Legal & General* was granted deposit-taking facilities by the Bank of England. In 1998 *Standard Life* established *Standard Life Bank* and *Prudential* set up what was to become the largest online bank, *Egg*, which it sold in 2007. Retailers too were casting eyes on financial services; Marks & Spencer gained deposit-taking facilities in 1987, and some of the major supermarkets too diversified into financial services, including insurance.

1988 brought new concerns for the life industry when a study conducted by Peat Marwick McLintock for the Securities and Investments Board recommended the disclosure of expenses and charges on life policies.

The fall in interest rates in the 1990s forced life offices to reduce bonus rates, causing a crisis, as policyholders found that the expected maturity returns on with-profits policies were insufficient to cover outstanding mortgages. The response of some companies was to close their life funds; between 1995 and 2004 67 offices did so (O'Brien and Diacon, 2005). Apart from *Equitable Life*, the most notable was *Royal Sun Alliance*, which closed and transferred its life funds in 2004. Consequently the life market in 2005 was substantially different to what it had been in 1979 (see Table 6.7); like general insurance, there have been considerable changes in the ranking of companies writing long-term assurance.

The market was also transformed by a series of mergers (see Appendix 3) in the 1990s. Some companies active in acquiring companies were bancassurers that saw life business as attractive with the increasing demand for pension provision, or wished to acquire a company's marketing expertise. Medium-sized offices, on the other hand, were seeking to gain economies of scale.

Regulation

The regulation of life offices dated from the Life Assurance Companies Acts, 1870 and 1872, and subsequent Acts imposed more stringent regulations regarding the authorisation, accounting, fitness of controllers, owners and managers, and the winding-up of companies. First the Board of Trade and later the Department of Trade and Industry acted as supervisor until 1st December 2001, when responsibility for the regulation of insurers was transferred to the *Financial Services Authority (FSA)* under the terms of the Financial Services and Markets Act, 2000.

The Financial Services Act, 1986, extended regulation to cover the activities of persons and companies engaged in advising on, arranging deals in or managing 'investments', so extending beyond life offices to embrace intermediaries too by setting up a system of self-regulatory organisations (SROs) overseen by the *Securities and Investments Board (SIB)*. It specified that intermediaries should be either authorised as 'independent intermediaries' or act as tied company representatives. The *Financial Intermediaries, Managers, and Brokers Regulatory Authority (FIMBRA)* became responsible for the authorisation of independent intermediaries. The activities of life offices were covered by the *Investment Management Regulatory Organisation (IMRO)* and the *Life Assurance and Unit Trust Regulatory Organisation (LAUTRO)*. In December 2001 the FSA assumed responsibility for the regulation of insurers and intermediaries and the SROs were wound up. However, the FSA regulatory regime covered not only the authorisation of life offices but the marketing of their 'investment' products too.

Complaints regarding mis-selling

The Financial Services Act, 1986, opened the way for *LAUTRO* and later the FSA, the Financial Ombudsman Service (FOS) and other bodies to deal with customer complaints against companies. The *Insurance Ombudsman Bureau* had handled individual complaints since 1981, though the Ombudsman had only limited powers in relation to life insurance. A considerable rise in policyholder complaints was stimulated not only by the creation of the FOS and legal changes but also by increased consumer knowledge spurred on by newspaper columns in the daily and Sunday papers, as well as by non-governmental organisations, such as the Consumers' Association and the Citizens' Advice Bureau. Many complaints were made regarding the cover provided by critical illness insurances and the mis-selling of personal pensions and endowments, which became one of the major issues of the late 1990s.

The 1980s and 1990s had seen increased popularity in the selling of low-cost with-profits endowment mortgages, and by 2004 some 8.5m policies were in force with the expectation of policyholders that the policy proceeds on maturity would repay their loan. By the late 1990s with-profits bonus rates were falling because investment returns were below those expected by life companies. In 1999 ABI members began regular re-projection exercises, notifying policyholders whether their policies were on track to meet the payment target, though warning letters gave little specific information on what action policyholders should take. Consequently, the volume of complaints to the FOS increased massively, reaching 69,700 by 2004–05, a fivefold rise in two years.

The regulator began to warn about inadequate marketing processes and market observers noted that '... the commission earned on endowments was far greater than for setting up a capital repayment mortgage with decreasing term assurance' (Samuel, 2003, p. 3).

The FSA found that by 2005 2.2m households with endowment policies faced an average shortfall of £7,200 (FSA, 2005, p. 12) and that 50–60 per cent of policyholders believed that their policy was mis-sold. By the end of 2004 major firms handled more than 695,000 complaints and paid some £1.1bn in redress.

The FSA, having carried out extensive supervisory activity, moved to establish 'appropriate complaints handling standards and working with firms to ensure that any increase in complaints can be handled by them fairly effectively and promptly' (FSA, July 2005, p. 3).

470,000 households complained to their insurer or to the Financial Services Ombudsman and from 2000 to 2007 the FSA fined nine firms for 'procedural deficiencies resulting in "mis-selling," "defective complaints handling," and the "mishandling of complaints,"' with fines totalling £5.2m.

The Treasury Committee that examined the matter was highly critical of the industry's investment action, its slowness in responding to regulatory pressure to improve its sales process and its commission arrangements (Treasury, 2004). The Committee concluded 'that the best available evidence suggests that mortgage endowment policies are currently showing a shortfall, of around £40bn' (Treasury, p. 25).

As noted above, the other major source of complaints regarding mis-selling was personal pensions. Following the enactment of the Social Security Act, 1986, between 1988 and 1994 the insurance industry sold over 5m personal pension plans. The House of Commons Treasury Committee found 'that many of these involved bad advice given to customers by financial advisors and insurers' (Treasury Committee, 1998, vol. 2, para. 6). Personal pensions were inappropriately sold to persons who were already members of good occupational pension schemes (Treasury, 1998, vol. 1, p. xvi). The Committee concluded that the regulatory system had failed to prevent misselling because firms did not abide by the rules. Subsequently the FSA calculated the cost of redress to 645,000 priority victims of up to £1,164m in March 1998. Later payments to others, and administrative and compensation costs, were put in the £8.4bn–£11.1bn range by the FSA (Treasury, 1998, p. 25).

The other debacle of the 1990s was the announcement in January 1994 by *Equitable Life* that it planned to cut the size of the final bonuses payable to with-profits policyholders with guaranteed annuity rate policies that it had begun to market in 1957. The House of Lords ruled against that decision in December 2000, and in 2001 *Equitable* was forced to close to new business. A report by Lord Penrose published in 2004 concluded that, while the regulatory system had failed policyholders, the 'society was the author of its own misfortunes' (Essen, 2008). Despite strong lobbying by policyholders' action groups, the Treasury refused to accept responsibility and pay compensation. Then in July 2008 the Parliamentary Ombudsman concluded that there had been maladministration 'in the form of serial regulatory failure' and recommended that:

1. the public bodies should apologise, and
2. the government should establish and fund a compensation scheme to provide compensation to individuals who had been affected (Parliamentary Ombudsman, 2008). The government delayed until the autumn its response, which was not available at the time of writing.

Mutual life offices

A major change to the UK life market was the demise of mutual life companies that had included many of the country's largest, best-performing life offices. Comparison of the performance of mutual vis-à-vis the proprietary life offices was fraught with difficulties but there was evidence that mutuals as a group provided better returns to with-profits policyholders (Carter, 1993). Unable to raise extra funds from shareholders to enable them to compete more effectively and finance their expansion, many offices demutualised. The outcome was not what had been expected; instead it left them vulnerable to takeover, mainly by banks and building societies and overseas companies, most notably the following:

Company	*Acquiring company*
FS Assurance	Britannia Building Society* (1989)
London Life	Australian Mutual Provident* (1989)
Scottish Mutual	Abbey National plc (1991)
Scottish Equitable	AEGON (1994)
Clerical Medical & General	Halifax (1996)
Scottish Amicable	Prudential (1997)
Scottish Widows	Lloyds TSB (2000)
Scottish Life	Royal London Mutual* (2001)

*mutual organisations

Other mutual companies that were demutualised or taken over before 1991 were *Boots Life*, *Federation Mutual* and *Pioneer Mutual*. At 31 December

1991 there were 27 mutual life offices and two mutual composite companies authorised to transact long-term insurance business with a 46.9 per cent share of total UK ordinary life premiums. Almost all had disappeared as independent companies by the end of the century, leaving only ten mutuals remaining, including the *National Farmers Mutual*, *Royal London Mutual*, *Norwich Union Life* (demutualised in 2000), the *Wesleyan* and *Standard Life* (demutualised in 2006). However, in 2005, two former mutual companies, *Scottish Equitable* (acquired by AEGON in 1994) and *Scottish Widows* (acquired by Lloyds TSB in 2000), together with *Standard Life* and *Norwich Union* (as part of the *Aviva* group), still ranked among the top ten leading life offices (see Table 6.7). The dramatic decline in the market share of the mutuals is shown in Figure 6.4.

Not only mutual companies were involved in mergers: during the 15 years from 1985 to 2000 around 30 proprietary companies were taken over too as companies sought to achieve the size necessary to compete in a highly competitive market and foreign companies sought to enter or expand in the UK (see Table 6.6).

Foreign-controlled companies were estimated to have had a 21.1 per cent share of new UK long-term regular premiums and a 31.5 per cent share of new single premiums in 2000 (ABI, 2001, Table 39). The increase in the UK market share of foreign-controlled companies is shown in Figure 6.5.

The closure of life funds and mergers substantially changed the UK life insurance market, as shown by the changes in the leading companies given in Table 6.7, and the fall in the number of UK companies, including composites, authorised to transact life insurance from 244 in 1990 to 203 in 1999 (ABI, 2001, Table 121).

A feature of the market resulting from the closure of many life funds has been the emergence of a number of 'closed fund consolidators' (firms with a

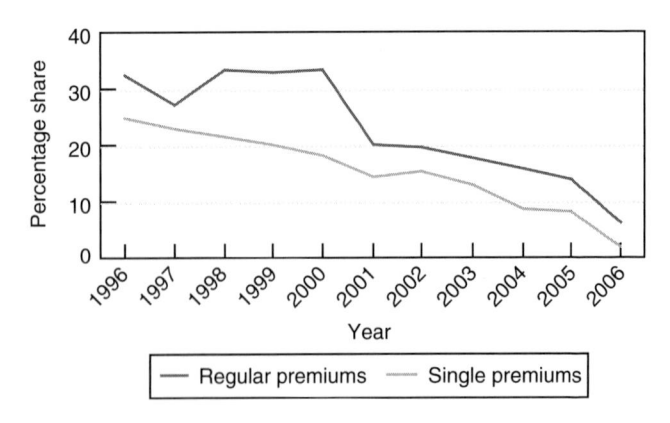

Figure 6.4 Mutual companies' share of new life business 1996–2006
Source: ABI.

Table 6.6 UK life funds acquired by foreign companies 1985–2000

Year	Acquired company	Acquiring company
1985	Albany Life Trident Life British National Life	Metropolitan Life (USA) New Zealand Insce Corp Citicorp (USA)
1986	Langham Life	Imperial Life of Canada
1987	Equity & Law	Compagnie du Midi (France)
1989	London Life Property Equity & Life Pearl	Australian Mutual Provident Eurolife (Gibraltar) Australian Mutual Provident
1992	Sun Life National Mutual Life	Union des Assurances de Paris Credit Suisse
1994	Scottish Equitable	AEGON (Netherlands)
1996	Colonial Mutual Life	Credit Suisse
1997	Threadneedle Pensions	Zurich Financial Services
1998	Eagle Star Allied Dunbar NPI	Zurich Financial Services Zurich Financial Services Australian Mutual Provident
1999	Guardian Royal Exchange	AXA (France)
2002	National Mutual Life	Swiss Re
2004	Crown Life Gresham Life	Swiss Re Swiss Re

Source: Post Magazine Insurance Directory, list of amalgamated companies (various issues) and Historical company changes, 2005.

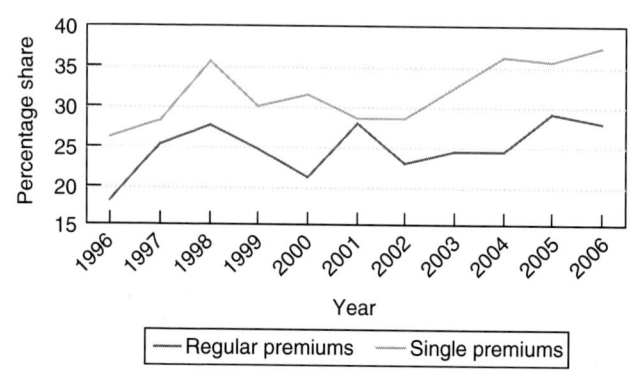

Figure 6.5 Foreign-controlled companies' share of UK life new premiums 1996–2006
Note: Covers new premiums for individual life and pensions business.
Source: Association of British Insurers.

Table 6.7 Leading companies' worldwide long-term insurance premiums

	1979 (£m)		2005 (£m)
Prudential	675.5	Prudential	15,028.0
Standard Life	558.7	Aviva	14,671.0
Legal & General	482.0	Schroder Hermes	9,550.8
Norwich Union	298.8	Managed Pension Funds	8,098.9
Commercial Union	290.5	UBS Global Asset Man	3,966.8
Scottish Equitable	287.0	Scottish Widows	3,669.6
Scottish Widows	252.7	Old Mutual	3,586.0
GRE	176.6	Standard Life	3,516.0
Eagle Star	175.4	Legal & General	3,344.0
Royal	139.3	Scottish Equitable	3,089.5
TOTAL	3,336.5		68,520.6

Sources: Carter, R.L. (1980) and *Insurance Company Performance 2007*, Centre for Risk and Insurance Studies, Nottingham University Business School, 2008.

strategy of acquiring closed funds), foremost of which have been *Resolution* and the *Pearl Group*, which at end 2004 owned 12 and seven closed firms respectively (O'Brien and Diacon, 2005).

Pensions business

Pensions business comprises both individual pensions and occupational pensions, though many of the latter are self-administered with life offices providing only group life cover to protect the fund against the mortality risk and investment and other management services. The performance of both types of business during the second half of the twentieth century was heavily influenced by a succession of government pension policies, plans and fiscal measures.

Individual pensions

The sale of deferred annuities to provide for retirement was boosted by the Income and Corporation Taxes Act, 1970, which introduced the so-called s.226 pensions that enabled policyholders to claim tax relief on contributions. Although they became available to any individual who had earnings but no pension arrangement, they were mainly purchased by the self-employed.

In response to criticisms regarding the inadequacy of the basic State pension the government enacted the Social Security Pensions Act, 1975, introducing a second-tier State Earnings Related Pension Scheme (SERPS), requiring all employees to be covered, which became operative in 1978. However, a large boost for individual pensions came when the government sought to shift some of the burden of pension provision to the private sector; the Social Security Act, 1986, replaced the old Section 226 retirement annuities with personal pension plans, which could be taken out by any working person who was not a member of an occupational pension scheme. The Act also (i) reduced the SERPS benefits, and (ii) allowed employees to contract out of SERPS and transfer from occupational pension schemes in favour of personal pensions. This produced a frenzy of selling, and in many instances mis-selling, of personal pensions. The Finance Act, 1987, allowed employees to purchase Free Standing Additional Voluntary Contributions (FSAVCs). Figure 6.6 does not show the full picture because it shows only regular premium income whereas a substantial amount of personal pensions business was single premiums. Nevertheless it clearly shows the surge in business after 1987.

New business premiums rose from £1,014m in 1985 to £1,628m in 1988 and to £2,844 in 1989. Eventually the aggressive selling brought accusations of mis-selling, which the regulators failed to rectify until the mid-1990s, when they required offices to review past sales and pay compensation to affected policyholders with a huge cost to insurers. That, together with the *Equitable Life*'s financial difficulties of December 2000, badly undermined public confidence so that new individual pensions premiums fell from £2,233m in 2002 to £1,859m in 2003, though sales later recovered.

1986 also brought new competition for life offices when building societies were allowed to offer personal pensions, though they failed to make

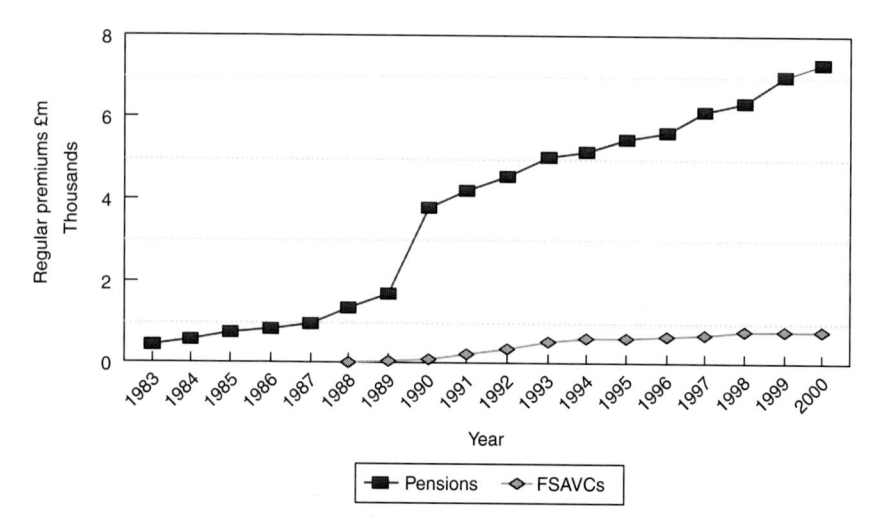

Figure 6.6 Regular premiums for individual and personal pensions
Note: 1983–1990 relates to individual pensions, 1990–2000 relates to personal pensions.
Source: Association of British Insurers.

much impact. The 'Big Bang' (the introduction of dual capacity on the Stock Exchange) stimulated further changes in financial markets.

The Finance Act, 2000, introduced stakeholder pensions that are low-cost, simple contracts. Many offices, however, were reluctant to market them, seeing that they offered poor profitability prospects.

Increasing longevity became a growing problem for the providers of pensions contracts. When there became evidence of differing mortality rates in different parts of the country, the *Prudential* in 2008, followed by other large life companies, including *Legal & General* and *Norwich Union*, began to use proposers' postcodes, which give an indication of their likely lifestyles and life expectancies, as a rating factor for annuities (Financial Times, 2008).

Occupational pensions

Life offices first became involved in group pensions business in the late nineteenth century with the sale of endowment assurances and annuities to companies as part of their pensions arrangements, but there was a marked change in strategy when in 1927 the Metropolitan Life of New York entered the UK market to offer group life and pensions contracts. Within a few months several British companies began to compete for the business too, and Legal and General became dominant in the 1930s (Hannah, 1986). However, the Finance Act, 1921, encouraged companies to set up their own self-administered schemes with help from consulting actuaries. Only the largest organisations possessed the resources and expertise to manage a scheme, so that smaller firms turned to life offices to provide insured schemes and life offices offered the self-administered schemes the opportunity to insure the mortality risk under group life insurances, and also buy in actuarial and administrative services.

The changing politico-social environment after 1945 brought an expansion of occupational pension schemes by extending membership beyond clerical and other staff to blue-collar workers.

The most important influences affecting occupational pension schemes in the second half of the century, and the success of life offices, were:

1. The economy;
2. Government pensions policies and plans; and
3. Increasing longevity.

The Finance Act, 1956, benefited life insurers by limiting the tax on annuities to only the interest element, enabling insurers to cut premiums for group pensions. Next the Finance Act, 1970, regularised the position regarding the payment of tax-free lump sums, which stimulated the growth of pension schemes so that by the 1970s pension funds accounted for a substantial share of total savings.

The acknowledged inadequacy of the basic State pension became a major political issue after the 1950s, with both Labour and Conservative governments proposing various schemes. The Social Security Act 1973 forced pension schemes to preserve pensions after five years of contributions. However, it was not until 1975 that Mrs Castle implemented the basic proposals of the 1969 Crossman plan by introducing an earnings-related pensions scheme (SERPS) in the Social Security Act, 1975. The requirements set for contracting out made occupational pension funds improve pension benefits, albeit at higher cost.

The introduction of SERPS and the provisions for companies to contract out resulted in most large pension schemes deciding to contract out, but many smaller and medium-sized companies did not do so. The Social Security Act, 1986, also allowed employees to elect to effect personal pensions rather than being members of their employers' occupational pension scheme, thereby reducing the size of the pension funds.

The difficult economic conditions in the early 1990s, and the fall in interest rates and increasing longevity, profoundly affected pension funds. Some funds failed while others were closed to new entrants or were changed to defined benefit schemes that shifted the investment and longevity risk to individuals. Figure 6.7 shows the performance of occupational pensions business written by life offices; unfortunately premiums for managed fund business are not available for earlier years. The shift to defined contribution schemes has been marked by a reduction in contribution levels by employers.

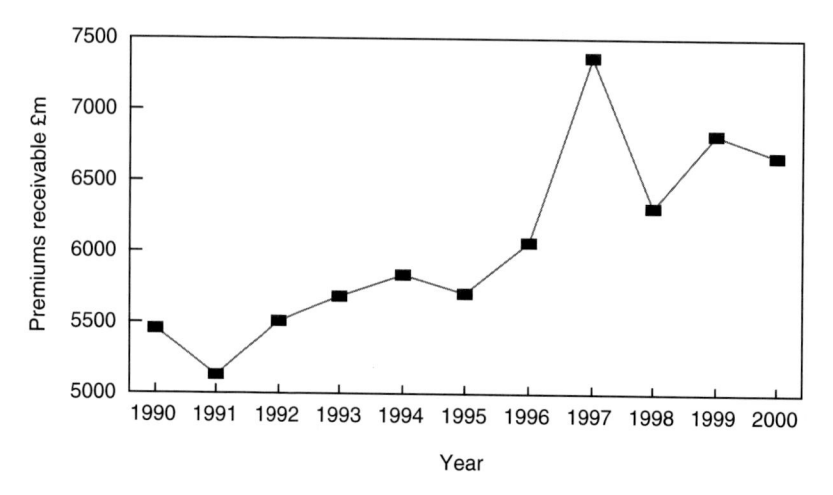

Figure 6.7 Premiums receivable for occupational pensions and group life schemes
Source: Association of British Insurers.

Overseas business

As noted in Chapter 11, companies were forced to leave many countries in the 1960s and 1970s, so that by 1980 overseas business accounted for only 14.3 per cent of ABI member companies' ordinary long-term net premium income. However, the major UK companies were looking to obtain a share of the huge United States life market[2], through the acquisition of American companies, notably:

- Legal & General acquired *Banner Life* in 1982 and in 1989 *William Penn Life of New York*;
- Prudential acquired *Jackson Life* in 1986; *and*
- Royal acquired *Maccabees Life Insce Co* in 1988;
- UK life offices continued to look to the United States as a source of business, and *Aviva* acquired *AmerUS Group* in 2006.

The growth and composition of UK life insurers' overseas business from 1996 to 2006 is given in Tables 6.8 and 6.9, though it should be appreciated that the figures are affected not just by the growth of business but by exchange rate movements too.

The opportunity for expansion overseas came when in the mid-1970s some countries began to relax their restrictions on foreign insurers, but it

Table 6.8 ABI member companies' long-term premiums

	UK (£m)	USA (£m)	EU (£m)	Rest of world (£m)	Total (£m)
1980	6,035	n.a.	537	323	6,895
1985	13,715	142	931	1,268	16,056
1990	32,196	1,828	1,995	2,774	38,793
1995	46,082	2,798	4,654	3,862	57,396
2000	127,754	5,596	7,993	6,880	148,223
2006	144,803	7,187	12,536	9,572	174,098

Source: Association of British Insurers.

Table 6.9 Overseas net long-term insurance premiums 1996–2006

Year	Channel Islands	EU	Rest of Europe	USA	Canada	Australia and New Zealand	China	Other Asia	Other	Total
1996	492	5,734	100	3,813	925	1,490		271	1,156	13,981
2000	1,789	7,993	788	5,596	1,558	545	90	1,406	702	20,467
2003	665	11,188	823	4,922	1,257	356	691	1,931	591	22,424
2006	2,742	12,536	81	7,187	2,067	67	1,242	3,005	367	29,295

Source: Association of British Insurers.

was not until the end of the multilateral negotiations leading in 1993 to the General Agreement on Trade in Services and the creation of the World Trade Organisation that an increasing number of countries opened up their markets. Given the highly developed, competitive market at home some UK life offices and Lloyd's were quick to seize the opportunities presented to re-enter overseas markets, particularly in Asia and the Far East. The three leading UK life offices moved into China and the Far East as follows:

1994 – *Prudential* established *Prudential Corporation Asia* with headquarters in Hong Kong and by 2007 obtained 45 per cent of its new business from Asia, including Vietnam where it is the market leader (compared with 31 per cent from the UK).
1999 – *Standard Life* established *Standard Life Asia* in Hong Kong. In 2000 it entered into an Indian joint venture and did the same in China in 2003. *Aviva* too established a strong presence in Asia, including the new rapidly industrialising India and China.

The results of those moves can be seen in Table 6.9, which shows the rapid increase in business from China and Asia since 2000, which seems destined to continue to increase in importance for UK life offices for the foreseeable future. Regarding 2007, Swiss Re observed that 'Life insurance premiums in China grew strongly (+19%) in 2007, versus 8.7% in 2006...In India the growth of life business...slowed down to a more sustainable rate of 14.2% in 2007. Private sector companies continued to gain market share with new products and distribution channels...Premiums in Vietnam also increased sharply in 2007, its first year of WTO membership' (Swiss Re, 2008, p. 23).

The creation of a single European market enabled UK companies to expand their business in Europe, though some of the growth for the EU and the decline in premiums from the rest of Europe shown in Table 6.9 can be attributed to the enlargement of the EU, but the EU became the largest regional source of business for UK companies' overseas branches and subsidiaries.

Business in the USA and Canada grew substantially too from the mid-1980s, following the acquisition of American companies.

African premiums fell each year to an insignificant £21m in 2006, but the most significant reduction in business was from Australasia.

Overall overseas premium income grew at an annual average rate of 7.5 per cent between 1996 and 2006 (see Table 6.8), so that by 2000 overseas business accounted for almost 14 per cent of the companies' total ordinary long-term premium income, with the EU and the United States respectively accounting for 39 per cent and 27 per cent of the total overseas business. Since 2000 overseas business has continued to grow in importance to reach 18 per cent of total worldwide long-term premiums.

7
Commercial Insurances

Whereas Chapter 5 dealt with personal insurances, this chapter will cover the developments in commercial and industrial insurance. Commercial insurance, excluding reinsurance and marine, aviation and transport (MAT) insurance with UK premiums of around £13.3bn in 2007 (see Appendix 4), generates only about one-half of the premiums for personal insurances, but the complexity of many of the risks insured requires considerable underwriting expertise and underwriting capacity. The continuing unprofitability of its commercial lines accounts persuaded the *Prudential* in 1991 to limit its general insurance business to personal non-life insurances, and withdraw from all commercial lines.

The Great Train Robbery in 1963, involving a claim of £2.6m, was the most high-profile crime of the decade, but was just a part of a general rise in crime, including theft of and from vehicles, burglary, the theft of cash in transit and arson, which resulted in rising claims for commercial insurers, and later insurance fraud was rising too. Another feature of the 1990s was the rise of the 'compensation culture', which impacted on liability insurers.

Property (fire) insurance

Fire insurance had been the largest class of business until the 1930s, when it was overtaken by motor insurance, of which commercial vehicles and fleets formed an important component. Then the growth in the post-war economy (industrial production rose by 20 per cent between 1946 and 1954), and in the size of industrial plants in many industries, resulted in a growth in demand for commercial and industrial property insurances. On the other hand, companies were appointing insurance managers, who, with brokers, were becoming more demanding in what they expected of insurers. Separate sums insured had always been required for each separate fire risk, but in the 1950s there was a demand for (a) 'blanket' insurances covering all property in one sum insured, starting first with 'stock floaters' covering stock at different locations and then spreading to the insurance of buildings and of machinery and other contents too, and (b) cover based on the cost of reinstating lost and damaged property, though some doubted the wisdom of insurers changing from an indemnity to a reinstatement basis (Carter, 1962). The 1953 East Coast floods stimulated a demand for cover against an increasing range of perils. This was putting pressure on the continuance of the fire tariffs, which tended to be inflexible in their operation. Insurers were also incurring increasingly large industrial fire losses: the growth of industrial plants and the more complex, expensive machinery and plant installed in them resulted in several fires, each costing over £1 million, in the 1950s. Limited market capacity to handle very large risks was forcing the tariff companies to relax the 65/35 per cent rule that had precluded tariff companies from participating in co-insured risks unless they held at least a 65 per cent share. Furthermore the adverse underwriting results were forcing all sections of the market, including Lloyd's, to draw closer together.

By the 1980s it had become the practice in some markets for major industrial undertakings to arrange for 'industrial all risks' policies to provide cover for physical loss or damage and/or consequential loss following thereon. UK insurers faced a demand for such covers when arranging international insurance programmes for very large industrial or commercial organisations and conglomerates.

The minimum price agreements (the tariffs)

By the mid-1960s insurers were complaining about soaring fire losses, which reached new records. The total number of fires rose from around 350,000 in the early 1980s to 467,000 in 1990; and the proportion attributed to malicious or doubtful ignition rose from under 15 per cent to over 20 per cent. Consequently fire insurance deteriorated from a profit to a substantial underwriting loss in 1962.

The tariffs had for long sustained a degree of market stability but lacked flexibility in that premium rates could not be changed fast enough to meet changing risk factors. Consequently the tariffs were already coming under pressure in the 1960s. Since 1945 one new tariff company and 28 independents had entered the fire market, of which 11 had started in 1960 or later (Monopolies Commission, 1972). The *General Accident*'s takeover of the tariff company *Yorkshire* in 1967 further weakened support for the tariffs; *Yorkshire* itself said that in due course it would abandon its tariff structure, following the example of the *Insurance Company of North America*, which some years earlier had withdrawn from the British tariff associations to successfully pursue an independent course (Carter, 1967). In 1968 there were 105 companies writing UK direct fire insurance, of which 29 were tariff and 76 independent (25 were foreign companies), plus Lloyd's, generating a total premium income of £164.6m, their respective market shares being tariff companies 63 per cent, independents 30 per cent, Lloyd's 7 per cent. The size distribution of the companies was as shown in Table 7.1, and the

Table 7.1 The UK direct fire insurance market 1968

Premium income	Tariff companies No. of companies	%[a]	Independent companies No. of companies	%[a]
Less than £100k	15	0.6	44	0.9
£100k–1m	3	0.6	22	5
£1–2m	2	2	4	4
£2–5m	2	4	4	9
£5–10m	3	11	1	5
Over £10m	4	49	1	9

Note: [a] % of total company premium income.
Source: Monopolies Commission, 1972.

Table 7.2 Net written UK fire premiums

	£m
1956	55*
1960	70*
1965	112*
1985	2,860
1990	5,462
1995	6,239
2000	6,910

Note: *relates only to ABI members but includes Lloyd's from 1985.
Source: Association of British Insurers.

growth of UK fire premium income, which includes household insurances, is shown in Table 7.2.

The market power of the tariff companies was demonstrated in December 1963, when mounting fire losses led to the FOC arbitrarily imposing a 15 per cent surcharge on fire premium rates for most industrial and commercial premises, despite being vigorously opposed by major industrial groups. Confronted by the countervailing power of major buyers, the FOC modified the surcharge to selective percentage adjustments that recognised the benefits of fire protection. The government responded in 1968 by referring the supply of fire insurance to the Monopolies Commission. The FOC voluntarily abandoned the domestic fire tariff as from 1 January 1971, leading to keener competition.

The Commission's report, published in August 1972, criticised the FOC's Co-insurance Agreement with its 65/35 per cent rule as a restrictive practice that constrained independents from competing by precluding tariff companies from participating in the large co-insured risks unless at least

65 per cent was placed with tariff companies. However, the growing size of the leading non-tariff companies and new overseas entrants meant that they could handle increasingly larger risks without tariff support. Nevertheless, some support for the commercial and industrial tariffs came for various reasons from some independent insurers, who, economic theory predicted, could take advantage, at least for the smaller trade risks, of a substantial increase in demand by offering a small reduction in price (Leftwich, 1966, ch. 11), though the FOC argued that the independents could provide cover for 95 per cent of all commercial and industrial risks without the support of tariff companies.

The independents offered some support for the tariffs as providing a desirable measure of market stability, and some said that they used the tariff premium rates as a basis for their own rating. One independent was quoted as saying:

> On the whole it [the tariff system] has proved beneficial because as the result of its influence a reliable, stable and financially secure market has developed, which is of inestimable value to the economic well-being of the community'. (Monopolies Commission, 1972, para. 242)

The independents also praised the FOC for encouraging fire prevention.

Nevertheless, when the Commission reported in 1972 it found that the commercial tariffs operated against the public interest, and though

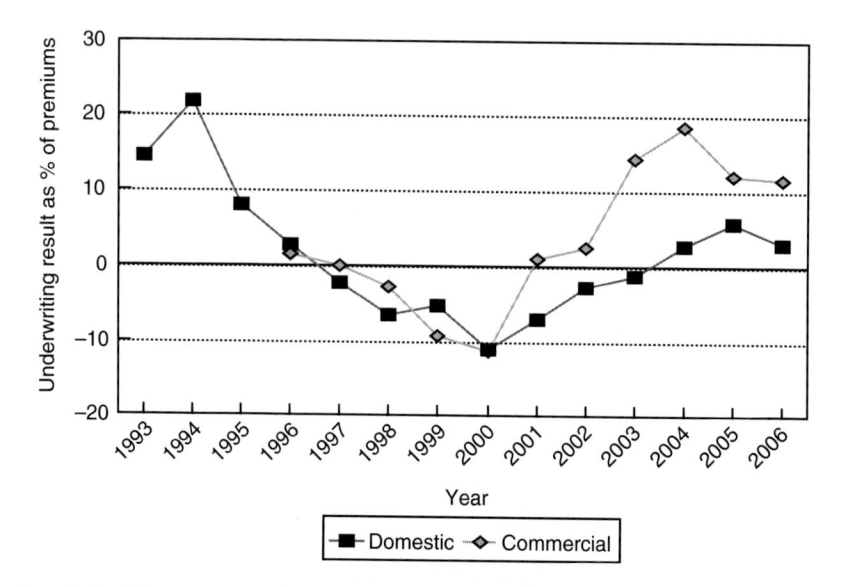

Figure 7.1 UK property underwriting results 1993–2006
Source: Association of British Insurers, 'UK Property underwriting ratios'.

it recommended their termination they were kept in force until 1985. However, by 1972 they had already become less effective as large buyers exercised their power to obtain rating and other concessions.

1974 was a bad year for UK fire insurers with the disastrous fire and explosion at the Flixborough chemical plant. The five leading UK companies reported that the Flixborough explosion cost them a total of £8.5 million after reinsurance recoveries, of which the *Guardian Royal Exchange* alone paid £2.8 million (Carter, 1975).[1] Underwriters had begun to base their underwriting decisions, including the amounts to be retained before reinsurance, on their estimates of Estimated Maximum Losses (EMLs). They were forced to reassess those estimates; when compared with an EML of 20 per cent the actual loss at Flixborough amounted to 80 per cent of the total value at risk (Hickmott, 1977). The performance of UK property insurance from 1993–2000 is shown in Figure 7.1. Fire business accounts for the bulk of property premiums. As can be seen, both domestic and commercial business incurred underwriting losses from 1998 to 2000.

'Consequential loss' (CL) insurance

This very successful innovative product, later called 'business interruption' insurance, to cover loss of profits and increases in the cost of working following a fire, had been written before the World War I, and the Fire Offices Committee had formed the Consequential Loss Committee in 1909 to operate a tariff. Interest in and demand for consequential loss insurance grew during the 1950s and encouraged the Corporation of Insurance Brokers to form the *Consequential Loss Society* in 1954 to provide a forum for discussion and learning.

Alongside the demand for CL insurance there developed engineering interruption insurance to provide cover for business interruption losses caused by accidents to machinery and the failure of public power supplies.

UK companies' gross written UK premiums for consequential loss peaked at £559m in 2003 but then fell back to £485m in 2005 (Association of British Insurers, 2001).

Commercial motor

Commercial motor business includes fleets and other, mainly small trade, vehicles. The first insurance for commercial vehicles was written in 1906, and by 1914 there were 82,000 goods vehicles licensed in Britain. That number quickly rose after 1954 (see Figure 7.2).

By 2000 the number of licensed commercial vehicles (excluding light goods vehicles) had risen to 418,000, and in 2000 the total premiums of £2,324m accounted for one-quarter of the companies' total UK motor gross written premiums. Premiums in 1980 for vehicle fleets of £225m were

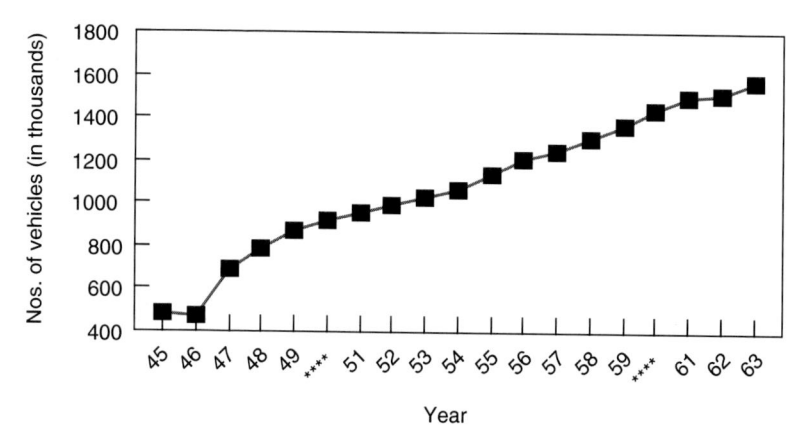

Figure 7.2 Commercial vehicles licensed 1945–63
Source: *Annual Abstract of Statistics* (various editions).

Table 7.3 UK motor revenue account (£m)

	Net written premiums		Underwriting result	
Year	Commercial	Domestic	Commercial	Domestic
1993	1,725	4,699	−45	136
1994	1,657	4,714	34	263
1995	1,544	4,378	−42	−40
1996	1,719	4,178	−174	−522
1997	1,691	4,402	−284	−878
1998	1,842	4,669	−519	−959
1999	1,944	5,099	−434	−876
2000	2,157	5,490	−278	−638

Source: Association of British Insurers, 2001, extracted from Table 56.

estimated to have accounted for around 14 per cent of the total UK company motor market (CII, 1981). The motor tariff was abandoned at the end of 1968, so, like private motor insurance, competition increased for commercial motor business too. As shown by Table 7.3, the business consistently incurred underwriting losses in the 1990s.

Credit insurance

As noted in Chapter 1, credit insurance commenced at the end of the nineteenth century. During the second half of the twentieth century there was some consolidation among credit insurers offering cover to multinational groups. However, some general insurers entered the market to start writing a credit account.

Credit risks fall into two categories – (i) buyer default, and (ii) political risks for exports. There was a small market, including Lloyd's and some international insurers, prepared to cover both risks, but in the UK the main supplier of political risk insurance was the government's *Export Credits Guarantee Department (ECGD)*. That situation changed in 1991 when *ECGD's Insurance Service Group*, which was responsible for credit insurance for exports sold on short-term credit terms, was privatised and sold to *NCM Credit*. At the same time ECGD introduced a Surplus Reinsurance Agreement to provide reinsurance to private sector providers of short-term trade credit insurance (see chapter 16 regarding responses to the 2008 financial crisis).

The UK's leading credit insurer *Trade Indemnity* was acquired in 1998 by *Groupe Euler* and its name was changed from *Euler Trade Indemnity* to *Euler Hermes UK* when bought by *Allianz*. In 2000 the aggregate gross written premiums for trade credit insurance was £319.1m, almost a fifth more than in 1995 (ABI, 2001, Table 82), and it increased to £323.4m in 2006.

Marine insurance

Marine insurance covers hull, cargo, liability, and war risks and offshore oil-rigs.

In 1945 the companies' premium income was £22.6m, increasing to £1,084m in 1999 (ABI, 2001, Tables 93–95). The business is written by both Lloyd's syndicates and companies but Lloyd's continues to have the largest market share, controlling £1,332m of the total £1,673m UK net written MAT premiums in 1999 (ABI, 2001, Table 41); Lloyd's estimated that its share of total world marine net premiums fell from 21.8 per cent in 1987 down to 7.9 per cent in 1999 (Lloyd's, 2001, Table 4.2).

Throughout the second half of the twentieth century the business was adversely affected by:

(i) Intense competition from new international markets and over-capacity; almost every year from 1966 until the mid-1980s one or more of the leading companies' chairmen in their annual report and accounts blamed competition for the losses sustained. Initially it was hull business that suffered most, but later cargo business too felt the strain as the volume of business fell due to the formation of captive insurers (Carter, 1976, p. 1,904). Only in three years did all of the leading companies report an underwriting profit. The aggregate figures for the leading companies are shown in Table 7.4; the UK company market as a whole incurred underwriting losses every year during the 1990s (ABI, 2001, Table 91). Lloyd's was more successful, reporting underwriting profits on ships damage and liability each year from 1980 until 1987 (Lloyd's, 1984, Table 1.8);

Table 7.4 Performance of leading companies transacting marine insurance 1958–69

	Premiums £m	Transferred to P&L (% premiums)
1958	49.7	4.8
1959	51.8	5.6
1960	54.7	7.5
1061	61.0	8.4
1962	60.5	8.6
1963	63.5	8.0
1964	66.4	7.3
1965	65.7	2.0
1966	72.2	−5.3
1967	84.8	−6.1
1968	107.9	−6.2
1969	124.2	1.1

Note: 1958–64 Performance of 12 leading companies, 1965–69 ten leading companies.

Sources: 1958–64 Savory Milln, *Insurance Share Annual, 1968*. 1965–69 R.L. Carter, 1971.

(ii) Inflation, which particularly affected hull risks because of delays in repairs being undertaken;
(iii) Economic recessions reducing the demand for shipping;
(iv) The weakness of the £ sterling, which increased claims costs on overseas business; and
(v) The increasing size of individual risks; values at risk rose as larger ships, such as supertankers and container ships, carried more cargo. In the mid-1970s insurers were concerned by the delays in handling ships in the ports of the OPEC countries. The *Phoenix* chairman expressed concern in the company's 1981 report and accounts regarding the liabilities arising from accumulations of risk in the North Sea, citing the *Stratfjord oil platform* as being insured for close to $2 billion. That concern was justified in 1988 when the *Piper Alpha* oil platform was destroyed by an explosion killing 167 men and causing an insured loss of £1.7 billion.

Aviation insurance

Aviation is one of the UK's fastest-growing industries. The number of aircraft landings and departures increased from 607,000 in 1970 to 1.98m in 2000, and the number of passengers passing through airports rose from 31.6m to 179.9m during the same period.

Insurance against the loss of or damage to aircraft hulls and liabilities to passengers and third parties had been transacted primarily by marine underwriters shortly after the first successful crossing of the Channel, and Lloyd's had issued its first aviation policy in 1911. The business took off at the end of World War I when air passenger travel was expanded, and the early 1930s were the heyday of dirigibles until the loss of the *R.101* in 1930 and of the *Hindenburg* in 1937. The *International Union of Marine Insurance* set up an aviation committee in 1934 by which date 'eight European aviation insurance companies and pools were formally established'. However, 'the London insurance market is still the largest single centre for aviation insurance' (Wikipedia, 2008), with Lloyd's estimating that its share of total world aviation premiums rose from 22 per cent in 1995 to 24 per cent in 1999 (Lloyd's, 2001, Table 4.2).

Market entry and competition

After World War I new companies entered the market, including *Aviation and General* in 1919 (though it was wound up in 1927), and an association of *Eagle Star, Excess* and various Lloyd's underwriters formed the *Aviation Insurance Association*, which was dissolved in 1923 (CII, 1968, p. 149). In 1922 the *British Aviation Insurance*, led by Captain Lamplugh, was formed through the merger of *White Cross* and *Union of Canton*. Personal accident insurance for passengers was first arranged at around the same time.

Specialist underwriters soon dominated the market. The *British Aviation Insurance Co. Ltd*, formed in 1931 to write aviation insurance, soon became the foremost company, and London became the leading world aviation insurance market. The *United States Aircraft Insurance Group*, formed in 1928, became a competitor in the United States and in the early 1930s European insurers entered the market. In 1935 the *Aviation & General Insurance Co. Ltd* was formed by a group of composite offices and brokers.

After World War II competition and underwriting losses in the London Market increased with the entry of some insurance companies and new Lloyd's specialist syndicates. The formation of the *Aviation Insurance Offices Association* in 1949 enabled underwriters to pool experience, though the Association did not operate a tariff. The 'joint hull and respect the lead' market agreement formulated in 1958 to eliminate the irresponsible actions of some underwriters survived until the 1960s, and premium rates fell (CII, 1968, p. 163). From then on company chairmen regularly complained of over-capacity, competition and underwriting losses, though occasionally they reported small profits. Unfortunately separate underwriting results are not available for companies' aviation business before 1996, but each year from 1996 to 2000 produced a small underwriting loss (ABI, 2001, Table 93), though Lloyd's succeeded in earning profits from 1982 until 1989 inclusive (Lloyd's, 1994, Table 1.7).

New types of insurance

Imperial Airways, formed in 1924, obtained an excess of loss insurance for its fleet (CII, 1968, p. 152). In the mid-1930s cover was made available to aircraft builders for loss of or damage to an aircraft. Next Lloyd's underwriters in 1946 introduced 'loss of licence' insurance to protect pilots, navigators and others against the failure to renew their licence on medical grounds.

The introduction of new jet-propelled passenger aircraft in the 1950s brought about the formation of more commercial airlines using aircraft that increased considerably in speed, range, size, value and passenger loads. The scope of aviation insurance extended to include helicopters and, since the 1960s, the manufacturers and operators of space satellites.

Potential liabilities to passengers and third parties also were rising. Liability to passengers travelling internationally and for goods carried by air had been established under the Warsaw Convention, 1929, and the limits of compensation were raised by the Hague protocol, 1955. Consequently there was a growing demand for insurance from companies operating, manufacturing, refuelling and servicing aircraft. Aviation developed into a major class of business; Lloyd's, a major player in the market, increased its global net premiums from £120m in 1980 to £324m in 1990 and to £464m in 2007.

The hijacking of four jetliners at Dawson's Field in 1970 and the collision of two aircraft on the ground at Tenerife airport in 1977 brutally demonstrated the potential losses, which continued to escalate. By the end of the century the value of a wide-bodied jet could be in excess of US$200 million for each hull plus a third party limit of $2 billion (Carter et al., 2000, p. 646). Cover for such amounts stretched the capacity of the international market, including reinsurance, and in 1990 to help to meet such demand *British Aviation, Aviation and General* and the aviation offices of the *Commercial Union, Eagle Star* and the *General Accident* combined to form the *British Aviation Insurance Group*. More companies joined as members and in 2000, in order to provide the whole range of services required by the international aviation industry, the group bought the American company *Associated Aviation Underwriters* to form *Global Aerospace*.

In 2000 aviation business accounted for one-quarter of companies' MAT net written premiums, but well over one-third of Lloyd's MAT premiums. Table 7.5 shows that aviation premiums for both the companies and Lloyd's

Table 7.5 Worldwide aviation net premiums (£m)

	Companies	Lloyd's
1987	276	538
1995	517	747
1996	418	628
1997	385	585
1998	304	469
1999	249	568

Sources: ABI, 2001, Table 90. Lloyd's, 2001, Table 4.2.

fell between 1995 and 1999, though as noted above Lloyd's still increased its share of the world aviation insurance market.

Engineering insurance

As noted in Chapter 1, engineering insurance commenced in the nineteenth century. The Engineering Offices Association was formed in 1920 to administer a tariff that operated until 1971. The major composite companies moved into the market early in the twentieth century either by setting up their own departments or by acquiring the specialist companies (see Chapter 1).

The business from the first developed in response to legislation, with the Factories Act, 1961, laying down regulations regarding the types of plant requiring to be inspected at specified intervals, which were amended by the Health and Safety at Work, etc. Act, 1974. It was an evolving process as new regulations were issued in the 1980s.

Traditionally engineering had been a niche market, but that changed in the 1980s with the development of industrial all risks property and business interruption insurances including some forms of coverage traditionally provided by engineering insurers. Also third party cover became absorbed into general public liability policies. That tended to reduce the premiums for engineering all risks insurance, so that companies' total gross premiums fell (see Table 7.6).

In addition to 'All Risks' insurances other engineering business generated gross written premiums of £248 million in 1999 (ABI, 2001, Table 135).

Insurers embraced information technology to speed up the service for customers, including the speedier provision of inspection reports. The market too changed with the mergers of engineering insurers in the late 1990s. In 1996 *British Engine* was acquired by *Vulcan* and the engineering subsidiaries of *Commercial Union* and *General Accident* were combined after their parent companies merged.

Table 7.6 Companies' premiums for engineering all risks

Year	Gross written premiums (£000)
1994	30,982
1995	21,495
1996	26,120
1997	21,549
1998	21,315
1999	18,158

Source: Association of British Insurers, 2001, Table 88.

New risks

The second half of the century saw much product innovation in response to changing economic, social, legal and technological conditions, as demonstrated by the two following examples, although in general the premium income generated was comparatively small.

Kidnap and Ransom

This cover became available on the Lloyd's market in the 1930s, but it was during the 1970s that the security of personnel became of increasing concern for international business corporations, non-governmental organisations and high-profile wealthy individuals and tourists.[2] It led to an increase in demand for insurance to cover ransom and extortion money and other risks in respect of terrorist and criminal acts. A key feature of such insurance was the emphasis placed on preventive security.

A variation on kidnap and ransom insurance was *product extortion and contamination insurance*, which also developed from rising criminal and political activity.

Unauthorised trading

The trader Nick Leeson, who brought about the collapse of Barings in 1985, John Rusnak of the Allied Irish Bank who lost $750m on poor investments in 2002, and the Société Générale $7bn fraud in 2008 dramatically exposed the vulnerability of banks and other institutions to the risk of potential losses arising from the activity of staff. The insurance industry responded in 1998 by launching an insurance to provide financial protection against reckless, unauthorised trading by a company's officers and full-time salaried staff that is concealed from the management.

Liability insurance

Workmen's compensation and public liability insurances were both products of the late nineteenth century, and the latter had been a major class of business for insurers throughout the first half of the twentieth century. Liability insurance was a difficult class of business during the second half of the twentieth century, producing underwriting losses each year of the last two decades (ABI, 2001, Table 75).

When the Workmen's Compensation Act, 1923, was passed insurance was not made compulsory for employers. All changed with the enactment of the National Insurance (Industrial Injuries) Act, 1946, providing compulsory social insurance against personal injury and industrial diseases caused by an accident in the course of employment. It left insurers only with insurance against employers' liability at tort, resulting in a substantial loss of premium income. In 1969 the Employers' Liability tariff was abolished and the Employers' Liability (Compulsory Insurance) Act was enacted, making it compulsory for every employer carrying on business in Great Britain to have employers' liability insurance. Originally a £2 million limit of indemnity was required but in 1999 it became compulsory for the insurance to have a limit of at least £5 million.

The massive liability losses suffered by insurers 20 or more years after going on risk arising out of exposure to asbestos made insurers more reluctant to write the business. UK employers' liability insurance incurred underwriting losses amounting to 39 per cent of net premiums in 1999 and 66 per cent in 2000 (ABI, 2001, Table 75). Consequently, in 2002 and 2003 employers' liability insurance became difficult to obtain at acceptable rates for high risk activities, such as sub-contractors and tradesmen in the building/construction trades. Demolition, asbestos, scaffolding and related trades found it almost impossible to obtain insurance; the situation subsequently eased.

Products Liability

The Sale of Goods Act, 1893, and the Supply of Goods (Implied Terms) Act, 1973, imposed on manufacturers and sellers a contractual liability for injury or damage arising out of the sale of defective goods. The Consumer Protection Act, 1987, which implemented the EC Directive on products liability, imposed a strict liability on manufacturers, importers, producers and suppliers for personal injury or damage caused by defective products, further stimulating demand for insurance protection.

The need for several manufacturers in the 1970s to recall potentially dangerous products created a demand for *product recall insurance.* New Acts (such as the Riding Establishments Act, 1970, that made insurance compulsory for riding establishments, the Hotel Proprietors Act, 1956, and the Occupiers' Liability Act, 1957) also extended the demand for *public liability insurance.* Following the abolition of the Employers' Liability tariff some insurers began to issue combined liability policies covering employers', public and products liability.

By the 1980s the focus of interest for liability insurers had become much wider, reflecting the growing complexity and more demanding legislative requirements. Subsequently the insurance industry developed new forms of liability covers, notably:

Professional indemnity insurance. The contractual standard of care between a professional man and his client was laid down in a number of cases[3] and the Latent Damages Act, 1986, extended the liability of professionals. Consequently in the 1970s and 1980s claims against professional people increased as society became more litigious, all of which bolstered the demand for insurance from professional and other persons supplying a skill or a service in exchange for a fee who sought to protect themselves against claims for negligence and breach of contract. The Insurance Brokers

Registration Council made it compulsory for registered brokers to effect professional indemnity insurance to indemnify themselves against any claims for damages for breach of professional duty. Insurance brokers encountered difficulties in complying with the IBRC rules, a problem that has persisted. Other professions have sought to overcome their problems in obtaining PI insurance by forming mutual insurance companies, including:

  i. *Bar Mutual* which was established in 1987 by the Bar Council to provide compulsory PI insurance for all barristers in England and Wales
  ii. *Housing Associations Mutual Insurance Association* established in 1987 to provide PI insurance for the in-house design and technical practices of housing associations
  iii. *PAMIA* established in 1989 to provide PI insurance for patent agents and trademark agents in private practice
  iv. *The Solicitors Indemnity Mutual Insurance Association* to provide PI insurance for solicitors in excess of the compulsory level required by the Law Society.

Contractor's design and construct risk is a form of professional indemnity insurance provided for contractors who themselves, rather than an independent architect or engineer, are responsible for the design of a new building.

Pollution (environmental impairment) insurance was introduced in the late 1980s. The Environment Protection Act, 1990, and the Water Resources Act, 1991, imposed liability for environmental offences and the remediation of contamination. The EU Environmental Directive 2004/35/EC firmly established the 'polluter pays' principle, prompting the rise of the environmental liability market in London.

A problem for insurers is to assess potential liabilities because it may be several years before bodily injury following an incident becomes manifest. Also, to avoid liability for seepage occurring over a long period of time, insurers generally sought to restrict their liability by covering only 'sudden and unforeseen' incidents, and place a cap on clean-up costs.

UK general liability net premiums rose from £1.1 bn in 1990 to £1.6bn in 1998 but fell back to £1.1bn by 2000; an underwriting loss was sustained in each of the 11 years (ABI, 1990–2000, Table 75).

Nuclear risks insurance

Since the advent of nuclear energy the insurance of atomic risks has been written in Britain by a pooling arrangement of insurance companies and Lloyd's underwriters operated by *Nuclear Risk Insurers*, formerly the *British Insurance (Atomic Energy) Committee*.

This was constituted in 1957 to insure the public liability and material damage risks of 'atomic installations' covering atomic reactors and atomic power stations or plant, or any other premises or facilities concerned with the production of atomic energy or other processes incidental thereto. *NRI* is an FSA-authorised insurance intermediary acting on behalf of over 20 British insurance companies and Lloyd's underwriters. Its £400 million block of risk transfer capacity is the largest in the world.

Minor radioactive hazards arising from isotopes, X-ray machines and particle accelerators are insured in the market by *NRI*. During the construction period of nuclear stations the risks insured by contractors' all risks policies are handled by conventional insurers, with *NRI* commencing cover once the site becomes active. However, *NRI* has expanded to include all risks related to nuclear energy, including contractors and suppliers to the nuclear industry. There are separate pools for home, foreign and Canadian risks.

The risks written through *NRI* are (i) liability risks to comply with the requirements of nuclear legislation; material damage for UK nuclear installations; (ii) business interruption; and (iii) mechanical and electrical breakdown of parts of a nuclear reactor. NRI developed balance sheet protection cover for power station operators combining property 'all risks', machinery breakdown and business interruption. Sixty to 65 per cent of *NRI*'s income comes from facultative reinsurance acceptances from foreign nuclear pools. The premium income collected from UK risks is placed 100 per cent with UK-based insurers. The nuclear industry's loss ratio has been favourable, although, given the potential catastrophic nature of a major nuclear accident such as Chernobyl, insurers' losses could far exceed the total premiums.

Construction and erection insurance

This class of business developed as the result of the huge post-war construction projects, and the issue in 1950 of standard forms of construction contracts requiring contractors to insure contract works. Some large contractors established their own captive insurance companies to write the business.

Insurances were arranged in the joint names of the employer and the contractor to cover the contractor's responsibilities for the works as stipulated in standard conditions of contract such as the ICE (Institute of Civil Engineers) contract and the JCT (Standard Form of Building Contract). Originally cover was provided on a specified perils basis but later 'all risks' cover was required in contracts and granted by insurers. Table 7.7 shows gross premiums written during the 1990s and claims incurred, which would have resulted in an underwriting loss certainly in 1994 and 1995.

Decennial liability insurance

Otherwise known as *latent defects insurance*, this was a non-cancellable ten-year (sometimes extended to 12 years) insurance introduced to cover losses that may be incurred by owners or leaseholders due to damage to their building arising during the duration of the insurance that may be caused after completion by latent defects in design, materials or construction.

Table 7.7 Worldwide contractors' all risks insurance

	Gross written premiums (£m)	Gross claims (£m)	% of premiums
1994	108.4	94.2	89.9
1995	101.4	93.4	92.1
1996	106.8	61.5	57.5
1997	114.1	66.6	58.4
1998	109.0	73.5	67.4
1999	104.3	64.8	62.1

Source: Association of British Insurers (1990–2000), Table 88.

There was a specialist market for the insurance, but with a large share of the cover for private residential buildings being provided by the National House Building Council insurance scheme.

Directors' and officers' liability insurance

Whereas until the mid-1980s there were few instances in Britain of company directors and officers being sued for breaches in the performance of their duties, in 1980 the situation began to change with the new Companies Act, the Company Securities (Insider Dealing) Act, 1985, and subsequent company legislation that added to directors' potential liabilities. Directors owe a duty of care to the company, its members, employees and third parties. It is generally agreed that a company is not precluded from purchasing insurance in its own name for the benefit of directors and officers acting in their personal capacity. Thus there was created a demand for D and O insurance, which indemnifies:

i. directors and officers in their personal capacity when they cannot claim an indemnity from the company; and
ii. the company in respect of loss where it is required or permitted to indemnify a director or officer.

Details of market premiums were not published by the Association of British Insurers until 2003, rising from £168m in 2003 to £175m in 2007. Estimates by Datamonitor were substantially higher figures.

Employment practices liability insurance

This cover was introduced to the UK by two American insurers in 1999 in response to the enactment of more stringent employment practice legislation. The cover is to indemnify the policyholder against any claim by an employee, and in some cases by an ex-employee, customer or supplier, alleging unfair employment practice by the company or by its directors, officers and employees (e.g. unfair dismissal, discrimination, sexual harassment, and breach of contract).

Infringement of industrial property rights

Intellectual property rights such as a patent, copyright, design, a trademark or trade name are of considerable commercial value, infringement of which may result in substantial financial loss. This is another new form of legal liability insurance, usually to cover defence and pursuit costs, the latter enabling policyholders, with the insurer's consent, to enforce their rights that may have been infringed by a third party.

Legal expenses

Legal expenses insurance to cover legal expenses in pursuit of or in defence of claims or criminal charges was slow to develop in Britain, other than as part of the cover provided by liability insurances, but in 1974 *Phoenix* in association with the *Deutscher Automobil Schutz Allgemeine Rechtsschutz-Versicherungs* formed *DAS Legal Expenses Insurance* to provide cover on a stand-alone basis. The market by 1999 generated £102m gross earned premiums, of which £25m related to non-motor commercial policies.

Medical malpractice

In the UK the provision of medical malpractice insurance has three segments: state provision, mutual assistance and commercial insurance, reflecting in some measure the provision of medical care in this country. These are the NHS Litigation Authority (NHSLA), the three medical defence societies operating on an advisory/discretionary basis and the commercial insurance sector.

By far the largest provider is the NHS Litigation Authority (NHSLA), established in 1995 to handle medical negligence claims made against NHS bodies in England and their healthcare professionals as well as other staff, which number close to 1 million in the UK. The NHSLA operates with the intention of avoiding the costly route of litigation, preferring Alternative Dispute Resolution (ADR) methods, and in 2006–07 96 per cent of the 5,426 claims it received were settled by a non-litigious route. Besides dealing with claims, the NHSLA also has an active risk management programme to help to raise standards of care in the NHS. It estimated its total liabilities were £9.1bn in 2007, if it had to pay out all claims immediately. The NHSLA is a risk pool and its income is provided by the NHS Trusts on a pay-as-you-go basis. It is not an insurer and uses no commercial reinsurance (NHSLA).

Although all NHS employees are covered by NHSLA for medical malpractice and negligence disputes, the cover does not extend to their outside, private work. To meet the potential liabilities in the private sector, for over a century medical and dental professionals and persons working in complementary healthcare used one of three mutual defence societies to support them in court cases, and represent them in disputes with patients.

The *Medical Defence Union (MDU)* was established in 1885 as a medical defence organisation. Its subsidiary *MDU Services Ltd* is an insurance intermediary established to arrange and administer for members malpractice insurance issued by *SCOR Insurance (UK)* and the *International Insurance Company of Hannover Ltd*. It provides insurance for 50 per cent of UK medical personnel for their liability in connection with non-NHS work or other risks not covered by the NHSLA.

The *Medical Protection Society* has 245,000 members in over 20 markets. It is not an insurer but provides legal defence and advice on a discretionary basis and paid claims and legal costs of £115m in 2006.

In Scotland the *Medical & Dental Defence Union of Scotland (MDDU)* is a mutual organisation that offers legal and advisory support for its members but not malpractice insurance, merely discretionary medico-legal advice and support.

The rapid rise in claims resulted in the withdrawal of private insurance and reinsurance capacity in medical malpractice, especially in the US and some European countries. This often led to the lack of availability of covers even at very high premium rates for specialist doctors such as obstetricians and anaesthetists. It was a problem that the creation of the NHSLA largely overcame in the UK.

In 2006 the Post Magazine Insurance Directory listed 12 companies offering medical malpractice cover and there were some 20 Lloyd's syndicates also active in this field.

Advances in technology

The rapid advances in technology that occurred created new industries and new risks for organisations, including:

Aquacultural insurance. The development of fish farming gave rise to a demand in the 1970s for this new class of business, which expanded in the 1990s. The cover was to protect against unforeseen and sudden stock mortality.

The rapid development of information technology, including the use of the internet, has played an important role in the administration and distribution of insurance business. However, it also created a demand for insurance against the associated risks, including:

(i) *Computer and computer records insurance*: The increasingly widespread use of computers led to a demand for insurance against:
    (a) physical loss or damage involving the computer;
    (b) losses arising through business interruption as the result of such damage or the failure of public utilities;

(c) legal liability for breach of professional duty in the performance of computer operations for clients.

Companies' 1999 gross written premiums for computer policies were £33.8m (ABI, 2001, Table 88).

(ii) Internet liability: During 1999 some companies and Lloyd's syndicates launched a new form of liability insurance to provide cover for website owners, producers and others against such risks as defamation arising out of the use of the internet, unauthorised access to records, the infringement of intellectual property rights, the failure of web sites and for breach of duty and damage resulting from the downloading of a virus from their emails.

(iii) Loss or theft of electronic information: This form of cover was launched by a broker with a panel of insurers to cover loss of, or theft of, electronic information (including intellectual property), loss of income due to network and website disruption, theft of credit card details, third party financial losses, breach of privacy and defamation, copyright infringement and false advertising.

(iv) Privacy and network security insurance: Criminal activity has brought into being new forms of insurance. The rise in the number of breaches of security resulting in the loss of confidential information, with a number of high-profile cases in Britain in 2006 and 2007 involving banks, the Inland Revenue and other bodies caused companies to seek insurance against the resulting substantial costs and expenses, including litigation expenses. Consequently the industry devised a new form of insurance, including within the cover:
  (i) third party privacy liability covering sums the insured is legally liable to pay as damages and claims expenses as the result of a breach of privacy;
  (ii) privacy regulatory defence to cover the defence of a regulatory action or complaint, including indemnity for a penalty imposed by a regulatory authority;
  (iii) credit monitoring, crisis management and customer notification expenses; and
  (iv) security liability covering sums the insured is legally obliged to pay as damages and claims expenses arising out of computer attacks.

Terrorism

The IRA spread their terror campaign to mainland Britain in the 1970s, carrying out a variety of bomb attacks over the next 20 years. In 1971 a bomb exploded in the Post Office Tower and four car bombs were planted in London to be followed in 1974 with the pub bombings in Birmingham. Spectacularly, in October 1984, a bomb exploded in the Grand Hotel in Brighton during the Conservative Party Conference. London Bridge Station was bombed in 1992, followed by a large bomb in St Mary Axe in the City of London destroying the Baltic Exchange and damaging surrounding buildings, causing in total £800 million of damage. In April 1993 another huge bomb was detonated in the City at Bishopsgate, causing approximately £1 billion of damage, presenting the insurance industry with huge claims. Insurers had excluded from policies issued in Northern Ireland damage resulting from acts of terrorism soon after the start of the 'troubles'. However, in 1992 and particularly after the 1993 bomb, insurers and reinsurers questioned whether they could continue to cover terrorist losses to commercial property in the rest of the United Kingdom. Following negotiations with the government a solution was sought with the formation in 1993 of a new mutual company, *Pool Re*. Member companies, in return for an additional premium, would include terrorism cover in their insurance against damage to commercial property caused by an act of terrorism and for business interruption following such damage, and the government was required to repay funds drawn down to pay very large claims that would exhaust *Pool Re*'s funds. The company incurred losses of £262 million for the Bishopsgate bomb and in 1996 incurred losses of £108m for the London Docklands bomb and £234 million in respect of the Manchester City bomb, but it did not need to seek any recovery from the government (Pool Re). Similar organisations have been established in other countries, such as GAREAT in France and EXTREMUS in Germany.

Following the 2001 attack on the Twin Towers in New York, the American government passed the Terrorism Risk Insurance Act of 2002 so that for future acts of foreign terrorism the federal government would provide a financial backstop for losses up to a certain limit. This enabled insurers to continue to offer coverage at a reasonable price. So-called 'domestic' terrorism lay outside the scope of the Act. That Act was modified by TRIPRA in 2007, which was extended to include domestic terrorism. The New York 2001 World Trade Center terrorist disaster forced insurers and international reinsurers to review their situation and reinsurers generally inserted a terrorist exclusion clause in their contracts.

Specialist insurers, particularly in the London Market, had offered stand-alone terrorism insurance for many years, but there was little demand until after 9/11; demand surged when insurers found an opportunity to compete with *Pool Re* for terrorism insurance in the UK. The private market is not bound by *Pool Re*'s restrictions, such as *Pool Re* members not being permitted to choose which properties to insure for terrorism. Also private insurers will cover overseas risks.

Lloyd's syndicates led the development of the private terrorism market, but the market has broadened to include other specialist insurers in the USA and Bermuda. The London Market's terrorism property insurance wording T3/LMA3030 enables a company to buy back the terrorism exclusion that now appears in all property insurances. It provides cover against physical loss or physical damage caused by an act of terrorism or sabotage as defined, including

> the use of force or violence, by persons or groups of persons acting alone or in connection with any action(s) committed for political, religious or ideological purposes. (LMA, 2006)

The London Market

The London Market has continued to evolve from marine insurance written by Lloyd's. In time companies were allowed to write marine insurance; new specialist marine companies were established and the *Institute of London Underwriters* was formed in 1884 to represent their interests. Thus by the end of the nineteenth century London had grown into a global market. In 1887 Cuthbert Heath wrote the first Lloyd's non-marine insurance and Lloyd's non-marine market was formally established in 1903 to work alongside the marine market. After the 1940s the market received a boost from the process of nationalisation and domestication pursued by many countries that then needed to buy more reinsurance from abroad, including from the UK companies they had earlier expelled.

Nevertheless, until the early 1970s the market remained centred around Lloyd's. The increase in the volume of business flowing into the market led to the development of a non-Lloyd's sector as many insurance and reinsurance companies, mainly from overseas, entered the market in the 1970s and 1980s by opening offices in the City (Holmes, 2002). Today the business written falls into the following lines:

- *Home-Foreign*, which comprises direct insurances and facultative reinsurances written in the UK for property and casualty risks situated abroad
- *Treaty reinsurance and retrocession* of non-marine risks
- *Marine, Aviation and Transport* business, including MAT reinsurance.

The market specialises in international large complex risks and reinsurance. It comprises Lloyd's of London, UK companies, including UK subsidiaries and branches of foreign companies, the mutual marine Protection and Indemnity (P & I) clubs, and brokers transacting both direct and reinsurance business. The current structure of the market in relation to both direct insurance and reinsurance business is shown in Figure 7.3; captive insurance companies could be shown as both buyers and sellers of reinsurance. The market's main participants are shown in Table 7.8.

At its peak in the mid-1980s there were almost 200 companies operating in the market. After the losses incurred, mainly from American catastrophe and liability (notably from asbestosis) business, in 1989 and the following three years over 50 companies either went into liquidation or voluntarily

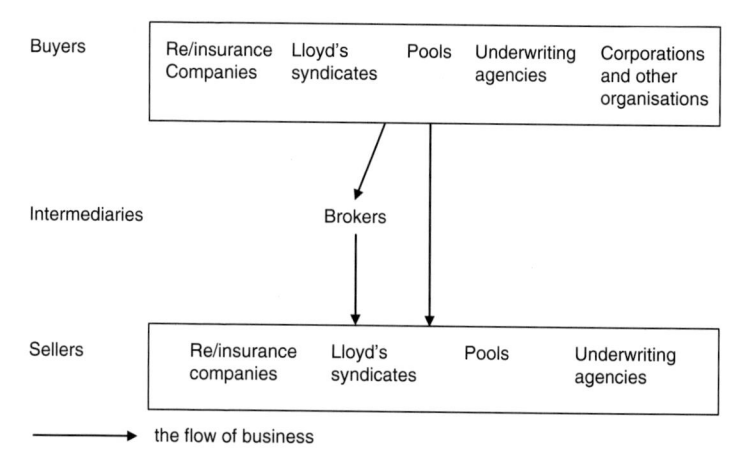

Figure 7.3 The London insurance market

Table 7.8 The London Market premiums for all lines

	Gross premiums written (£m)		
	1990	1995	2000
Insurance companies	6,068	7,494	n.a.
P & I clubs	603	775	n.a.
Lloyd's	5,729	6,766	n.a.
Total gross premiums	12,390	15,035	17,773
Net premiums	8,077	10,808	11,128

Source: R.L. Carter and P. Falush, 1995, 2000 – Association of British Insurers, *Insurance Statistics Year Book, 1990–2000*.

withdrew from the market (Carter and Falush, (1995)). In 1990 *London United Investments* went into administration and its *KWELM* insurance company subsidiaries (*Kingscroft, Wallbrook, El Paso, Lime Street* and *Mutual Re*) were placed in run-off. By 1995 the number of independently operating companies and groups had fallen from about 170 to around 114 highly capitalised groups, so that there was no significant loss of underwriting capacity. Moreover, London was able to attract a number of new companies to the market, so that in 2002 it was comprised of 86 Lloyd's syndicates and over 100 companies with a total market gross premium income of approximately £14.9 billion (Ross, 2002). Lloyd's too was undergoing a transformation, as Names with unlimited liability for their underwriting debts were being replaced from 1994 by limited liability corporate members, including UK and overseas insurance companies (see Chapter 10).

Table 7.9 shows that companies are now larger writers of non-MAT treaty reinsurance than Lloyd's, though Lloyd's has retained its lead in MAT business. Apart from 1997, every year from 1993 to 2000 the industry incurred an underwriting loss on non-MAT reinsurance (ABI, 2001, Table 47).

Over the years the market has been badly hit by American natural disasters, starting with the 1906 San Francisco earthquake and fire, and culminating with hurricanes Katrina, Rita and Wilma in 2005, which caused estimated insured losses of US$45bn, $10bn and $10bn respectively. (Swiss Re, 2006). It was estimated that 45 per cent of the 2005 US catastrophe losses of $62.1bn were paid by overseas reinsurers, including London (Hartwig, 2007).

A unique feature of the market is the LMX market, which comprises Lloyd's and company reinsurers. The reinsurers involved sought to reinsure each other on an excess of loss programme basis. The aim was to arbitrage the account written by arranging the outwards reinsurance at a lower premium rate than that prevailing on the inwards business and also to hold a relatively low retention. The excess of loss treaty reinsurance programmes include insurance, reinsurance and even retrocession business. The LMX market reinsures marine and non-marine business and the reinsurers involved usually specialise in this market and the business is placed by brokers with speciality knowledge. LMX underwriting has resulted in spectacular losses for Lloyd's and companies.

The Swiss Re in 1995 concluded in its study of the London Market that:

> Given its outstanding insurance know-how, the excellent working conditions of its brokers, its traditionally good access to international business and its proximity to an important banking centre, the London market...will continue to be a major centre for insurance in the future too. (Swiss Re, 1995)

The market has had to cope with many challenges since then.

Competition has increased from Bermuda and the Dublin International Financial Services Centre, and since the 1980s from the development of new financial instruments allowing the transfer of risks to capital markets. Major international insurers and reinsurers have been attracted to Dublin as a base for their European operations since it was set up with EU approval

Table 7.9 London Market net written premiums 2000 split by insurer (£ million)

	Home-foreign	Non-MAT reinsurance	MAT	Total
ABI companies	843	1,857	−116	2,584
Lloyd's	3,149	1,544	1,322	6,015
Other	47	2,015	467	2,529

Source: Association of British Insurers, 2001, Table 41.

in 1987. Bermuda has developed from being the largest location for captive insurers into a major international reinsurance market. Following the withdrawal of reinsurance capacity from London and other markets after a series of major catastrophes in the late 1980s and early 1990s, Bermuda was able to attract the capital for the formation of new companies. It has become a leading market for both catastrophe and financial reinsurance. Annual surveys undertaken by the US Department of Commerce of reinsurance purchased from abroad by insurers and reinsurers resident in the United States show that Bermuda overtook the UK as the largest supplier in 1981, and since then Bermuda has become the dominant supplier (see Figure 7.4); in 2000 Bermuda's reported share of total US reinsurance premiums paid abroad was 38.3 per cent against 13.4 per cent for the UK. The UK figures include both companies and Lloyd's but do not include Lloyd's very substantial surplus lines business.

As noted above, a number of natural catastrophes in America produced large losses for London insurers. Moreover, the attack on the Twin Towers on 11 September 2001 resulted in record massive insured losses totalling an estimated £30–35 billion not only for American primary insurers and reinsurers but for the international market too; Lloyd's of London alone paid gross direct and reinsurance claims before reinsurance recoveries of around US$5 billion (The Economist, 2004). Not only individual risks but also concentrations of risks exposed to natural and man-made disasters have become larger, for example, the total value insured of the Florida coastal exposure in 2004 was estimated at $1,937.3bn (Hartwig, 2007).

Both the Lloyd's and company markets have become more concentrated with reductions in the numbers of syndicates, underwriting agents and

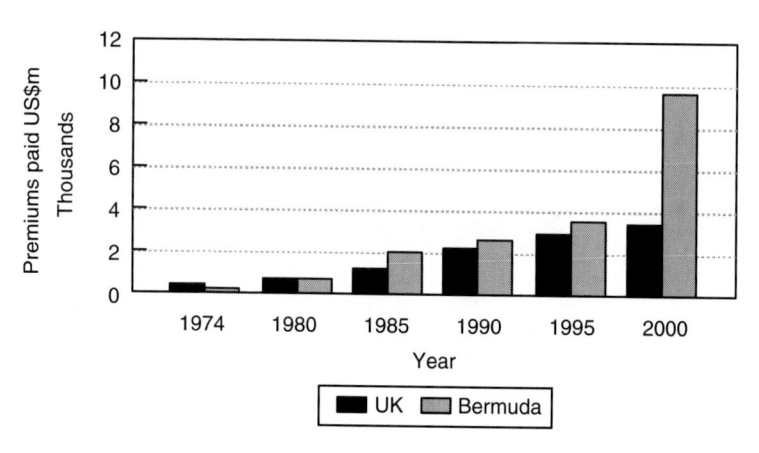

Figure 7.4 Premiums paid by insurers and reinsurers resident in the USA for reinsurance purchased from the UK and Bermuda

Source: US Department of Commerce.

companies, so creating larger, more highly capitalised insurers capable of writing larger risks. Nevertheless, London still remains essentially a subscription market where capacity can be mobilised with large risks being shared by a number of (re)insurers from both the company and Lloyd's markets.

Brokers

Like insurers, the broking sector also became more concentrated due to mergers first among the major brokers and in the last decade of the twentieth century among small to medium-sized broking firms too. Following the acquisition of Lloyd's broker *Minet Holdings* by the American *St Paul Companies* in 1987, *AXA* in 2007 started a new wave of insurers acquiring commercial brokers, including *Smart & Cook* and *Layton Blackham*, who were ranked amongst the UK's top 50 brokers. Brokers remain the largest source of commercial insurances (see Figure 7.5).

All of the developments noted above are clear evidence of the skill and innovative success of both companies and brokers operating in the London Market. Nevertheless, in order to compete internationally the market has had to look for ways to improve efficiency, which has encouraged closer cooperation between companies and Lloyd's. The Market Reform Group (MRG) formed by Lloyd's, companies and brokers aimed at identifying

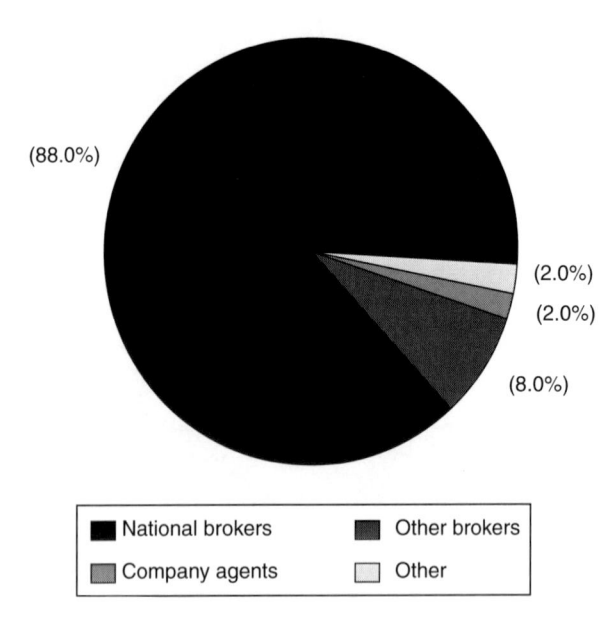

Figure 7.5 Sources of UK commercial lines business 2000
Source: Association of British Insurers, 2001, Table 106.

market inefficiencies and to develop solutions to deliver a more competitive service, such as the 1995 'contract certainty' initiative to ensure the more rapid production of contract documents. The MRG has developed further initiatives since 2000, such as the merging in 2001 of the former separate company and Lloyd's market bureaux into a single bureau *Insure* managed by *Xchanging Insurance Services*. An Electronic Claim Files depository and the Insurers' Market repository were set up in 2006 to provide insurers, reinsurers, Lloyd's managing agents and brokers with a single integrated claims adjusting and processing service and for the processing and settlement of premiums. Efforts were continuing to develop an electronic placing service for the whole market, using ACORD standards.

Insurance fraud

The growth of insurance fraud has not been confined to personal insurances. A 2005 report prepared for the Association of British Insurers (ABI, 2005) found that fraud was widespread among firms too. It found that all types of commercial claims fraud cost £550 million every year, which 'equated to 5% on a typical commercial premium', being similar to personal lines claims (ABI, 2005). Up to 15 per cent of the fraudulent claims arose from the exaggeration of genuine accidents, though other frauds included inventing a claim or withholding information on an application for insurance. Fraud can also arise because customers, suppliers and employees make claims against companies that are passed on to insurers. 'Nearly a quarter (22%) of employees thought it would be easy to exaggerate a genuine illness suffered in the workplace to gain compensation' (ABI, 2005, p. 3).

An aim of insurance fraud prevention in commercial lines was to disrupt organised criminal gangs networks. Cross-analysis revealed many fraudulent attempts by questioning claimants and bringing prosecutions. ABI research estimated that undetected commercial fraud amounted to £0.6bn during 2006, equivalent to 6 per cent of premiums. It also estimated that 11 per cent of the ten million claims paid by the industry are fraudulent, with most coming from property covers (0.5m) followed by motor (0.2m) and other classes (0.4m, including personal accident and pecuniary loss) (ABI, 2007a). The industry claimed that in 2006 it prevented £489m worth of fraud, a threefold increase from 2003.

8
Reinsurance

Reinsurance is essentially an international business conducted by Lloyd's, professional reinsurers (that is, companies specialising in reinsurance) and some direct insurers. It was estimated that in 1965 there were almost 200 professional reinsurers operating in the world (Neave, 1976, p. 55). The market has grown considerably since then. The bulk of the business is non-life, though life reassurance is transacted too.

The origins of facultative reinsurance[1] go back to the fourteenth century (Golding, 1927). Treaty surplus reinsurance written in Britain dated from 1821 (Raynes, 1968, p. 327), with the first recorded marine reinsurance dating from 1370 (Carter et al., 2000, p. 12). The treaty became the predominant form of reinsurance in the twentieth century, and practices were changed to reduce the costs of administering treaties, such as the abandonment of ceding companies providing bordereaux detailing risks ceded, and improved accounting. Also the switch to non-proportional reinsurance reduced administration costs. By the end of the century non-MAT treaty business accounted for over 70 per cent of the business written by companies on the London Market (see Table 8.1). Despite the disadvantages of facultative reinsurance, the growth in high-severity risks and in the size of individual risks in the second half of the century helped to reinvigorate facultative business (Carter et al., 2000, p. 321), but market premiums are not available because neither Lloyd's nor the companies publish separate figures for facultative reinsurance. However, *LIRMA* estimated that its member companies' aggregate facultative non-marine premiums in 1996 were £355m (Carter and Falush, 1995).

The first specialist reinsurance company, the *Kölnische Rücksversicherungs Gesellschaft*, commenced business in Germany in 1852, but the first professional reinsurer formed in Britain in 1867 survived for only three years. Several other companies too were formed but they too were short-lived (Golding, 1927); they included:

	Established	Wound up
Reinsurance Fire & Life	1867	1870
London & General Fire Reinsurance	1873	1874

Fire Reinsurance	1874	1882
London Reinsurance	1875	1881
Fire Guarantee	1875	1876
British Fire Reinsurance	1880	1886
Equitable Fire Reinsurance	1880	1884
Economic Reinsurance	1888	1894
Law Investment & Reinsurance	1892	1907
City Reinsurance	1894	1895
Fire Reinsurance of London	1895	1904 (acquired by King Insce)

A number of companies were formed during World War I when British insurers were forced to rearrange their reinsurances during the period of hostilities, but again most were short-lived, notably:

Globe Reinsurance	1914	1917
British Reinsurances	1918	1921
First National Reinsurance	1919	1922
Associated reinsurers	1919	1933

However, by the end of the first quarter of the twentieth century reinsurance was well established in Britain. Cuthbert Heath had written Lloyd's first reinsurance on American risks in the 1880s (Lloyd's, 2008), and the following first long-surviving professional reinsurance companies were formed:

1869 *London Guarantee & Accident Co.*, later renamed *London Guarantee & Reinsurance Co.* and acquired by the *Phoenix* in 1922;
1907 *Mercantile and General Reinsurance Co.*;
1908 *British and European*, acquired by *British General* in 1918;
1919 *Victory Reinsurance Co.*

The major direct insurers wrote reinsurance too, usually through a separate department and later through specialist subsidiaries.

Table 8.1 Business written on the London Market 2000

	Non-MAT reinsurance (£m)	Marine, aviation and transport	Home-foreign (£m)
ABI member companies	1,857	−116	843
P& I clubs and others	2,015	467	47
Lloyd's	1,544	1,322	3,149
TOTAL	5,416	1,673	4,039

Source: Association of British Insurers, 2001, Table 41.

During the late 1960s, the 1970s and the 1980s many new British and foreign-owned companies entered the London Market to write reinsurance business; at its peak in the mid-1980s there were 'over 200, including all of the world's major reinsurance companies, writing reinsurance business in London' (Carter and Falush, 1995). The London Market was truly international in regards to both its participants and the business written. One of the most significant new entrants was the *NW Re*, a part of the *Norwich Winterthur Group* formed in 1986 as a joint venture between *Norwich Union Fire*, *Winterthur* of Switzerland and *Chiyoda* of Japan; it quickly grew to become a major international reinsurer.

In 1968 the *Mercantile & General Re* was acquired by the *Prudential* which sold it to *Swiss Re* in 1996. *Victory Re* too was taken over in 1991 by the Dutch company *NRG*. So Britain lost its two major reinsurance companies.

Table 8.2 shows the breakdown and development of UK companies' reinsurance premiums. The overseas premiums would have been adversely affected by the strengthening of the external value of the £ sterling.

After World War II international business was presenting various new problems, notably:

1. Besides the loss of business caused by communist countries nationalising their industries, the United Nations Conference on Trade and Development (UNCTAD) encouraged developing countries to domesticate their business, place restrictions on reinsurance being ceded abroad and form regional reinsurance companies and pools to write reinsurance that formerly would have gone to international reinsurers (Carter and Dickinson, 1992, p. 43), which, however, did benefit to some extent from local companies' needs to purchase more reinsurance.
2. As the use of treaty reinsurance increased internationally, so too did the direct insurers' demand reciprocity (that is, a ceding company requiring the reinsurer to exchange some reinsurance business in return for the

Table 8.2   Breakdown of UK companies' reinsurance net premiums (£m)

	UK premiums	Overseas premiums	Total
1994	1,270	1,198	2,468
1995	1,649	1,090	2,739
1996	1,759	1,030	2,789
1997	1,650	772	2,422
1998	1,633	666	2,299
1999	1,378	204	1,582
2000	1,858	217	2,075

Sources: ABI, 2001, Tables 100, 101, 102 and 103.

reinsurance being ceded). Eventually reciprocity fell away, partly because proportional reinsurance became less profitable and reinsurers did not have a favourable portfolio of business to exchange, and also because as insurance groups grew larger their reinsurance needs changed.
3. The Bretton Woods Agreement of 1944 had brought some degree of stability to the world's foreign exchange markets. Then the American decision to float the US dollar in 1971 plunged reinsurers into a new era of uncertainty (Carter et al., 2000) because:
    (a) a change in exchange rates and the settlement of a claim could increase the reinsurer's liability, and
    (b) when assets and/or liabilities are denominated in a foreign currency it exposes the reinsurer to a transactions and an economic exposure, calling for better foreign currency management.

Reinsurers responded by inserting 'Currency fluctuation' clauses into their non-proportional reinsurance contracts under which losses may be incurred in several currencies (Carter et al., 2000, p. 227).

During the 1970s there were a number of attempts in America to establish Insurance Exchanges largely modelled on Lloyd's of London. Of the three exchanges set up in Chicago, Miami and New York, today only the Illinois Insurance Exchange is still writing business but no longer writes reinsurance business.

Excess of loss reinsurance

London and Lloyd's in particular became the major market for excess of loss reinsurance. This form of reinsurance was pioneered by the Lloyd's underwriter, Cuthbert Heath, who perceived that insurers required catastrophe reinsurance to protect them against an accumulation of losses from a single catastrophic event such as the 1906 San Francisco earthquake. The new form of reinsurance was used by American companies from the 1920s. By the end of the century Lloyd's still had the largest shares of MAT reinsurance and non-proportional reinsurances written on the London Market (ABI, 2001).

Until the 1960s proportional reinsurance[2] was the predominant form of treaty reinsurance,[3] particularly by way of reciprocal exchanges of property quota shares between insurers and reinsurers. The 1980s and 1990s saw a switch to non-proportional (excess of loss)[4] reinsurance even for property accounts that traditionally had been reinsured by proportional treaties, resulting in non-proportional premiums exceeding proportional premiums (see Table 8.3), so that since the 1970s excess of loss has now become the most widely used form of reinsurance by UK companies for non-life business.

Table 8.3 Development of UK insurers' worldwide reinsurance net premiums (£m)

	Non-proportional	Proportional
1983	182	591
1985	407	681
1990	570	753
1991	796	837
1002	749	935
1993	800	802
1995	935	715
1996	897	862
1997	800	870
1998	732	871
1999	632	746
2000	875	982

Sources: 1983–93 ABI, 1993, Table 46. 1994–2000 ABI, 2001, Table 97 (excluding Lloyd's).

Resolution of disputes

Traditionally disputes relating to reinsurance contracts were settled through arbitration. However, an increasing (though still relatively small) number of disputes were taken to the courts after the 1960s, providing a growing body of case law on important issues. However, arbitration clauses are universally included in reinsurance contracts, and London Market insurers and reinsurers adopted as from January 1994 the ARIAS (AIDA Reinsurance and Insurance Arbitration Society (UK)) Rules for use by the parties to any reinsurance dispute. The Arbitration Act, 1996, considerably limits the powers of the courts to intervene.

Difficult decades – the 1980s and 1990s

The *Reinsurance Offices Association* was formed in 1968 to represent the interests of reinsurers operating on the London Market. It was merged into the *London International Insurance and Reinsurance Market Association* (*LIRMA*) in 1991, which in turn changed to the *International Underwriting Association* (*IUA*) in 1998 following *LIRMA*'s merger with the *Institute of London Underwriters* (*ILU*), whose members were London Market marine company insurers and reinsurers. In 2008 the *IUA* had 39 ordinary members, all operating in the London Market.

During the 1980s–1990s London Market reinsurers incurred very large losses mainly on American business. First a succession of major American hurricanes (Betsy in 1965, Camille in 1969, Celia in 1970, Gilbert in 1988, and Andrew in 1992) badly hit London's catastrophe excess of loss business. Then huge liability claims arising from asbestosis, pollution and tort reform, including the awarding of punitive damages and class actions in America, and disastrous individual losses (the *Piper Alpha oil rig*, 1988 and *Exxon Valdez*,[5] 1989) resulted in escalating losses, to the extent that some reinsurers, for example, Swiss *Re*, withdrew from writing American liability business.

A combination of losses on past and current, mainly American, business during 1988–92 resulted in Lloyd's alone incurring total losses of £7bn, which made the Council adopt drastic measures to protect its capital (see Chapter 10). Many companies similarly made large losses, and some 70 companies failed or withdrew from the London Market between 1988 and 1992. These included well-known companies owned by insurers such as *NW Re* (which had become the London Market company leader for excess of loss reinsurance), *Victory*, *Excess*, and *English & American*, which went into provisional liquidation in 1993. The British composite companies had a long history of writing reinsurance either as a reinsurance department or within a subsidiary company, for example, *British & European*, *Guildhall*, *London Guarantee & Reinsurance*, *Royal Re*, but virtually all withdrew from the market. The London Market was hit by a capacity crisis and this gave the opportunity for investors to put money into the capitalisation of new reinsurance companies located offshore in low-tax countries, notably Bermuda. Those new reinsurers maintained strong links with the London Market either by establishing branches in London, by becoming Lloyd's corporate members or by reinsuring Lloyd's and London Market companies. The next disasters to hit reinsurers were the 2001 terrorist attacks on the World Trade Center, New York, which caused the largest ever single insured loss event, and the 2005 hurricanes Katrina and Rita. Consequently UK reinsurers incurred underwriting losses on their worldwide reinsurance business every year in the 1990s ranging from £27m in 1997 up to £784m in 1992 (ABI, 2001, Table 98). During 1996 to 2006 ABI members' underwriting losses on the non-MAT reinsurance account totalled £2,448m or 10.9 per cent of worldwide premium income, with a deficit in all but one of the 11 years in this period. Lloyd's performed somewhat better, making an underwriting profit of £953m (2003–07) even after absorbing the £1.3bn underwriting loss in 2005 (Eyes on the Future, Lloyd's, 2007, p. 51).

The rapid rise in inflation worldwide following the 1972 oil crisis created new problems for insurers of those classes of business with claims exposed to inflation. Excess of loss reinsurers were exposed to disproportionately higher rises in claims costs than their reinsureds, because of:

1. more claims falling within the reinsurance treaty limits, and
2. the reinsurer having to bear the full cost of claims falling within the limits.

Therefore, Index (or Stability) clauses were introduced to share the burden more fairly (Carter *et al.*, 2000, p. 216).

Terrorism was generally covered in general property insurances before the 9/11 World Trade Center disaster of 2001, and stand-alone terrorism coverages had been offered by private insurers, notably Lloyd's, for many years. However, a new demand for insurance in Britain followed the IRA bombings in Birmingham and London in the 1980s. The government and the industry responded by forming *Pool Re* in 1993 as a mutual reinsurance company to reinsure its members against property damage and business interruption caused by an act of terrorism in England, Scotland or Wales. The 2005 World Trade Center disaster had a profound effect on reinsurance business, causing insurers and reinsurers to re-examine their exposures, and to reassess their attitude towards cover for terrorism. It also increased demand for private stand-alone terrorism coverages that was met largely by Lloyd's and later by specialist insurers in the USA and Bermuda (see Chapter 7).

Hurricanes Katrina and Rita in 2005 likewise made reinsurers reassess potential catastrophe exposures and encouraged improvements to catastrophe models used in underwriting such risks. They also reinforced concerns regarding global reinsurance market capacity, encouraging the mobilisation of capital market funds for the transfer of risks in the forms of weather derivatives, and securitisation (that is catastrophe bonds and swaps). It remains arguable whether such financial instruments are competitors of or complementary to traditional reinsurance, but demand remains strong for the catastrophe bonds.

The London Market

The UK market moved into the twenty-first century as it began the twentieth, without a major British-owned global reinsurance company, the *Mercantile & General Re* having been acquired by *Swiss Re* in 1996. However, the *Amlin Group*, writing reinsurance through its wholly owned syndicate 2001 at Lloyd's and *Amlin Bermuda*, developed into the world's 39th largest global reinsurance group by 2007 (Standard & Poor's, 2008). London remains a major, vibrant international reinsurance market, with new companies coming into the market (e.g. *Brit Insurance*, which was established in 1995, took over *Benfield Reinsurance* in 1999 and in 2006 was a lead investor in *Norton Re*, formed to write catastrophe retrocession business in Bermuda). Also all of the world's major global reinsurers have a presence in the market.

Although the number of active companies and Lloyd's syndicates has fallen, market capacity has been maintained by an increase in the average size of company and syndicate. The London Market remains the major lead reinsurance market, especially for marine and aviation business and risks that require strong underwriting expertise, such as catastrophe, kidnap and ransom, and terrorism risks. However, the company market has secured a

Table 8.4 Distribution of LIRMA member companies' reinsurance premiums 1996

Non-marine		Marine	
Proportional treaty	714	Proportional and non-proportional treaty	211
Non-proportional treaty	834	Aviation	58
Facultative	355		

Source: R.L. Carter and P. Falush, *The London Insurance Market* (London: London Insurance Market Strategy Committee, 1998).

substantial share of the reinsurance business placed on the London Market (see Table 8.1) and, though Lloyd's is still the largest marine market, the companies now control the largest share of non-MAT treaty reinsurance, of which non-proportional reinsurance represents the largest share.

The distribution of the companies' reinsurance business in 1996 is shown in Table 8.4.

International competition

The London Market faces keen competition from foreign (especially major American and European) reinsurers. Bermuda is now the main location of companies transacting financial reinsurance and it is a major international market for catastrophe reinsurance. In 1981 Bermuda overtook London as the largest supplier of reinsurance to insurers and reinsurers resident in the United States. According to the US Department of Commerce Bermuda had a 38.7 per cent share of total US reinsurance premiums paid to reinsurers resident abroad compared with the UK's 5.5 per cent share (US Department of Commerce, 2008).

The creation by the Irish government in Dublin of the International Financial Services Centre in 1987 created new competition for London, attracting international reinsurance companies to use it as their location for European business. Standard & Poor's listed 14 global reinsurers as being located in Ireland in 2006 (Standard & Poor's, 2008, p. 32), though all of the world's major global reinsurers are located in London.

Financial reinsurance

Although, as noted in Chapter 9, the first financial reinsurance contracts took the form of 'time and distance' covers written for Lloyd's underwriters in the early 1970s, financial reinsurance developed in low-tax centres, notably Bermuda, which attracted the capital for the formation of new companies specialising in the business. Despite objections from regulatory and fiscal authorities, finite reinsurance continues to grow, enabling insurers to spread their loss experience over longer periods, and offering cover for risks not handled by traditional reinsurances (see Chapter 9). As noted above, new forms of contract have been developed by brokers and investment banks transferring risk to the capital markets, including the securitising of insurance risks, and new products are still evolving.

As long as London possesses the skills and expertise to underwrite and manage reinsurance business it will remain the prime international reinsurance market; in 2006 Lloyd's alone received net earned premiums of £4,186m (Lloyd's, 2007, p. 78) with the ABI companies writing a further £1,990m (ABI Total Market or web xls Table 5).

9
Risk Management

Risk management

Companies and other organisations generally need to stabilise their finances, including revenues and profits, from year to year. Therefore, they need to protect themselves against major losses of assets that could expose them to the possibility of a substantial loss of business, so being unable to maintain dividends for shareholders, insolvency or hostile takeover. A problem is that some of the most potentially damaging risks are highly unpredictable. Insurance evolved as a means of protection against financial loss arising from the occurrence of uncertain events causing loss of or damage to property, business interruption or legal liability to compensate third parties for injury or damage.

The first steps for an organisation in the management of risks, including insurance purchasing decisions, are risk identification and evaluation. However, risk management as a formal discipline was only recognised in Britain after 1969, though practice long pre-dated this. For example, captive insurance companies were formed in the 1920s; in 1920 British Petroleum had formed the *Tanker Insurance Co. Ltd* to insure part of their own risks; in 1926 Nobel Industries had formed *Imperial Chemicals Insurance Co.* and other major corporations had followed suit. The origins of the Association of Insurance Managers in Industry and Commerce (founded in 1963) lay in regular meetings, beginning in 1952, of the insurance managers of leading UK industrial groups (Brighton *et al.*, 1991). Large buyers of insurance were then beginning to become more demanding in what they wanted from insurers. For example, they were asking for:

- engineering all risks insurances;
- blanket fire insurances covering all of a group's premises with one sum insured for buildings, one for machinery and plant and one for stock wherever located instead of separate sums insured for each 'fire risk'; and
- premiums that reflected their own loss experience.

Thus they were attacking the principles of the fire tariffs. Perhaps more fundamental from a risk management point of view was their increasing realisation that there were advantages to be gained from participating through 'self-insurance' arrangements in financing their high-frequency, low-severity losses to avoid the phenomenon of so-called 'pound swapping' with insurers. It was not only private companies that were beginning to retain a part of their own risks; a 1965 survey of local authorities showed that they too were tending to retain more risks and had established 'self-insurance' funds (Carter, 1965).

Frank Knight's seminal book *Risk, Uncertainty and Profit*, published in 1921, first distinguished uncertainty (which is not measurable) from risk, which can be measured. Other influential books and articles followed, the first specifically on the subject of risk management being Mehr and Hedges' *Risk Management in the Business Enterprise*, published in 1963; so that by the 1960s risk management was becoming widely taught in American universities and colleges (Crockford, 1982) and formally practised in North America. The Insurance Institute of America developed in 1966 a set of examinations that led to the designation 'Associate in Risk Management'. In 1962 Douglas Barlow, the insurance risk manager at Massey Ferguson, developed the idea of 'cost of risk'.

The concept of risk management spread to Britain following the publication of a booklet by W. Horrigan in 1969 and a series of articles following his visit to America with Dr Dinsdale (Horrigan, 1969).

AIMIC quickly after 1969 arranged special meetings for members at Nottingham University to explain the concept, and itself changed its name to *AIRMIC* (the Association of Insurance and Risk Managers in Industry & Commerce) in 1977.

The University of Nottingham in 1969 pioneered the teaching of and research into insurance and risk management in UK universities, to be followed by other institutions, notably the City University and the Glasgow College of Technology (now Glasgow Caledonian University), which introduced the first specialist risk management degree course. Research into risk management, insurance and economics was boosted by the formation in 1975 of the International Association for the Study of Insurance Economics (the Geneva Association). Then in 1982 the Chartered Insurance Institute introduced a risk management paper among its options for the Fellowship examinations.

The scope of risk management had been closely associated with insurance from its inception. However, the debate during the 1970s and 1980s was whether it should be confined to the management of 'pure' risks (which can only result in loss) or should embrace 'speculative' risks (which may cause profit or loss) too. Bannister and Bawcutt, for example, in 1981 argued that risk management should cover the control of all risks that may threaten an organisation's assets and earnings (Bannister and Bawcutt, 1981). Gradually, as new risks for organisations arose from changing business practices, such as reliance on 'just-in-time' component supply chains, new technology and the need for business continuity, so the latter view prevailed, giving rise to new concepts like emergency planning, enterprise risk management and continuity risk management.

Alternatives to insurance

The growth of the multinational corporations with larger, more complex geographically diversified risks subject to differing local regulations forced corporations to consider alternatives to insurance. Further stimulus to do so came from:

- fluctuations in premium rates in the course of the insurance cycles which undermined the annual financial stability companies sought from purchasing insurance;
- the withdrawal of insurance capacity for some risks, such as asbestosis, following catastrophic losses;
- the unwillingness of insurers to provide insurance against some new risks that they thought were too unpredictable to underwrite.

Loss prevention

The old adage 'prevention is better than cure' found a new resonance in the 1970s as governments focused on issues of safety that directed attention to the need for loss prevention and mitigation in the management of risks. It further stimulated interest in risk management. A powerful incentive was provided in the UK by the Health and Safety at Work Act, 1974, which (i) created the Health & Safety Executive with powers to investigate accidents and impose prohibition orders, and (ii) imposed new duties on all employers to ensure as far as is reasonably practicable the safety and welfare at work of employees and third parties. Breaches of the Act could result in prosecution and the imposition of prohibition orders on employers. Then the Consumer Protection Act, 1987, which implemented the EC Product Liability Directive, imposed a strict liability for personal injury and damage caused by a defective product.

In 1991, the *National Forum for Risk Management in the Public Sector (ALARM)* was established to make a positive contribution to loss reduction in the public sector, its members being local authorities, government departments, the emergency services, universities, etc.

Risk transfer through contract conditions

Contracts relating to the supply of goods or services and construction contracts frequently incorporated conditions known as indemnity, exclusion and hold-harmless clauses to transfer from one party to the counter-party the financial consequences of injury, loss or damage arising from the undertaking of the contract. For example, leases contained clauses typically requiring the tenant

> to keep the premises in good repair and condition and be responsible for any damage of whatsoever nature, and to indemnify the landlord in respect of any claim for injury to any person or damage to property arising out of the use and occupancy of the premises.

Similarly a specialised supplier of adhesives included in sales contracts a clause making customers satisfy themselves as to the suitability of the goods for any particular purpose. However, it was not possible to contract out of liability for death or personal injury caused by negligence.

The government intervened in 1977 to control the avoidance of liability by contractual terms by the enactment of the Unfair Contract Terms Act, 1977. Additional protection was provided for consumers by the Unfair Terms in Consumer Contracts Regulations, 1994, even though the Sale of Goods Act, 1979, had already extended the degree of protection for consumers. In 1999 the Office of Fair Trading examined 27 cases and required 144 standard contract terms to be abandoned.

Widening the scope of risk management

The 1990s brought new dimensions to risk management. The Cadbury Committee's report in 1992 on corporate governance suggested that an organisation's governing board is responsible for setting risk management policy, assuring that there is an understanding of all its risks, and overseeing the entire process. It considerably strengthened the role of risk management in all types of companies and other bodies, embracing operational, organisational, enterprise and other risks besides just insurable risks.

The increasing vulnerability of many organisations to disruptions to their activities encouraged the development of business continuity management, which is an ongoing process to deal with such threats to an organisation's reputation as product recall and exposure to terrorism, and product contamination. As part of an organisation's planning it may include emergency planning, including the adoption of such practices as the provision of back-up facilities for key information processing facilities.

Alternative risk transfer (ART)

The shortcomings of traditional insurance prompted the development of (a) alternative means of transferring risks to different third-party risk carriers and of (b) alternative products.

Mutual risk sharing

- The difficulty in obtaining, or the high cost of, insurance led some organisations to establish mutual insurance companies using professional third-party managers to share risks among themselves, and to obtain reinsurance protection against very high-value losses and/or accumulations of losses. For example, difficulties in obtaining professional indemnity insurance during the 1980s led to the following companies being established and managed by *Thomas Miller & Co. Ltd*.
- The *Solicitors Indemnity Mutual Insurance Association* set up in 1986 to provide top-up insurance for solicitors' professional indemnity risks above the Solicitors' Indemnity Fund.
- The *Bar Mutual Indemnity Fund* founded in 1988 as a compulsory scheme to insure the professional negligence risks of all practising barristers in England and Wales.

Pool Re was established as a mutual in 1993 with government support to provide funding for large-scale terrorism losses for commercial premises.

Self-insurance

As noted above, the retention by business and other organisations of some of their own risks using internal funds from which transfers could be made to general reserves in the event of loss was well-established by the 1960s. Mainly funds were used for high-frequency low-value risks where to insure would have meant repaying the insurer by way of higher premiums for losses sustained plus the insurer's expense/profit loading and later premium tax – a phenomenon called 'pound-swapping'.

Self-insurance had its limitations and disadvantages; for example, contributions to an internal fund did not qualify for tax deductibility like insurance premiums. So the next logical step was for an organisation to form its own subsidiary insurance company.

Captive insurance companies

A captive insurer is an insurance company established primarily to insure or reinsure the risks of its parent company and fellow subsidiaries, as part of their insurance programmes. A captive must be adequately capitalised and meet accounting and regulatory requirements. It becomes a more risky venture when a captive, without adequate management skills and experience, decides to write third-party business and some captives lost money doing so.

The primary reasons for the formation of captives have been attributed to 'the insensitivity of the insurance market to its customers' and the enterprise of Fred Reiss, who founded a captive management company in America in 1958 (Sennett, 1991). One of the risks in founding a captive is lack of management skill, which a third-party management company can supply.

Other risk management consultancy firms were established (some by the major brokers) to advise on various aspects of risk management, including the formation and management of captives. The growth of captive insurers threatened the volume of premiums paid to traditional insurers and it induced some insurance companies to take an interest in risk management; for example, in 1972 the *Sun Alliance & London* formed a risk management service available on a fee-paying basis.

More detailed reasons for the formation of captives that were given are:

(i) the high premium rates and lack of sensitivity to risk improvement with discounts limited to designated types of fire protection;
(ii) a captive offers a company the ability to retain the risk of high-frequency, low-value losses, which if insured cost more in the long run in premiums than the cost of claims;
(iii) insurers discouraging self-insurance, giving only small discounts for deductibles;
(iv) the difficulty of arranging coherent international programmes and global covers;
(v) captives could provide more flexible insurance coverages to better meet the needs of parent companies;
(vi) a captive provides access to the reinsurance market thereby bypassing higher-cost direct insurers;
(vii) it can help groups to increase their own insurance capacity by building up reserves;
(viii) to develop funds for handling 'uninsurable risks'.

The term 'captive' came into vogue in America in the 1950s–1960s, but there were cases of major industrial and commercial groups well before the 1960s establishing such companies, sometimes because of difficulties encountered and/or the cost involved in trying to place very hazardous risks on conventional insurance markets. In the UK notably:

> British Petroleum founded *Tanker Insurance Co.* in 1920
> Nobel Industries formed *Imperial Chemicals Insurance* in 1926
> BAT Industries formed *Tobacco Insurance* in 1929
> Unilever formed *Blackfriars* in 1937.

Generally those companies originally just wrote a small share of the group's insured risks, acting as a replacement for 'self insurance'.

Regarding point (vi) above, reinsurers were more sympathetic to demands for excess of loss covers and for premiums based on the reinsured's own loss experience. Goshay had suggested in 1964 that the *raison d' être* of a captive seemed to be its use as a reinsurance conduit (Goshay, 1964). In 1971 the Chairman of the Reinsurance Offices Association said that if the establishment of a captive was part of a programme of cutting losses through improved prevention, then reinsurers would be sympathetic and support their formation (Neave, 1971). However, a survey of UK-owned captives found that in 2005 there were 350 captives owned by FTSE 100 and FTSE 250 firms and that 59 per cent did not buy reinsurance and retained risk for their own accounts (Marsh, 2007). Collectively the captives surveyed had an annual premium income of over £650m.

The explosion in captives came in the 1970s when UK groups followed the Americans in establishing captives in offshore (low-tax) locations, and many more were formed in the 1980s. Since then growth has remained steady at between 12 and 18 each year, but being at its height during 'hard' market cycles (Marsh, 2007). Today captives are represented in all industry sectors, particularly financial services, manufacturing and service supply.

Guernsey had a long history of involvement with insurance, first in association with Lloyd's, then through the appointment on the island of agents to represent British and continental insurers, and during the nineteenth century through the formation of local mutual insurance companies (Ward, 1989). The first captive insurance company was established there in 1922 (Ward, 1989), and in the 1970s it became the favoured location for UK-owned captives with 219 companies (including PCCs) established there in 2007. The Isle of Man registered its first UK-owned captive in 1981 and 87 UK-owned captives were established there in 2007. The other main location of choice was Bermuda, although new captives have sought the same captive benefits nearer to home, including Dublin. Locations compete to attract captives. The choice for a company of where to locate a captive is determined by its objectives. There are regulatory cost advantages for a UK group locating a captive outside the EU, but in order to do business with an EU member country it then would have to use a fronting insurer.

The new breed of captives have tended to write mainly long-tail casualty business (besides short-tail property and business interruption risks), excess of loss insurances and reinsurances, and to provide cover for traditionally non-insurable risks, like product recall. Over 60 per cent of the captives surveyed by Marsh covered overseas risks.

The 1990s saw the formation of Protected Cell Companies (PCCs) run by a management company that give smaller companies access to the use of a captive, each member participating through its own managed cell. PCCs have been the fastest growing form of captive. New mutuals continue to be formed too. In September 2007 the *Fire and Rescue Authorities Mutual* was formed to cater for the needs of those types of organisation, and in 2007 a mutual was in the process of being formed for local authorities (Business Insurance, 2007).

Financial/finite risk insurance and reinsurance

The origins of financial reinsurance date back to the 'time and distance' contracts arranged by Lloyd's syndicates in the early 1970s. They were essentially tax deferral contracts more akin to banking arrangements in the form of funded or guaranteed profit contracts than insurance, because the reinsurer in return for a consideration undertook to repay all or most of it at one or more future dates. Such contracts were challenged by both regulatory and tax authorities on the grounds that they included no transfer of risk, which is the key element of an insurance contract.

Over time financial reinsurers responded with the development of *finite risk* contracts covering some element of underwriting, timing (speed of settlement), and finite risks. Instead of the liability of the reinsurer being capped in relation to the premium payable, the reinsurer's liability was set at a considerably higher level.

The new finite risk reinsurance contracts could be classified into (i) *retrospective loss contracts* under which the reinsurer assumed liability for outstanding claims incurred on portfolios of business written in previous years, and (ii) *prospective loss contracts* (including *finite quota share*), which, unlike conventional annual insurance contracts, are normally arranged on a multi-year basis, being designed to spread annual future net loss experience over time. Both include the transfer of finite and timing risks. Finite reinsurance contracts often include cover for traditionally non-insurable risks, such as credit, investment and exchange rate risks. Eventually *multi-trigger* policies were devised, the key feature of which is that a claim will be paid only if a non-insurance event (such as a fall in interest rates) occurs in addition to an insurance event. Thus, for example, a company may protect itself against an adverse insurance loss event occurring at a time when it suffers poor returns from export sales or higher import costs due to a deteriorating exchange rate.

Finite risk contracts again came under the scrutiny of tax and regulatory authorities in the late 1990s, although a 1998 report by the European Commission's Working Group on Financial Reinsurance recognised that finite risk reinsurance can confer benefits (EU, 1998). The issue came under close scrutiny again after the collapse of the Australian insurer *HIH* in 2002 following its acquisition of *FAI*, which had entered into a number of financial reinsurance agreements, and with the New York State's Attorney General's complaint in 2005 against *AIG* regarding the accounting treatment of financial reinsurance contracts. New financial reporting regulations have required greater transparency in financial reporting.

Capital market products

The occurrence of a series of major American natural catastrophes highlighted the huge potential exposures that were far beyond the limited resources of the insurance industry and turned attention to the need to tap into the far greater resources of the world's capital markets. Consequently insurance, which had been the traditional means of transferring the financial cost of uncertain losses, was confronted by new competition in the

1970s when brokers and various, especially American, financial institutions looked for ways of involving the stock markets in risk financing.

One development in the mid-1990s, initiated by the California Earthquake Authority in 1995, was their proposal for the *securitisation* of insurable risks, notably the issue of Catastrophe bonds, which enabled the risk of large exposures to be transferred into capital markets. The bondholder agrees that, in return for a prospectively higher rate of return than that available under normal corporate bonds, it will accept the risk of the loss of interest and/or capital if a specified loss event (or loss experience) materialises, costing the original risk-bearer or an insurer more than a pre-agreed amount. The notional value of the placing is put into a trust account to provide the issuer with funds in the event of a loss occurring. The high cost of creating a bond fell over time as parties gained more experience. Originally created to transfer catastrophe exposures, they have been used to protect portfolios of motor insurance and other classes of insurance.

Insurance derivatives

Financial derivatives are futures contracts to protect buyers against changes in prices or other variables. Insurance derivatives were developed to enable insurers to protect themselves against the risk of incurring large losses arising from randomly occurring catastrophes. The Chicago Board of Trade (CBOT) began trading in US catastrophe futures and options in December 1992. The CBOT contracts enabled the risk of loss to be transferred directly to the financial markets. The Northridge earthquake in January 1994 revealed that many claims were not reported during the claims reporting period used for calculating the index used for the CBOT contracts, so reducing their value as an effective hedge. Therefore, a second generation of contracts was launched in 1996, the 'PCS Cat Insurance Options', which trigger payments based on US regional loss indices produced by Property Claims Services.

Despite the early volumes of trade on the CBOT having reached substantial proportions, by 2001, faced with declining contracts traded, the CBOT ceased trading in them. Other organisations, however, commenced trading in insurance derivatives.

Catastrophe swaps

A screen-based Catastrophe Risk Exchange (CATEX) was set up in New York in 1996 to provide for the trading of risks. It was initially established to facilitate the swapping of catastrophe exposure by insurers and reinsurers.

Risk management at the start of the twenty-first century had progressed a long way since the 1960s and was still evolving.

10
Lloyd's of London

Lloyd's of London is undoubtedly Britain's best known and most historic insurance institution, which evolved in a rather piecemeal fashion during the past 320 years since its beginnings in Edward Lloyd's coffee house in the seventeenth century. The Lloyd's market developed sophisticated underwriting expertise and the ability to accept risks that no other insurer would entertain. Until the beginning of the twentieth century Lloyd's specialised in marine cargo and hull and war risk insurance. Lloyd's had policyholders in close to 200 countries.

Lloyd's progress was supported from its early years by the assembly of a global network of agents in most ports of the world, which not only helped the insurer with claims settlement and shipping and commercial information, but was also found useful for the British Foreign Office.

Readers not familiar with the working of the British insurance market should note that there is a fundamental difference between the financial structure of Lloyd's and that of a conventional insurance company. The operations of an insurance company rest on the capital subscribed by its shareholders, plus the retained profit over its past years of operations. Lloyd's is not an insurance company; the Corporation of Lloyd's itself writes no insurance business but provides the accommodation and services that members need to conduct their business. Lloyd's is an insurance market where individual underwriters accept risks from Lloyd's brokers on their members' (Names') behalf. Traditionally, until the end of the twentieth century, Lloyd's finances rested on its investors' personal assets, the wealth of the Names.

If an insurance company makes large losses and cannot pay its claims, it will go bankrupt. Lloyd's claims, however, were guaranteed by the personal wealth of the totality of its Names without limit. In other words, Lloyd's operated on the basis of unlimited liability, while insurance company claims settlement capacity is determined by the assets it has on its balance sheet, including its solvency margin.

While unlimited liability of Lloyd's Names was regarded as a major security benefit, the negative features of the traditional method of capital backing were not seriously tested until the late 1980s, when the huge property and liability losses incurred drove bankrupt many wealthy Names, including rich establishment figures. The adverse outcome of the unlimited liability regime gave a strong impetus to the reorganisation of Lloyd's in the 1990s. This led to the phasing out of unlimited liability and the introduction of corporate members, that is, shareholder-owned limited liability insurance vehicles, which now provide the overwhelming majority of the capital backing for Lloyd's. In 2007 corporate members contributed 93 per cent of Lloyd's market capacity, while the remaining 1,124 Names with unlimited liability were down to 7 per cent. No new Names have been admitted since 2003.

The security of Lloyd's policyholders is also supported by the Lloyd's Central Fund (£2,054m in excess of technical reserves in 2006), and further backing for claims in the US is available from the American deposits.

The early years of the twentieth century saw Lloyd's diversify beyond marine insurance to transact other classes of non-life insurance. The Committee accepted the first non-marine deposit in 1903, so establishing a non-marine market. The first reinsurance contract was written in 1903 and the first motor and aviation policies were issued in 1904 and 1911 respectively. A key figure in the growth of the non-marine business at Lloyd's was Cuthbert Heath, an innovative underwriter who wrote the first reinsurance policy in this market and also invented excess of loss reinsurance contracts. In 1908 the annual audit and premiums trust fund became compulsory under the Assurance Companies Acts, 1909.

The Lloyd's Act, 1911, extended the Society's objects to cover the carrying on of business of insurance of every description, and included the power to act as Trustee of any trust deed or guarantee furnished by any member under the provisions of the Assurance Companies Act, 1909, 'for the settlement of claims before any balance of profit could be distributed' (Cockerell, 1983).

The first time Lloyd's published aggregate premium figures was for 1913, when total premium income was £12,861,000, of which £8,861,000 was marine insurance. (It should be noted that Lloyd's – unlike insurance companies – publish premium income after the deduction of brokers' commissions.) After the end of World War I, the Chairman of Lloyd's drew attention to the widening of its business from a primarily marine account to other risks. In 1923 he said that 'non-marine guarantees at Lloyd's had grown from £366,000 from 1904 to £13m by 1921' (Wright and Fayle, 1928, p. 441).

Lloyd's Acts

In 1871 a private Act of Parliament, the Lloyd's Act, 1871, had given its 400 or so members (Names) powers to incorporate, with a formal organisational structure headed by an elected Committee of Lloyd's. The Society's powers were extended by the Lloyd's Act, 1925, when the Central Guarantee Fund was created. The Lloyd's Act, 1951, empowered the Society to borrow to raise funds for its new building, and extended its powers as trustee for trust deeds or guarantees, and it repealed the 1925 Act. The Lloyd's American Trust Fund was established for US dollar premiums in 1939.

A general meeting of members in 1978 agreed to the establishment of a working party to examine self-regulation at Lloyd's, and in 1979 Sir Henry Fisher was appointed as its chairman. The following year a Bill was drafted based on the Fisher proposals and the Lloyd's Act, 1982, was enacted, which defined the management structure and rules under which Lloyd's operates.

The major object of the Act was to establish a Council of Lloyd's, comprised of six working and six external members elected by Lloyd's members, six nominated members confirmed by the Governor of the Bank of England, and a Chairman and a Deputy Chairman elected annually from among the working members. The Council was made responsible for the management and supervision of the market, though it could delegate some of its responsibilities to committees, and defined its functions and powers. All members of the Council had to be approved by the FSA. The first Chief Executive was appointed at the Council's first meeting in 1983. Although Lloyd's excelled in many insurance fields, it remained a highly conservative body, and allowed the first female underwriting members to its floor only in the early 1970s.

The Treasury announced in March 2008 (Treasury, 2008) its intentions to amend various constitutional aspects of Lloyd's governance arrangements, including the abolition of the requirements for the Governor of the Bank of England's approval of nominated Council members, and the prohibition of associations between Lloyd's brokers and managing agents.

The Financial Services and Markets Act, 2000, transferred responsibility for the supervision of insurers to the FSA, and the independent regulation of Lloyd's by the FSA became effective from 30 November 2001.

The system of self-regulation was radically changed in January 2003 by the creation of the Lloyd's Franchise, which redefined the relationship between the Corporation of Lloyd's and the franchisees (the managing agencies). The aim was to create a market of independent businesses and to commercially manage the market to promote its overall profitability by analysing and controlling risk exposures. The Franchise Board set up by the Council in January 2003 has the task of seeking to maximise the long-term return to all capital providers by creating a disciplined marketplace. It is guided in that task by an Underwriting Advisory Committee, and the Market Supervision and Review Advisory Committee.

Another break with tradition occurred in January 2005, when Lloyd's switched from its traditional system of three-year accounting (whereby each underwriting year's accounts were closed at the end of three years) to a system of annual accounting on an International Accounting Standards basis, with annual profit distribution.

Renewal and reconstruction

The late 1980s and early 1990s were a traumatic time for Lloyd's, with its continued existence being threatened by mounting underwriting losses of over £7 billion, mainly on American property catastrophe and asbestosis and pollution liability insurance, plus some exceptionally large single losses, including the loss of the oil rig *Piper Alpha* in 1988. These losses emerged over a five year period, causing the worst results in Lloyd's over-300 year history. The Council in 1991 set up a Task Force under the chairmanship of Sir David Rowlands (who was appointed the first full-time remunerated Chairman of Lloyd's in 1993) to consider the Society's capital base and to identify a framework in which it should operate in the future. The *Reconstruction and Renewal Plan* that was published in February 1992 recommended a number of fundamental changes that formed the basis for a business plan published in 1993. The contentious proposal to admit corporate members with limited liability was implemented in 1994.

The number of active individual underwriting members fell from 26,019 in 1985 to 5,159 in 1999. To replace that loss of capital, in 1993 the members approved the admittance of the first corporate members, and in January 1994 25 were admitted. In 2007 there are 119 corporate members, contributing 82 per cent of the market's underwriting capacity.

Liability for 1992 and prior years' claims was undertaken by *Equitas*, a new reinsurance company formed in 1992. The Reconstruction and Renewal Settlement proposals were finally accepted by 95 per cent of the members in 1997. In 2007 there were 119 corporate members plus 892 Name corporate members (see Table 10.1) who together contributed 93 per cent of the market's underwriting capacity.

Table 10.1 Lloyd's membership

Year	Members	Corporate members
1899	714	
1910	667	
1930	1,412	
1950	2,743	
1960	4,808	
1970	6,001	
1980	18,552	
1990	34,146	
1994	31,789	95
2007	1,124	892[a] + 119[b]

Notes: [a] 892 Name company corporate members or Scottish Limited Partnerships, or Group Conversion Vehicles, or Limited Liability Partnerships (new for 2007).
[b] 119 other corporate members with limited liability.
Source: Lloyd's (1999).

The corporate members include UK listed insurers – companies listed on the London Stock Exchange that provided 39 per cent of the 2007 corporate capacity. The remaining capacity was contributed by some of the world's leading insurance and reinsurance groups, mainly from the US (17 per cent of corporate capacity) and Bermuda (5 per cent of corporate capacity), and other overseas insurers, including Australian and German. The competitive nature of Lloyd's insurers has been recognised by foreign companies since 2005, when several units (including *Atrium* and *Talbot*) were purchased by Bermuda insurance interests. 2008 also saw the purchase of one of the largest Lloyd's insurers, *Kiln*, by the largest Japanese non-life insurer *Tokio Marine and Nichido Fire* for £442m.

The Lloyd's market has since the 1990s been consolidating, like insurance markets worldwide. In 1985 there were 384 syndicates. The failure of some syndicates as the result of the 1988–92 losses and the merging of others reduced that number to 62 at the beginning of 2005. The number of managing agents has likewise fallen to 79 in 1999 from 306 in 1985 (see Table 10.2).

Traditionally only Lloyd's accredited brokers could place business at Lloyd's. Again mergers reduced their numbers, as shown in Table 10.2. As part of its Reconstruction and Renewal Plan Lloyd's sought to widen access to its market so that 22 of the 167 brokers in 2007 were overseas brokers and any broker could apply for provisional accreditation to gain access to the market. In 2008 the Treasury announced its intention to remove the restriction requiring managing agents to accept business only from a Lloyd's broker to open up access to the market for all intermediaries (Treasury, 2008).

Those reforms were advanced by the Government to amend the Lloyd's Act, 1982, with the aim of simplifying Lloyd's governance rules. The proposals also aimed to

> remove the restriction that requires managing agents generally to accept business only from a Lloyd's broker while retaining the class of "Lloyd's broker" for brokers that want to bear that title. (Treasury, 2008)

However, they also proposed to allow for the monitoring of conflicting interests between them.

Table 10.2 Lloyd's statistics

	Active underwriting members	No. of syndicates	Brokers	Managing agents
1980	18,522	437	266	192
2005	2,330	62	158	45

Source: Lloyd's (1999), Lloyd's *Market Results & Prospects, 2007*.

The principal objective of the proposals was to modernise the rules, and reduce unnecessary restrictions on how Lloyd's organises its affairs.

Since catastrophe excess of loss reinsurance was first devised by Cuthbert Heath following the 1906 San Francisco earthquake, Lloyd's has been a leading market for such business. It is not surprising, therefore, that the attack on the Twin Towers on 11 September 2001, which resulted in record massive insured losses totalling an estimated $30–35 billion, cost Lloyd's alone gross direct and reinsurance claims before reinsurance recoveries of around US$5 billion (*The Economist*, 2004).

Cooperation

The 1990s saw Lloyd's and the London Market companies drawing closer together to improve the operations and efficiency of the London Market.

The London Insurance Market Network (LIMNET) was formed by Lloyd's, the companies and brokers in 1987 to promote and facilitate the exploitation of IT on a marketwide basis. It proceeded to develop common standards and systems to process accounts, and settle balances, electronically. However, it was not successful in 1992 in developing widely utilised systems for the placing and closing of risks. Eventually the two formally separate Lloyd's and company bureaux were merged into *Xchanging Insurance Services*. An Electronic Claim Files (ECF) depository and the Insurers' Market repository (IMR) were set up in 2006 to provide insurers, reinsurers, Lloyd's managing agents and brokers with a single integrated claims adjusting and processing service. The aim in 2007 remained the development of an electronic placing and closing system.

Cooperation, however, was not confined just to IT. A long-standing criticism of the London Market was the delays in preparing contractual documents, so in 1995 the Market Reform Group, representing Lloyd's, the International Underwriters Association and brokers, cooperated to meet the deadline set by the FSA for the achievement of 'contract certainty'.

Geographical spread

Throughout its history Lloyd's derived the majority of its business from overseas clients, although the home market proportion – especially in direct business – increased substantially only in the post-war decades. However, there were major year-to-year fluctuations, as a consequence of changing local market conditions and regulatory restrictions.

Lloyd's had long written a relatively small amount of short-term life business and in 1971 it established *Lloyd's Life Assurance Co.* to be able to write long-term assurances. However, the company was sold to *Royal Insurance* in 1985, but a small number of syndicates (nine in 1994) wrote gross life premiums of £46m in 2007.

Table 10.3 Lloyd's gross premiums UK – overseas split (£m)

| | Direct and facultative || Reinsurance (excl. facultative) || Total |
	UK	Overseas	UK	Overseas	
1988	1,369	2,028	408	1,242	5,047
1998	1,988	2,699	258	1,329	6,274

Source: Statistics Relating to Lloyd's, Statutory Statement of Business.

Table 10.4 Territorial split of direct and facultative business 2000

Country	% of direct/facultative gross premiums
1. UK	36
2. US	28
3. Canada	3
4. Bermuda	2
5. France	1.9
6. Germany	1.7

Source: Statistics Relating to Lloyd's, 1999, Table 3.4.

The US had from Lloyd's early days been a major source of business for both direct and reinsurance business. The geographical detail for direct business is shown in Table 10.4, while in reinsurance the US participation was even stronger with a 45 per cent share.

Lloyd's continued to enter markets where for historical reasons it had little business, including China, where it opened an onshore reinsurance company, *Lloyd's Reinsurance Co. (China) Ltd* in Shanghai in 2007 after already having set up the Asia Platform in Singapore, which expanded to 13 syndicates in 2007. Lloyd's was also considering obtaining admitted status to several States in the US in order to broaden its coverage by writing more direct business (Insurance Day 17 July 2008).

Growth of business

During the post-war period Lloyd's grew rapidly, primarily in non-marine business. But marine insurance remained an important element throughout, and in 1987 the marine net premiums of £1,580m made it the second largest account, representing 31.5 per cent of its total business. This represented 21.8 per cent of global marine premiums (Statistics Relating to Lloyd's, 2001, p. 54). However, Lloyd's was not able to maintain this high share in later years and by 1999 its net marine premiums dropped to £633m, or only two-fifths of the 1987 figure, amounting to a 7.9 per cent world share. In the aviation business, however, Lloyd's fared much better, maintaining a global share between 21 and 34 per cent during the 1990s.

Treaty and facultative reinsurance fluctuated between 50 and 60 per cent of direct business written by Lloyd's, but was showing steep falls during the problem years of the late 1980s and early 1990s.

During most of the period from the middle of the twentieth century, the British insurance company market's non-life business showed a faster rate of premium growth than that of Lloyd's, as shown in Table 10.5. Companies expanded much more rapidly during the decade 1960–1970. Lloyd's performance was particularly weak during the 1990s, but it achieved quite a jump in premiums from 1980 to 1990 following the severe problems after 1988, which were followed by reconstruction.

From 2000 to 2006, however, Lloyd's premium income increased significantly, with a 105 per cent rise (to £12.7bn) while the company market developed less rapidly, with a 13 per cent rise (to £41.2bn) during the same period.

Table 10.6, showing the contributions of the different lines of business to the total UK non-life insurance transacted by Lloyd's and the company market respectively, highlights the importance of motor business and general liability for Lloyd's. However, Lloyd's controlled just under half of the companies' share in the UK property business. These proportions are likely to reflect Lloyd's absence of banking and building society connections, which play an important role in the placing of personal lines insurance of the household accounts.

Table 10.5 Comparison of Lloyd's – Companies' premium growth 1950–2000 worldwide non-life business

	Lloyd's net premiums (£m)	% change in ten year period	Insurance company market net premiums (£m)	% change in ten year period
1950	147	–	425	–
1960	255	73	924	117
1970	496	95	2,028	126
1980	1,862	275	8,147	291
1990	5,280	183	25,450	212
2000	6,203	18	36,649	44
Total increase 1950–2000 (%)	4,220	n.a.	8,623	n.a.

Sources: Statistics Relating to Lloyd's (various years), ABI (1985) General Business Key Statistics 1950–1985), ABI Insurance Statistics Yearbook (various years).

Table 10.6 Comparison of distribution of lines of business UK non-life market 2000

	% of Lloyd's total premiums	% of UK companies' total premiums
Accident and health	6.5	14.1
Motor	53.2	36.3
Property	14.5	28.7
General liability	18.3	7.9
Pecuniary loss	7.5	13.0
	100.0	100.0

Source: Lloyd's Market Reporting & Analysis Department.

Table 10.7 Lloyd's underwriting results 1996–2006

	Net premiums (£m)	Underwriting result (£m)
1996	4,810	575
1997	4,709	4
1998	4,869	−904
1999	5,785	−1,563
2000	6,203	−1,794
2001	6,930	−1396
2002	7,600	2,440
2003	9,063	3,250
2004	9,201	1,867
2005*	11,785	−1,388
2006*	12,688	2,142

Note: *Annual accounting results.
Source: Lloyd's, 2007, p. 15.

Following the Renewal and Reconstruction period business grew rapidly but underwriting profitability fluctuated sharply (see Table 10.7). After four years of very heavy losses during 1988–2001 – including its settlement of £1.98bn for the terrorist events of 9/11 – three profitable years followed, but the 2005 loss of £1,388m was mainly due to the severe American hurricane season, which cost Lloyd's £2.9bn. These sharp profits fluctuations indicate that Lloyd's is still heavily involved in high-risk high-rewards contracts, which seem to have caused many problems in recent years. A notable feature of Lloyd's progress after 2000 was the reduction in the purchase of reinsurance. Net retentions increased from 68.7 per cent of gross premiums in 2001 to 80.4 per cent of gross premiums in 2006, despite the wildly fluctuating underwriting performance.

11
International Business and Europe

At the commencement of the twentieth century British insurers already had a major overseas presence, not only in the countries of the Empire, but in the US, Europe and also on other Continents. Most of this was in non-life – fire, accident and marine – business with relatively few life operations. However, no statistical data exist covering this period, beyond some company information. In his history of the *Royal Exchange Assurance*, Supple quotes that by 1905 'the nine leading British companies which between them accounted for about two-thirds of all fire premiums, earned half their £15.6m premium income in the United States' (Supple, p. 213).

After a difficult interwar period, there was significant expansion during the post-war decades. UK companies substantially increased their global non-life insurance premium income, the share of overseas business being 66.7 per cent of the global total in 1956, the first year when relevant company market statistics were published, but the rapid growth of domestic business in the 1990s caused the overseas share to fall (see Tables 11.1 and 11.3). Lloyd's business was always predominantly from overseas sources, with the 1988 share standing at 66 per cent, which increased to 76 per cent by 2007 (see Tables 10.3 and 10.4 in Chapter 10). Companies achieved faster growth than Lloyd's in their global business over the second half of the twentieth century, though Lloyd's grew faster between 1961 and 1969. However, by 2006 companies' overseas income was down to 22.3 per cent of the companies' total non-life premiums due to their departure from several markets, the most important of which was the US.

Legislative obstacles

The companies soon encountered restrictive legislative difficulties in North America, Europe and some other countries (Raynes, 1968, p. 271). Nevertheless, the major companies and Lloyd's were writing a substantial volume of overseas business by 1900, so that overseas business accounted for some 60 per cent of British companies' total fire premium income. Over

Table 11.1 UK insurers' global net non-life premium income (£m)

	UK market*	O/seas market*	Total*	Lloyd's	Global total
1949	n.a.	n.a.	371	164	535
1961	331	652	983	346	1,329
1970	777	1,307	2,084	694	2,559
1990	15,542	9,944	25,486	6,058	31,544
2006	32,183	9,257	41,440	13,200	54,640

Note: *company premiums.
Sources: Association of British Insurers, 1985 (BIA member companies only). Lloyd's of London, Statistics Relating to Lloyd's 1999.

70 companies were operating in North America, with some such as *Liverpool London & Globe*, *Royal* and *Commercial Union* operating on a large scale, writing over $2 million fire net premiums in the United States and Canada (Noyes, 1953). British companies were writing the overwhelming share of American premiums placed with foreign companies.

Companies were also transacting a small amount of life business, particularly in North America and the English-speaking dominions, which became the main focus of the operations of some companies, such as *Gresham Life* and *Colonial Life* (Noyes, 1953). However, overseas the life premiums received remained small relative to marine and other non-life business.

World War I set back overseas business; markets in enemy countries were closed to UK insurers and international trade was disrupted. Nevertheless, in the immediate post-war boom motor and other new classes of business provided new opportunities for expanding overseas. The companies' international motor business net premium income was estimated to be £5.55m by 1920 compared with domestic premium income of £3.43m (Westall, 1998).

Nationalisation and domestication

The worldwide interwar years' recession adversely affected the growth of both British and overseas business. Then overseas operations were curtailed by World War II. Nevertheless, it has been estimated that in 1949 some 60 per cent of the total premiums written were derived from abroad (Noyes, 1953). However, the international political and economic climate was changing. The Soviet government's nationalisation of the Russian insurance industry in 1918 set a pattern after 1945 for other Communist governments, particularly those of China and Eastern Europe. Also many, mainly ex-colonial, developing countries, after gaining independence, wanted to build up and diversify their economies, including establishing their own local insurance markets to limit the outflow of funds. They were encouraged by the United Nations Conference on Trade and Development UNCTAD

(Malinowski, 1971), and they either:

- followed the Communist policy of nationalising their industries; or
- sought to domesticate their markets by imposing regulatory and/or exchange control restrictions or by imposing discriminatory taxation on foreign insurers and brokers operating in their countries; or
- limited foreign companies to minority shareholdings in former subsidiary companies (Carter and Dickinson, 1992).

So British insurers were excluded from, or faced restrictions on, their business in many countries, some of which, like India, had been an important source of business. Consequently during the 1960s the companies' overseas business grew more slowly than their domestic premiums (see Table 11.1).

However, obstacles to trade were not limited to just developing countries. Some industrialised countries protected their domestic insurers too, as the OECD were able to reveal in 1983 (OECD, 1983). For example, in 1985 the regulatory costs of entering the German market were described as substantial (Finsinger *et al.*, 1985), Japan strictly limited the entry of foreign companies (Carter and Dickinson, 1992), and a company wishing to establish a presence in the United States had to incur the costs of obtaining regulatory authorisation from each State in which it wished to operate. Foreign reinsurers had to deposit collateral funds in US trust funds to cover their liabilities to US cedants, which remains a contentious issue.

Consequently, focusing on developing countries, in 1970 the *Norwich Union* claimed in its annual report that it had been forced to withdraw from 22 countries. All other British companies were similarly affected; the *Phoenix*, for example, in the same year reported that it had had to leave Uganda, Sudan, Ethiopia, Morocco and Guyana, and had been required to reduce its shareholding in Peru. However, it did not mean a complete loss of business, because, as the chairman of the *Norwich Union* explained, 'paradoxically the nationalised industries often require to purchase far more reinsurance from outside the country'. Therefore, the major British companies sought to expand their reinsurance business, including some insurers setting up reinsurance subsidiaries, despite many countries also restricting the placing of reinsurances with foreign reinsurers (Carter and Dickinson, 1992). It was political considerations of a different nature, that is, the opposition to apartheid, that persuaded companies to curtail their activities in South Africa. As cited above, in 1956 overseas business accounted for 69.7 per cent of BIA members' total net general insurance written premiums, by 1975 it was down to 60.0 per cent and to 50.7 per cent in 1985 (ABI, 1985, Table 2).

The United States

The other difficult territory for British insurers was America, which for long had been the main source of overseas business. In 1968 the US fire, accident

Table 11.2 Aggregate American underwriting results of the seven leading British companies, 1962–83

US net premiums (£m)	US underwriting results (£m)	Worldwide underwriting results (£m)
11,974.7	−173.8	−573.9

Source: Authors' calculations from the seven leading companies' annual reports and accounts.

and motor premiums of ABI member companies amounted to over $1 billion. Continuing underwriting losses (see Table 11.2) in the USA were forcing the companies to review their business there. For example, in 1965 the hurricane Betsy and the Los Angeles riots exhausted the reinsurance facilities of the *Northern & Employers*, and cost the *Royal* $5.9m; Mr Orme of the *Royal* described the USA in 1965 as 'an era of profitless prosperity' (Royal, 1965). Subsequent natural disasters and heavy losses on liability business eventually forced some companies to leave some areas of the American market and/or lines of business. The aggregate results of the seven British companies writing the largest amounts of American non-life business (*Royal, Commercial Union, General Accident, Guardian Royal Exchange, Sun Alliance* and *Phoenix*) are shown in Table 11.2; the seven companies collectively made an underwriting profit in only five of the 20 years 1962–83 inclusive, and *Royal* achieved a profit in only three years. UK companies subsequently failed to achieve any consistent improvement in underwriting results; during the 1990s ABI member companies wrote aggregate US net non-motor premiums of £22,992m, on which they incurred an underwriting loss each year amounting in total to £4,200m, with the annual underwriting loss ratio ranging from 9 to 43 per cent (ABI, 2001, Table 67). It must be emphasised that trading results allowing for investment returns on technical reserves would have been rather more favourable, but published accounts did not provide that information.

Losses on American business were also the main cause of Lloyd's disastrous 1988–92 underwriting years' losses. In 1968 *Sun Alliance* sold its American subsidiary *Manhattan Guarantee*. Eventually, in 2006 even the *Royal Sun Alliance*, which had written a very large American account for a century, decided to sell all of its US business to a company formed by its former US managers. Consequently America fell from being the major single source of overseas business (33 per cent in 1975) to a mere 0.5 per cent by 2006 (see Table 11.3). The figures do not include American business written on a cross-frontier basis in London.

Conversely, the major British companies decided to expand in the American life market in the 1980s.

- In 1982 Legal & General acquired Banner Life;
- In 1986 Prudential acquired Jackson Life;

Table 11.3 Geographical breakdown of ABI member companies' non-life net general premium income

Year	UK (£m)	USA (£m)	EU (£m)	Rest of world (£m)	Total
1975	1,859	908	494	1,380	4,641
1980	4,295	1,317	823	1,712	8,147
1985	7,789	3,073	1,253	3,680	15,795
1990	15,542	3,090	2,491	4,363	25,486
1995	18,800	4,188	5,331	4,390	32,709
2000	24,278	4,948	5,278	3,752	38,257
2006	32,183	44	6,475	2,738	41,440

Source: Association of British Insurers.

Table 11.4 Geographical percentage breakdown of ABI members' ordinary long-term premium income

Year	UK (%)	U.S.A. (%)	EU (%)	Rest of World (%)
1980	87.5	n.a.	7.8	4.7
1985	85.4	0.9	5.8	7.9
1990	83.0	4.7	5.1	7.2
1995	80.3	4.9	8.1	6.7
2000	86.2	3.8	5.4	4.6
2006	83.2	4.1	7.2	5.5

Note: For monetary data see Table 6.8.
Source: Association of British Insurers.

- In 1988 Royal acquired Maccabees Life Insce Co.; and
- In 1989 Legal & General acquired William Penn Life of New York.

Therefore, within 20 years ABI members had built up a substantial volume of American life business (see Table 11.4).

By 2000 American business accounted for a quarter of all long-term business written overseas compared with 6 per cent in 1985.

Liberalisation of trade in insurance

The mid-1970s brought some easing of the political climate as first Egypt, after having nationalised its industry in 1956, allowed foreign insurers to participate in two new direct insurance companies incorporated under its 1974 Free Zone legislation, and South Korea followed by denationalising its state reinsurance corporation. After prolonged multilateral negotiations commencing in 1976, despite opposition from some developing nations, eventually at the end of the Uruguay Round of GATT negotiations a Final Act including provisions on services was agreed in December 1993. That provided for:

1. The creation of the General Agreement on Trade in Services (GATS) to provide 'most favoured nation' (MFN) treatment in relation to trade in services, including establishment. However, WTO members were to be allowed to impose or retain restrictions required for 'prudential regulation' of their industries. So began the process of eventually removing barriers to trade in services, and
2. The formation of the World Trade Organisation (WTO) as a permanent body to cover trade in services with the GATS Annex on Financial Services defining the scope of the GATS in relation to insurance.

The next important step was when the GATS/WTO Agreement on Financial Services (the Fifth Protocol to the GATS) was agreed in December 1997. When China joined the WTO an important new market was opened to international, including UK, insurance companies and Lloyd's. Both Lloyd's and the major UK life offices, notably *Prudential* and *Aviva*, were quick to seize the opportunities by establishing operations in China and India.

The US regulation requiring overseas reinsurers to deposit 100 per cent collateral in US trust funds to cover their liabilities to US cedants has been a long-running trade issue between America and the EU. Following the formation of the Transatlantic Economic Council after the EU–US Summit of April 2007, the Comité Europeen d'Assurances (CEA) was hopeful that the meetings would lead to regulatory reform creating a level playing field for EU reinsurers accepting US reinsurances.

The figures for the rest of the world in Tables 11.3 and 11.4 include important markets such as Australasia and Canada besides Africa and Asia, and were almost one-third higher in 2006 than in 2000.

Europe

Britain's entry into the European Community in 1973 generated much enthusiasm in the industry for expansion in Europe. It also had a profound impact on the regulation of the industry through the need to adopt the various Insurance Directives. EU countries accounted for almost 16 per cent of the UK industry's overseas non-life premiums by 1985, rising to almost three-quarters by 2006 when EU life premiums accounted for 43 per cent of total overseas premiums.

Before Britain entered the EEC a number of Directives had been issued by the Commission to further the creation of a single market in insurance.

The *1964 Reinsurance Directive* (64/225/EEC) gave Community reinsurers:

1. 'freedom of establishment' – the right of a reinsurer with a head office in one member state to establish agencies and branches in any other member state under the same conditions as a national reinsurer; and
2. 'freedom of services' – the right of a reinsurer established in any member country to conduct business with an insurer established in any other member state whether or not the reinsurer has an office there, and conversely the right of an insurer to reinsure directly with a reinsurer established in any other member state.

The 1925 interim report of the Clowson Interdepartmental Committee had recommended that reinsurance should be exempted from the UK insurance regulatory framework, but the recommendation was not adopted by Parliament, so that reinsurers established in Britain were subject to basically the same regulatory rules as direct insurers, unlike reinsurers in some member states, a situation that was not dealt with until 2005 by the *Reinsurance Directive* (2005/68/EU), which required the regulation of pure reinsurers to be implemented by all states by December 2007.

The *Motor Insurance Directives* (72/166/EEC and 72/430/EEC) were the first steps towards freeing the movement of vehicles in the European Union, and of establishing a single market for motor insurance.

Freedom of Establishment

UK insurers welcomed the first steps towards the creation of a single market in direct non-life insurance.

The *First Non-Life Insurance Directive* (73/239/EEC) and the *Non-Life Insurance Directive* (73/240/EEC) dealt with the achievement of 'freedom of establishment' for direct insurance, enabling an insurer with its head office in any member state to establish agencies or branches in another state. To avoid distortions arising from differing national supervisory legislation, the first directive set out the conditions for the establishment and operation of non-life insurance, including a minimum solvency margin that had to be incorporated into UK supervisory legislation.

The 1974 European Court of Justice decision in the case of *Reyners v Belgian State*, which dealt with 'freedom of establishment' under Article 54 of the Treaty of Rome, removed the need for a specific directive to confer 'freedom of establishment' for long-term assurance. So in 1979 the *Life Insurance Freedom of Establishment Directive* (79/267/EEC) merely facilitated establishment by laying down common community rules relating to the authorisation of companies, agencies and branches, solvency, and the separation of the management of the long-term and general insurance business of composite insurers. It also forbade the setting-up of new composite companies.

The large UK companies looked forward in the 1970s to expanding their business in Europe. *Royal* acquired a 10 per cent holding in the *Aachener und Münchener* in 1972, and the same year *Commercial Union* acquired the *Compagnia di Assicurazione da Milano*, followed in 1974 by the takeover of the large Dutch insurer *Delta Lloyd*. Also in 1974 *Royal* reorganised its Dutch business following the acquisition of *Boot & Pit* in 1973. Other companies too embarked on the acquisition of European insurers, but it was not a one-way process as European companies looked to the UK market (see Table 11.5). Moreover, trading conditions in the various European markets often proved to be difficult; for example, the French fire tariff was terminated in 1980.

The acquisition by *Allianz* of the composite insurer *Cornhill* in 1986 was a major development for the UK market, followed by the takeover of the *Eagle Star* by *Zurich Financial Services* in 1998. The most spectacular European

Table 11.5 British companies acquired by European companies

Year	Company acquired	Acquiring company
1967	Contingency	GAN (France)
1968	Life Association of Scotland	Nationale Nederlanden (Holland)
	Pendle	Ancienne Mutuelle (France)
1971	Triumph	Ennia NV (Holland)
1974	Moorgate	Pojhola of Helsinki (Finland)
	County Fire	Copenhagen Re (Denmark)
1979	Gresham Life	NV AMEV (Holland)
1980	Dog Breeders Insce	Generali Group (Italy)
1981	Provident Life Assocn	Winterthur Swiss
1984	Economic	Hafnia Group (Denmark)
1986	Cornhill	Allianz (Germany)
1987	City of Westminster	Assurances Generales de France
	Equity & Law Life	Compagnie du Midi (France)
1988	Sentry	Assurance Generales de France
1989	DAS Legal	Deutscher Automobil Schutz
	National Insce & Guarantee	Skandia International (Sweden)
	Prolific Group	Hafnia (Denmark)
1994	Scottish Equitable	AEGON (Holland) acquired an interest
1996	Provincial	UAP (France)
1997	Threadneedle	Zurich Financial Services
1998	Eagle Star	Zurich Financial Services
	Trade Indemnity	Groupe Euler
	Euler Trade Indemnity	Allianz
1999	Guardian Royal Exchange	AXA (France)

Source: Post Magazine Insurance Directory list of companies amalgamated.

Table 11.6 Foreign share of the UK general insurance market
Net premiums written (excluding Lloyd's)

	Motor, fire and accident (%)	MAT and reinsurance (%)	Total (%)
1990	18.5	45.7	23.7
1995	26.7	54.9	32.1
2000	37.3	84.9	42.2
2005	41.3	89.1	49.9

Note: Includes companies, friendly societies and P & I Clubs.
Source: Association of British Insurers, 2001, Table 108.

acquisition occurred in 1999 when the venerable *Guardian Royal Exchange* was acquired by *AXA*. Combined with the acquisition of other UK companies by other foreign insurers, the foreign share of the UK company market rose substantially (see Table 11.6).

Freedom of services

It took a long time before agreement could be reached on conferring 'freedom of services' – the right for insurers to sell their services across national frontiers and for a client in one member state to buy insurance services from an insurer with a head office in another member state but without an office in the country of the client. The 1978 *Co-insurance Directive* (78/473/EEC) was an interim measure to provide freedom of services for risks that were large enough to require the participation of several insurers. However, it had little effect on the amount of cross-frontier business transacted because of disagreements regarding the interpretation of the directive, including the location of the leading insurer.

Full freedom for all non-life direct insurances was achieved only in 1992 with the *Third Non-life Insurance (Framework) Directive* (92/49/EEC). The directive introduced the principle of 'home' country control of insurers, and prohibited national provisions requiring prior approval of policy terms or premium rates. The directive was brought into force in the UK by the *Insurance Companies (Amendment) Regulations*.

The 1992 Third *Life Insurance (Framework) Directive* closely followed the terms of the non-life directive and came into force in July 1994 (with time extensions for a few countries). It completed the creation of the 'single market' for insurance.

Intermediaries

The *Insurance Intermediaries Directive* (77/92EEC) adopted in 1976 permitted insurance brokers and insurance agents who are EEC nationals to operate on an establishment or services basis throughout the Community. It was repealed by the 2002 *Insurance Mediation Directive* (2002/92/EC), which was aimed at harmonising national rules on the regulation of brokers and limited authorisation as brokers to those established in the Community with adequate training and experience. It was implemented in the UK in 2005.

Other directives have been adopted covering such matters as accounting for insurance undertakings, insurance groups, and the winding-up of insurance undertakings.

As shown by Tables 11.3 and 11.4, following the opening up of European markets and the enlargement of the EU, UK companies have considerably expanded their business in Europe. The EU share of overseas total general insurance premiums has risen from 18 per cent in 1975 to 71 per cent in 2006. The equivalent figures for overseas long-term insurance were 25 per cent and 43 per cent, making Europe the largest source of overseas business for UK insurers. The contribution of individual EU countries to the total business written in the EU is shown in Figures 11.1 and 11.2. The Netherlands, Ireland and France have large shares of both non-life and life business, and Belgium is an important contributor to non-life business but not to life.

Details of underwriting results for EU non-life business are not available before 1994. From 1993 to 2000 the companies made an underwriting loss of £1,012m, on net premiums of £16,781m, or 5.5 per cent of net premiums. The results of individual countries are not known.

It should be noted, however, that Europe was just one of the regions of interest to British insurers during the last quarter of the twentieth century. ABI information shows that, despite the withdrawals from many markets in

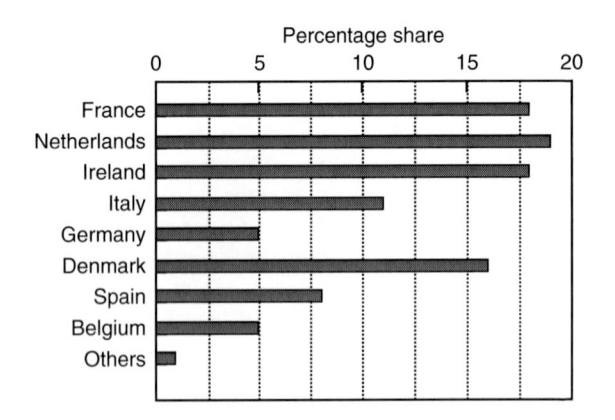

Figure 11.1 Shares of ABI companies' total EU net Non-life insurance premiums 2000
Source: Association of British Insurers 2001, Table 51.

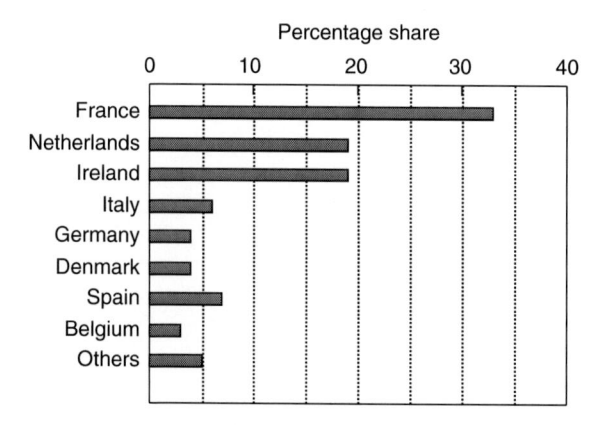

Figure 11.2 Shares of ABI companies' total EU Ordinary life premiums 2000
Source: Association of British Insurers 2001, Table 5.

earlier years, in 1992 its member companies or affiliates were represented in 122 countries. The highest numbers of companies outside Europe were situated in Australia with 40 followed by Canada (39) and the entrepôt markets of Hong Kong (34) and Singapore (23) (ABI, 1992).

Part III
Market Infrastructure

12
Competition and Mergers

Competition

Non-life business

Apart from government anti-inflationary measures in the 1970s restricting the size and timing of rate increases for motor insurance, the UK government, unlike those of some other countries, such as Germany, never sought to constrain competition that might undermine the security of insurers by regulating premium rates, policy cover or policy conditions for any class of insurance business. Instead the philosophy behind UK insurance regulation from the outset was 'freedom with publicity', that is, accounts and statements had to be published annually so that the public could judge for themselves the security of insurance companies, which were then free to conduct their business as they judged best.

Consequently the UK has always had a competitive insurance market, but a key factor affecting competition is the degree of uncertainty in the fixing of premium rates because of the uncertainty in the estimation of future claims costs, and potential investment earnings on funds. A company's existing claims data may be misleading because of (i) small sample size, (ii) changing risk factors, and (iii) delays in the settlement of claims that for some classes of insurance sometimes may take several years to settle. Therefore, estimated future claims costs may be under- or overestimated, leading to variations between insurers in premium rates. Not surprisingly, since the nineteenth century at times of intense competition insurers colluded to constrain competition through the establishment of tariff (i.e. minimum rate) associations to control premium rates and conditions for fire and certain classes of accident insurance (see Chapter 13).

Such cooperation brought some benefits for both insurers and policyholders, such as market stability, the encouragement of technical research, the pooling of underwriting information and advice into hazards (such as fire safety by the *Fire Prevention Association* formed by insurers in 1946). It also had the disadvantages of encouraging collusive behaviour, complacency, poor expense control, the failure to pay sufficient attention to consumers' interests and needs, and inflexibility and delays in changing rates and conditions in response to changing risk factors. In other words, the tariffs mainly served the interest of insurers rather the public interest.

Throughout the first half of the twentieth Century, the tariff companies' domination of the market ensured a large measure of market stability. However, by the late 1950s the maintenance and enforcement of the tariffs came increasingly under threat. Large industrial groups were beginning to challenge the fire tariffs as many sought both to retain ('self-insure') their high-frequency, low-value risks, and also to demand premiums more closely related to their own individual loss experience. However, the tariff companies still controlled the overwhelming share of the market in the mid-1950s, with the major independents largely content to follow the tariffs while seeking to attract business by offering small discounts from tariff rates and more generous no-claims discounts for motor and household insurances, but generally they did not fundamentally seek to undermine the tariffs. Moreover, the FOC retained sufficient power in the fire market to impose an arbitrary 15 per cent surcharge in 1963 on industrial and commercial tariff premiums, which in 1965, under pressure from large buyers, was modified to selective percentage adjustments to both tariff and non-tariff risks.

Motor insurance

The influence of the tariff companies, however, was declining in the early 1960s. Car ownership continued to rise, attracting to the expanding insurance market new small companies, which sought to exploit the weaknesses and inflexibility of the motor tariff and competed vigorously on price. Whereas the major independent companies were still content to largely follow the tariff, the newer companies attempted to identify and attract the 'good' risks and avoid the 'high' risks like young inexperienced drivers and high-powered sports cars, a process that was aided by the inflexibility of the tariffs. For example, if as shown in Figure 12.1 the tariff combined equally sized risk groups A and B, the failure to recognise their differing loss expectancies of £100 and £80 respectively would produce an average loss expectancy of £90, on which the premium rate would be based. Recognising that risk group B had a lower loss expectancy, the new non-tariff companies sought to attract that business with premiums based on the lower loss expectancy of £80, leaving the tariff companies with the higher risk group A at an inadequate premium. The tariff rates were based on cars and geographical areas, but the new non-tariff companies looked to other risk factors; the *Midland Northern & Scottish*, for example, introduced its 'Alpha' plan with premium rates based on drivers.

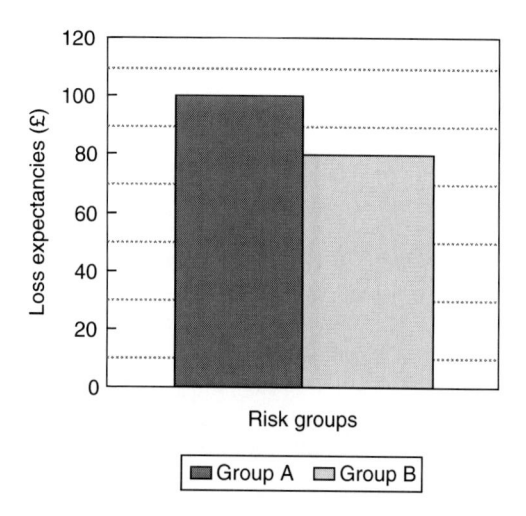

Figure 12.1 Classification of risks
Source: Authors' data.

Inevitably, as more companies entered the market, the intensifying competition culminated in the failure of most of the new entrants, including the *Irish American*, the *London & Cheshire* and most notoriously the *Fire Auto and Marine*, established in 1963 by the entrepreneur Dr Emil Savundra (see Chapter 5). Having grown rapidly for three years, it went into liquidation in 1986, leaving around 280,000 motorists without insurance cover, and Savundra was eventually arrested and convicted. The company's advertising slogan in 1965 had been, 'We've got them worried' – too true! The government proceeded to strengthen regulation by enacting the Part II of the Companies Act, 1967.

The British Insurance Association, in an attempt to restore some stability to the market, responded in 1965 with the adoption of a report by McKinsey & Co. to establish the Motor Risks Statistical Bureau. Its objective was to try to modify competition through the pooling by companies of loss statistics to facilitate sounder underwriting throughout the market.

Following a long-standing propensity for companies to combine whenever trading conditions became difficult, the major tariff companies sought to strengthen their positions in the 1960s with a series of mergers. The Accident Offices Association, under pressure from the ten leading tariff companies, despite the opposition of some of its smaller members, abandoned the motor tariff on 31 December 1968 to the delight of some members and the trepidation of others (Carter, 1969). The market plunged into a period of intense competition, making underwriting losses of 7.3, 14.5 and 8.6 per cent in 1969, 1970 and 1971 respectively (ABI, 1985). The Chairman of the independent *Eagle Star* commented in its 1969 annual report and accounts:

> A loss on motor business was the result of rate-cutting launched by some sections of the motor market at the beginning of 1969, despite clear indications that the cost of claims was rising steeply.

And the General Manager of the *Friends Provident & Century* (one of the smaller tariff companies) said at the 1969 Conference of the Chartered Insurance Institute:

> In these days of mergers there was developing a considerable deterioration in the amount of co-operation between companies. Certain big companies have steam-rollered over things in recent months. (Carter, 1979, p. 15)

The continuing competition brought the collapse in 1971 of the large mushrooming independent motor insurer *Vehicle & General*. It involved other motor insurers in substantial additional costs in providing cover for and compensating *V & G*'s million policyholders. Again the government sought to control insurance companies more rigorously by enacting the Insurance Companies Amendment Act, 1973.

However, there were signs that more stringent underwriting by companies was beginning to work at a time of rising inflation, and the market achieved a small underwriting profit in 1973.Then it lapsed back into a small loss in 1975 because attempts to increase premiums were more than offset by rising inflation and government control for several years over the size and timing of rate increases. Moreover, competition remained keen as companies sought to retain market share in a rapidly growing market: the net UK motor premium income of the member companies of the British Insurance Association rose from £130 million in 1961 to £628m in 1975. Some companies were keen to obtain investment income, given the prevailing high rates of interest, apparently ignoring the fact that claims costs were inflating at an even faster rate. Consequently, apart from 1976, the market continued to incur underwriting losses for most of the remainder of the century. The problem for companies was whether to write business that would be unprofitable or accept the increase in expense ratios that would ensue from turning away business.

Advances in information technology brought about the next surge in competition with the formation of *Direct Line* in 1984, using the most advanced information technology then available to cut out intermediaries and commissions by direct selling to the public by telephone of motor insurance (and later other personal insurances and financial services), using advanced underwriting software to provide quotations. Companies embarked too on extensive television advertising campaigns.

In the 1990s the internet opened up a new marketing channel that lowered entry barriers for new companies. The success of other new companies founded to exploit the opportunities offered by information technology (e.g. *Churchill* and *E-sure*) in due course forced established companies to adopt the same methods, including the formation of direct dealing subsidiaries, notably *Norwich Union Direct* and *Royal Sun Alliance's 'More than'*.

Fire insurance

Fire insurance had been for two centuries the mainstay of the UK non-life industry and remained so until the 1960s. Underpinned by the Fire Offices Committee's UK and overseas fire tariffs, the companies' worldwide fire business consistently returned a profit from the date of the San Francisco earthquake in 1906 until 1962. In 1968 105 companies plus Lloyd's (with a 7 per cent share of total premium income) were operating in the UK direct fire insurance market, but the Monopolies Commission found that the market was highly concentrated, with five companies controlling 58 per cent of the total companies' premium income. The tariff sector was even more concentrated, with the leading four companies' premiums amounting to £110m out of the total £153m premiums written by tariff companies (see Table 7.1). The premium income of the independent companies amounted to £104m, but they had limited opportunities for effective competition due to the FOC's restrictive 65/35 per cent rule, which precluded any tariff company from participating in the large co-insured risks unless at least 65 per cent was placed with tariff companies. However, the growing size of the leading non-tariff companies, new overseas entrants and Lloyd's meant that they could handle increasingly larger risks without tariff support. The supply of fire insurance was referred in 1968 to the Monopolies Commission, which argued that, though aggregate demand is price inelastic, the demand for the individual firm is highly elastic. The Commission required the tariff companies to explain their competitive behaviour. It led to the abandonment of the household tariff in 1970, but, despite the Commission finding in 1972 that the commercial tariffs operated against the public interest (Monopolies Commission, 1972), the industrial fire tariffs were kept in force until 1985. Perhaps not surprisingly, the Commission received substantial support for the maintenance of the tariffs from the main independent companies, who, economic theory predicted, could take advantage, at least for small trade risks, of a substantial increase in demand by offering a small reduction in price. No tariffs have operated since 1985 for any class of insurance.

Following the ending of the household tariff, there was keen competition for business, but underwriting results were undermined more by inflation and rising burglary and subsidence losses than by competitive pressures. Eventually in the 1970s most companies introduced the index-linking of sums insured. Although the commercial fire tariff was not abandoned until

1985, there was growing competition for fire business at a time of rising fire losses leading to underwriting losses. As noted above, major industrial groups began to exercise their countervailing power to demand special terms from insurers, including partial insurance arrangements (that is, first loss covers and large deductibles) and experience-related premiums.

Other classes of business were adversely affected by new legislation. For example, the Health & Safety at Work Act, 1974, which had increased employers' duty of care to employees and third parties, led to an increase in employers' liability claims, which, generally taking a long time to settle, were badly affected by inflation.

The gradual creation of the single European market from 1974:

1. provided access for British insurers and brokers to formerly closed European markets, but
2. also opened up the British market to the entry of European insurers.

The London Market

The number of British and foreign companies, including subsidiaries of overseas leading insurance and reinsurance companies, operating in the London Market had grown rapidly in the 1980s, reaching over 200 companies by the mid-1980s. However, Lloyd's and the London Market companies were facing increasing competition from abroad, including the rapidly growing Bermuda market, which according to the US Department of Commerce overtook the UK in 1981 as a supplier of reinsurance to insurers and reinsurers resident in America, and in the 1990s from Dublin, which proved attractive for foreign insurers and reinsurers as a base for their European operations. At the end of the decade and in the early 1990s the Market was badly hit by huge losses incurred on American catastrophe and liability reinsurances, resulting in the forced or voluntary withdrawal of some 70 companies and the near collapse of Lloyd's. Twenty-six companies were wound up between 1989 and 1995, and many more were taken over. The Lloyd's rescue plan, which introduced limited liability corporate members, was followed by a consolidation of syndicates as underwriting agencies created syndicates capable of accepting larger risks. The company market too consolidated into a smaller number of larger companies; the takeover of British reinsurers and the withdrawal of others left the London market dominated by foreign companies.

Life business

Life business was growing rapidly during the 1980s and 1990s at a time of intense competition from inside and outside the industry (see Table 12.1).

Collusion between life offices never extended to the setting up of a premium rating tariff, but the Life Offices' Association (LOA) did impose limits on commission rates and the timing of the payment of commissions to intermediaries.

Table 12.1 ABI member companies' long-tem premiums

	UK (£m)	USA (£m)	EU (£m)	Rest of world (£m)	Total (£m)
1980	6,035	n.a.	537	323	6,895
1985	13,715	142	931	1,268	16,056
1990	32,196	1,828	1,995	2,774	38,793
1995	46,082	2,798	4,654	3,862	57,396
2000	127,754	5,596	7,993	6,880	148,223
2006	144,803	7,187	12,536	9,572	174,098

Source: Association of British Insurers.

With-profits business had become the most important source of business, but by the 1960s bonus rates were lagging behind the investment earnings of the life offices, though as a partial solution in the late 1960s life offices introduced terminal bonuses to give maturing policies some benefit of the capital growth of investments. Nevertheless, the way was open for new product competition with the introduction of unit-linked life insurances, where the policyholder shared directly in the underlying investment performance of the funds, which on a rising Stock Market proved to be very popular. Moreover, the new companies (notably *Abbey Life* – formed in 1961 – and *Hambro Life*) and other companies employing their own direct sales forces led to *Equity and Law* asking the LOA in 1971 for the commissions agreement to be relaxed. When that request was rejected *Equity and Law* resigned its membership, but the agreement was not finally abandoned until 1982.

New competition came from outside the industry as unit trust companies (for example, the *M & G Group*, which formed *M & G Life Assurance* in 1961) and banks established their own life offices (Barclays Bank had established *Barclays Life Assurance Co.* in 1965 and Lloyds TSB established *Black Horse Life Assurance Co.* in 1973). Banks entered into relationships with insurers (replacing the agencies that had traditionally been the domain of bank managers). To try to counter the new competition some life offices as early as 1968 set up their own unit trusts. Also to help to counter the competition from unit-linked insurances, in 1969 *Royal* introduced a new product (life policies linked to building society deposits) and entered into arrangements with 20 building societies to market it (see Chapter 6).

The 'financial services revolution' of the 1980s transformed financial markets and created new threats and opportunities for life offices (see Chapter 6). The Financial Services Act, 1986, reorganised the market in two ways. First, it required the polarisation of persons advising on or dealing in 'investment business' into tied representatives and independent intermediaries (called independent financial advisers (IFAs)). Secondly, it set up the *Securities and Investment Board* (*SIB*) and new self-regulatory organisations (the *Financial Intermediaries, Managers and Brokers Regulatory Association* (*FIMBRA*), the *Life Assurance and Unit Trust Regulatory Authority* (*LAUTRO*) and the *Investment Managers Regulatory Organisation* (*IMRO*)), which intermediaries and the life offices had to join, a situation that lasted until the enactment of the Financial Services and Markets Act, 2000, when the supervisory role passed to the FSA. In the succeeding years new products, first developed in America, were brought to the market (e.g. universal life and critical illness policies).

The main threat to and opportunity for the established life insurance market at the time was seen to be 'bancassurance' – the provision of insurance products by banks – seeking to exploit the synergies and the cost advantage of having large customer databases and large numbers of customers with whom they had regular contact, though sales did not necessarily take place through their branches. Life insurers too were equally anxious to gain access to that distribution channel and some diversified into banking services. However, the subject is discussed more fully in Chapters 6 and 14. In Britain product complexity and regulatory requirements and the success of direct distribution channels, notably by telephone and the internet, have limited the penetration of bancassurance (Swiss Re, 2007). Bancassurers gained most success in selling simple life and non-life products, with in 2006 an estimated 10 per cent share of non-life business and a 20.3 per cent share of life business (Swiss Re, 2007). However, by 2007 banks and building societies had increased their share of general insurance retail sales to 16 per cent (ABI, 2008). IFAs were far more successful in retaining control of the more complex life and pensions products with a 75 per cent share of life and pensions business in 2007 (ABI, 2008). By the end of the decade new models were being tried by banks, including joint ventures and multi-supplier strategies.

The introduction of personal pensions in 1987 brought a massive growth of new business; the total number of new individual pension contracts sold rose from 912,000 in 1987 to 2,592,000 in 1988 (ABI, 1993). Many thousands of individuals (such as nurses and teachers) were encouraged to opt out of secure occupational pension schemes in favour of personal pensions, leading to complaints of mis-selling by overenthusiastic, commission-remunerated salesmen. Consequently the number of new personal pensions sold fell sharply in the second half of the 1990s.

The performance of the life offices during the remaining years of the century was determined mainly by economic conditions and government policies, notably:

- changes to the state pensions scheme and changing provisions regarding occupational, self-employed and personal pensions;
- the introduction of MIRAS (mortgage interest relief at source) in 1983, which increased the demand for mortgages, endowment and mortgage protection policies;

- the withdrawal of LAPR (life assurance premium relief) on all new qualifying policies taken out after 13 March 1984 to put life assurance on a level playing field with other forms of saving.

Mergers

The data on companies amalgamated and companies wound up shown below is compiled from the lists of 'Amalgamated Companies' and 'Historical Company Changes' published in the Post Magazine's *Insurance Directory*. Although the data on mergers and acquisitions shown in the tables and graphs below may not be fully comprehensive, they are a good record of the amount of activity each year.

Numerous companies were merged and wound up in the first two decades of the twentieth century, including during World War I, though on a smaller scale than during the preceding years (see Figure 12.2). Gross domestic product at fixed prices had remained virtually unchanged since the end of the nineteenth century, shipbuilding was in decline and unemployment, which had doubled in 1909 and 1910, rose to 1½ million, making trading conditions difficult for insurers. The number of companies leaving the insurance industry rose, with 17 companies being amalgamated and 11 wound up in 1909, and 17 being amalgamated and 21 wound up in 1910. However, of the 204 companies amalgamated from 1900 to 1920, most involved small

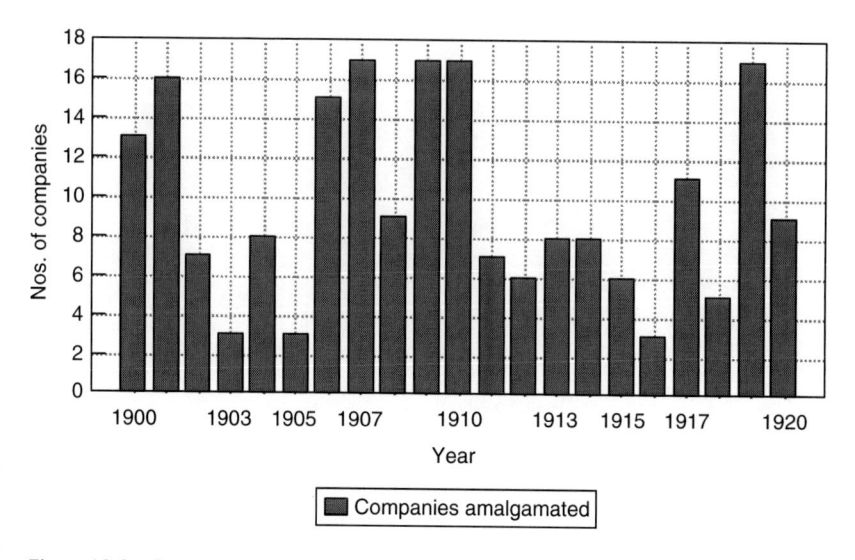

Figure 12.2 Companies amalgamated 1900–20
Source: *Post Magazine Insurance Directory*, authors' calculations.

companies, including 31 small, local plate glass insurance companies often merging with a neighbouring company. The prime purpose of some mergers was that of the old-established fire offices seeking to grow and diversify into other classes of business. They acquired life offices and companies that had been established to write the new classes of insurance, as shown in Table 12.2. In principle, diversifying should have enabled them to achieve more stable underwriting profits because the underwriting results for the different classes of insurance were not correlated. On the other hand, in 1905 the *Commercial Union* acquired the venerable fire office the *Hand-in-Hand*, which had been established in 1696.

As shown by Figure 12.3, during the 25 years from 1920 there was less merger activity, and again many of the companies involved were small, local,

Table 12.2 Acquisitions of companies by major companies

Date acquired	Company acquired	Acquiring company
1900	Equitable Plate Glass	Northern
	Lion Life & Accident	Ocean Accident & Guarantee
1901	United Kent Life	Royal
	Universal Life	North British & Mercantile
1902	National Guardian Life	National Union
	Imperial Life	Alliance
1904	Scottish Employers Liability	London & Lancashire Fire
1906	Accident Insce Co. No. 2	Commercial Union
	Provident Life	Alliance
1907	Employers Liability	Ocean Accident & Guarantee
	Employers Mutual	Vulcan Boiler
	Equitable Fire & Accident	London & Lancashire
	Globe Accident	Commercial Union
	Goldsmiths & General Burglary	Guardian
	Lancs & Yorks Accident	Scottish Union & National
	Scottish County & Mercantile	Commercial Union
	Standard Marine	London & Lancashire
	Pelican & British Empire Life	Phoenix
1908	Norwich & London Accident	Norwich Union Fire
1909	British & Foreign Marine	Royal
	Law Life	Phoenix
	Rock Life	Law Union & Crown
	Scottish Livestock	General Accident
1910	Alliance Plate Glass	Commercial Union
	London & General Plate Glass	Guardian
	Railway Passengers	North British & Mercantile

Source: Post Magazine Insurance Directory, authors' calculations.

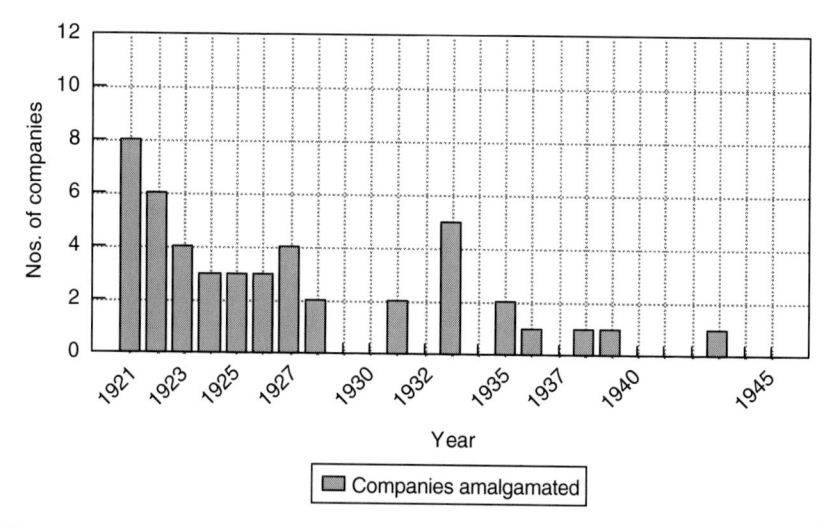

Figure 12.3 Companies amalgamated 1921–45
Source: *Post Magazine Insurance Directory*, authors' calculations.

specialist or plate glass companies, but the major companies were still expanding their ranges of activities through acquisitions to strengthen their status as composite insurers, for example in:

- 1922 the *Phoenix* acquired the *London Guarantee and Accident*
  Provincial took over the *Monument*
- 1923 *General Accident* acquired the *English*
- 1924 *Commercial Union* acquired the *West of Scotland*
- 1926 *General Accident* took over *General Life*
  Commercial Union acquired the *Liverpool Marine and General*
- 1927 *Royal Exchange* acquired the *Motor Union*
  Sun acquired the *National Parcels*
- 1931 *London Assurance* acquired the *Guildhall*
- 1933 *Phoenix* acquired *Tariff Reinsurance*.

During World War II there was very little merger activity, as shown by Figure 12.3. The next wave of mergers came in response to the intense market competition during the 1960s (see Figure 12.4) following a plethora of new companies having been enticed to enter the market by the large increase in demand for motor insurance. After the collapse of the *Fire Auto & Marine* in 1966, 22 companies were wound up between 1967 and 1971, including over a dozen of the new motor insurers, and another 28 were taken over. *Eagle Star* and *General Accident* were particularly active been 1967 and 1970, each taking over several companies, including marine insurers.

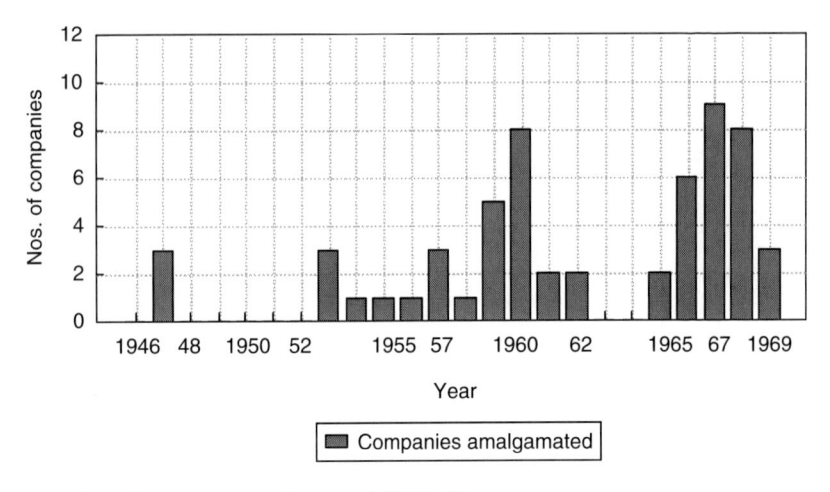

Figure 12.4 Companies amalgamated 1946–69
Source: *Post Magazine Insurance Directory*, authors' calculations.

The 1960s saw the disappearance as independent entities of some of the country's oldest companies, as the major companies took over weaker companies and specialist companies to improve the cost structure of the merged company. For example, a feature of the *Guardian Royal Exchange* merger was the reduction in the combined staff numbers of the two companies. Peter Dugdale, the Managing Director, referred to the unification of the branch network, the creation of a joint brand image and the reduction in the staff numbers of the two companies from 11,500 to 7,500 by 1970 (Dugdale, 1983).

Europe was moving towards the creation of a single market, presenting the prospect of increasing competition at home, where the tariffs were coming under threat, and in Europe, where eventually government controls on premium rates and policy covers had to be abandoned. As noted above, the major companies saw mergers as a means of achieving economies of scale and of meeting the intensifying competition at home by giving them greater financial strength and geographical spread to provide a genuinely international service for major industrial groups that were beginning to look for insurers capable of supplying global covers for their home and overseas associates and subsidiaries. The major mergers are recorded in Table 12.3. By acquiring *Midland Assurance* in 1959 the *Eagle Star* acquired a large employer's liability insurance account. Other mergers provided the acquiring company, including the UK's then largest life office *Prudential*, with access to the life and non-life international reinsurance markets[1]. The most interesting acquisition was in 1967 by the independent *General Accident* of the *Yorkshire*, which besides being a tariff company also wrote a large life account (see Chapter 7).

Table 12.3 Mergers of major companies 1959–68

Date acquired	Company acquired	Acquiring company
1959	Alliance	Sun
	Scottish Union & National	Norwich Union Fire
	Maritime	Norwich Union Fire
	Midland	Eagle Star
1960	Employers Liability	Northern
1961	London & Lancashire	Royal
1965	London	Sun Alliance
1966	Home & Overseas	Eagle Star
1967	Yorkshire	General Accident
1968	Mercantile & General Reinsurance	Prudential
	Northern & Employers	Commercial Union

Source: Extracted from *Post Magazine Insurance Directory* 'Tables of companies amalgamated'.

Whether the mergers were successful in improving companies' performance is questionable, though they did not appear to make it worse. However, Carter commented at the time:

the performance of some merged groups suggests that sometimes mergers have consumed management time and energy which could have been better used in improving their own business and in introducing modern management techniques to their companies. (Carter, 1970)

The 1970s brought a new round of consolidation in the industry with the major companies again on the acquisition trail (see Table 12.4). *Phoenix*, which had acquired *Bradford* and *Pennine* in 1971, was itself acquired by *Sun Alliance & London* in 1984, together with the *Century*, so that again old established companies lost their independence while extending the *Sun Alliance & London*'s international business and life accounts. In 1984 life office *Legal & General* followed *Prudential*'s lead in acquiring a reinsurance company (*Victory Re*), and the American conglomerate *ITT* diversified by acquiring two UK general insurers, the *London & Edinburgh* (1972) and the *Excess* in 1973.

After the UK industry's euphoria about Britain joining the EEC in 1973, the British companies quickly found themselves at a disadvantage in competing against their European competitors, which, having operated in highly regulated, protected markets, had been able to build up large reserves and were acquiring financially weaker British companies (see Table 12.5). The most notable European acquisitions were those of two of the leading UK companies, *Guardian Royal Exchange* by *AXA* in 1999 and *Eagle Star* by *Zurich Financial Services* in 1998 (see Figure 12.5).

162 The British Insurance Industry Since 1900

Table 12.4 Mergers and acquisitions by major UK insurance companies 1970–84

Date of acquisition	Acquired company	Acquiring company
1971	Bradford Pennine	Phoenix
1973	Victory Re	Legal & General
1984	Phoenix	Sun Alliance & London
	Century	Sun Alliance & London

Source: Extracted from *Post Magazine Insurance Directory* 'Tables of companies amalgamated'.

Table 12.5 British companies acquired by European companies

Year	Company acquired	Acquiring company
1967	Contingency	GAN (France)
1968	Life Association of Scotland	Nationale Nederlanden (Holland)
	Pendle	Ancienne Mutuelle (France)
1971	Triumph	Ennia NV (Holland)
1974	Moorgate	Pojhola of Helsinki (Finland)
	County Fire	Copenhagen Re (Denmark)
1979	Gresham Life	NV AMEV (Holland)
1980	Dog Breeders Insce	Generali Group (Italy)
1981	Provident Life Assocn	Winterthur Swiss
1984	Economic	Hafnia Group (Denmark)
1986	Cornhill	Allianz (Germany)
1987	City of Westminster	Assurances Generales de France
	Equity & Law Life	Compagnie du Midi (France)
1988	Sentry	Assurance Generales de France
1989	DAS Legal Expenses	Deutscher Automobil Schutz
	National Insce & Guarantee	Skandia International (Sweden)
	Prolific Group	Hafnia (Denmark)
1994	Scottish Equitable	AEGON (Holland) acquired an interest
1996	Provincial	UAP (France)
1997	Threadneedle	Zurich Financial Services
1998	Eagle Star	Zurich Financial Services
	Trade Indemnity	Groupe Euler
	Euler Trade Indemnity	Allianz
1999	Guardian Royal Exchange	AXA (France)

Source: Extracted from *Post Magazine Insurance Directory* 'Tables of companies amalgamated'.

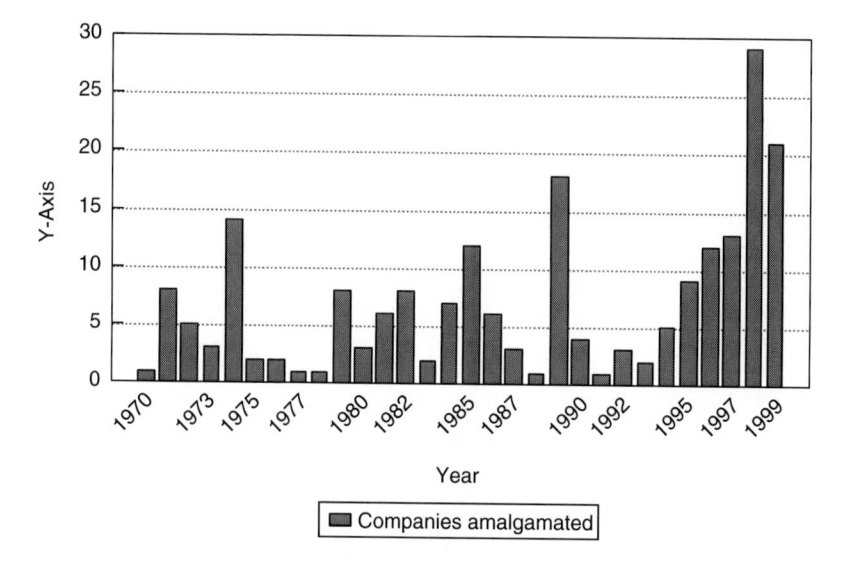

Figure 12.5 Companies amalgamated 1970–99
Source: Post Magazine Insurance Directory, authors' calculations.

Mergers of major companies in the 1990s

Despite mergers and acquisitions being subject to statutory control by both the UK and EU competition authorities, and intervention by the FSA that could impose requirements on the merged businesses, the 1990s brought another fever of merger and acquisition activity. The major British companies aimed to secure economies of scale and the ability to compete against their powerful international competitors when in:

- 1996 the *Royal* merged with *Sun Alliance & London* to form *Royal Sun Alliance*;
- 1998 *Commercial Union merged with the General Accident* to form the *CGU*;
- 1999 *CGU* merged with *Norwich Union* to form *CGNU*, which was changed to *Aviva* in 2002.

Thus the UK non-life market became dominated by two giant groups. Both of the first two mergers above were expected to achieve considerable cost savings, including staff cuts.

One of the aims of the *RSA* merger was to become the largest composite insurer and one of the country's top life insurers and fund managers. It is ironic, therefore, that in less than ten years, during the 2004 with-profits crisis, the group closed its life funds and transferred its life companies and funds to *Resolution Life*. In 2005 Britannic acquired *Resolution Life*, which changed its name to *Resolution PLC*. Closed fund managers *Resolution* and *Pearl Group* went on to manage many other closed funds (O'Brien and Diacon, 2005).

RSA quickly took another major step to improve its portfolio of business. As long ago as 1965 the *Royal*'s Chairman in his annual report had described American business as 'an era of profitless prosperity', so it was perhaps surprising that it took another 40 years to persuade it to sell its often loss-making non-life US business in 2006 to a company formed by its US management team.

Throughout Europe the creation of the single market and the convergence of financial markets had stimulated companies into large numbers of acquisitions, with the largest number involving British companies, including the acquisition of life offices by banks, building societies and other institutions (Cummins and Weiss, 2004). The most commonly given reason for a merger is to achieve economies of scale, but in diversifying mergers, such as a bank buying an insurer, there may be economies of scope.

The demutualisation of mutual life offices in the 1980s and 1990s gave banks the opportunity to acquire a life office, beginning with *Abbey National*'s acquisition of *Scottish Mutual* in 1992 (see Chapter 6). In 1999 two other banks were involved in the acquisition of life offices – *Halifax* acquired *Clerical Medical Investments* and *Lloyds TSB* acquired *Scottish Widows*. *Royal Bank of Scotland*, which had pioneered the technique of direct dealing through call centres, expanded its non-life interests, acquiring *Privilege* in 1998, *UK Insurance* in 1999 and *Churchill Insurance* and the *National Insurance & Guarantee* in 2003.

Table 12.5 records UK companies acquired by European insurers over the last four decades of the twentieth century.

Numbers of companies

It is relevant in the context of competitive market conditions to review the number of insurers that were active during the past decade (see Table 12.6). The number of authorised insurers was well over 1,000 in 2007, with the 786 non-life companies being the largest group. The increase in the total since 1998 owes much to the impact of the 1992 Third Insurance Directives creating a single market for the European Economic Area (EEA). The companies listed under 'other' include branches of EEA insurers with head offices in other European countries as well as companies from other markets. The strongest rise in total numbers was in non-life companies, with 786 being authorised by the FSA in 2007. Of this total 402 were EEA firms and 57 from further afield. Thus the majority of the growth was due to EEA company arrivals. It is notable that the UK-based non-life companies declined by 25 per cent since 1998, probably due to mergers and foreign acquisitions.

Life company numbers increased, again due to foreign, mostly EEA entrants, while UK numbers dropped by 28 per cent. The steepest contraction

Table 12.6 Authorised insurance companies

		1998	2007
Life companies	UK firms	162	121
	Others[a]	14 (4)	94 (83)
	Total life	176	215
Composites	UK firms	55	19
	Others[a]	7 (4)	28 (26)
	Total composites	62	47
Non-life companies	UK firms	451	384
	Other[a]	143 (73)	402 (345)
	Total non-life	594	786
Total	UK firms	668	524
	Other	164	524
	Total	832	1,048

Note: [a] Number of firms in brackets are EEA firms with head offices outside the UK.
Source: FSA figures as at 31 March.

was in the composites, where the rise in new entrants did not offset the contraction in UK authorisations.

It should be noted that the above figures exclude the mutual sector, such as industrial provident societies and friendly societies (registered under the Provident Societies Act 1965), which between them numbered 10,634 in 2007. These figures give an indication of the abundance of small regional suppliers of insurance products and the consequent competitive nature of the British market.

Insurance buyers often deal with insurance intermediaries. The FSA listed 8,353 general insurance brokers in 2007, a decline from the 10,833 two years before.

Intermediaries

Mergers have not been confined to insurers; there have also been many mergers of broking firms.

The 1980s and 1990s saw merger activity resulting in the creation of a few very large global broking groups, notably the *Marsh & McLennan Cos.*, *Aon Corporation* and *Willis Group Holdings*, which operate internationally and have become the world's three largest brokers.

Among the major UK brokers operating in the London market, the most important mergers occurred in 1980 when the two American mega-brokers *Marsh McLellan* and *Aon* acquired leading UK brokers, gaining the advantage of direct access to the Lloyd's market. *Marsh McLellan*, which had earlier merged with American brokers *Johnson & Higgins*, acquired the largest

UK broker *C T Bowring & Co.* UK broker *Willis Faber & Dumas*, which had been formed in 1928 as the result of the merger of *Willis Faber* with *Dumas & Wylie Willis* in 1987, acquired *Stewart Wrightson* (which itself in the late 1960s had acquired the old established Lloyd's broker *Bray Gibb*) and in the early 1990s *Willis* merged with the American broker *Corroon Black*. A further takeover of a large UK broker by an American broker occurred in 2006 when *Lockton* acquired *Alexander Forbes*.

The domination of the handling of large commercial insurances by the large broking groups encouraged the development of niche players providing specialist insurance products often for affinity groups, such as *Towergate*, which have the advantages of flexibility and specialism. Also the expansion of direct dealing by insurers and the regulation of intermediaries by the FSA following the enactment of the Financial Services and Markets Act, 2000, led to some consolidation of small–medium general insurance intermediaries. Some joined networks, such as *HLA Global* and *Broker Worldwide*, to provide them with compliance and other common services, and access to a panel of insurers with whom they had negotiated products. Others sold out to larger firms, notably the *Folgate Partnership*, which, after having made a substantial number of acquisitions during 2003 and 2004, itself merged in 2005 with *Towergate*, which through further acquisitions became the largest independently owned insurance organisation incorporating an underwriting division that acts as a virtual insurer. Other consolidators include the *Jelf Group* and the *Oval Group*, which was founded in 2003 with the backing of *Caledonian Investments* and set about acquiring regional broking companies and a Lloyd's broker.

The other major development around the turn of the century was the acquisition by insurers of retail brokers, notably:

- *Norwich Union* acquired *Hill House Hammond*, though it disposed of the company in 2006;
- *Sun Alliance & London* acquired an interest in *Swintons* in 1988.

Prudential, on the other hand, chose to sever all of its links with brokers in 1991 when it restricted its general insurance business to personal insurances handled by its direct sales force.

In 1987 the American insurance group *St Paul Companies* had acquired a Lloyd's broker, and some major brokers owned insurance companies. However, in 2007 *AXA* initiated a round of insurers acquiring commercial lines brokers with the takeover of *Stuart Alexander, Latham Blackham* and *Smart & Cook*, and in 2008 of the *SBJ Group*. The expansion of an insurer into broking raised questions of relationships with other brokers that may provide it with business and of fair competition, and of channel conflict within the same ownership.

The 1990s brought a new channel of distribution into being – the internet. And it led to the emergence of both on-line insurers and brokers such as *Oval On-line* catering for commercial insurances, and particularly the emergence of so-called aggregators, such as *Confused* and *Money Supermarket*, that is, companies that acquire a panel of insurers and then advertise on television the opportunity for consumers to obtain price comparisons. The entry of major retailers Dixons and Tesco (with *Tesco Compare*) into the price comparison websites intensified the competition between the aggregators. Brokers, especially small and medium brokers, have criticised them for not providing clients with full comparisons of policy cover, of insurers' reputations for claims handling, etc., which is part of the role of a broker, and calling for FSA regulation. Not all insurers are prepared to participate in aggregators' panels of insurers; in 2008 *Norwich Union* announced its intention to withdraw from all price comparison websites but to provide its customers on-line and by telephone with the prices and details of the cover of its competitors.

13
Trade Associations and Other Bodies

This chapter briefly explains the formation and objectives of the associations that have performed important roles in the development of the insurance industry during the twentieth century. They can be classified as falling into four categories:

1. those formed to control competition (the collusive associations);
2. those formed to ensure market cooperation in regards to a particular issue, or to represent the interests of their members to government and regulatory bodies, in some cases in response to public pressure (the cooperative associations);
3. those formed as the result of government action, including the enactment of various Acts (the quasi-official associations); and
4. educational and training bodies.

Collusive bodies

Both life and non-life insurance at times have been excessively competitive. Professors Brown and Wiseman's claim that the 'propensity to combine' has been 'as pervasive as the propensity to compete' (Phelps Brown and Wiseman, 1966, p. 122) has been true of the insurance industry. It was as early as the nineteenth century that Scottish offices colluded to fix fire premium rates for flax and cotton mills and other types of premises with the formation in Edinburgh of the *Association of Managers of Fire Insurance Offices* in 1829 (Raynes, 1968, p. 331). The *Scottish Fire Insurance Managers* was formed to administer the tariffs (Raynes, 1968, p. 337).

The *Life Offices Association* (*LOA*) was established in 1848 to represent the interests of life offices in England, having been influenced by the Scottish equivalent *ASLO* (Raynes, 1968, p. 347). Although not attempting to control premiums, the Association did enforce an agreement on the amount and timing of payment of commissions to agents. The *LOA* and *ASLO* worked closely together, until the *LOA* was merged into the *ABI* in 1985.

The *Associated Scottish Life Offices* (*ASLO*) was formed in 1841 and remained independent when the *LOA* was merged into the *Association of British Insurers* (*ABI*) in 1985. Today it discusses matters of general interest to the industry, and sometimes passes on its views to the ABI.

The *Institute of London Underwriters* (*ILU*) was founded by marine insurance companies in 1884. Its Joint Hull and War Risks Committees, on which Lloyd's was represented, *recommended* premium rates and surcharges for hull and war risks. In 1998 the *ILU* was merged with the *London Insurance & Reinsurance Market Association* (*LIRMA*) to form the *International Underwriting Association* (*IUA*).

The *Fire Offices Committee* (*FOC*) was formed in 1868 to formulate and enforce minimum premium rates for fire insurance, followed the next year by the *Fire Offices Committee (Foreign)*.

The FOC in 1968 had 110 members. Its member companies, the tariff companies, dominated the practice of fire insurance at home and in many overseas territories for over 100 years. It exercised considerable market power for over 100 years, controlling competition to bring stability to the market but at the cost of complacency and a lack of flexibility in altering premium rates quickly in response to changing risk factors. Reference to the Monopolies Commission (see Chapter 7) led to the FOC's demise in 1985 when it was merged into the new *Association of British Insurers*.

The *Accident Offices Association* (*AOA*), the accident counterpart to the FOC, was formed in 1906 by 24 companies that wished to provide uniform premium rates and conditions for workmen's compensation insurance. The Association adopted a workmen's compensation tariff in 1909, a motor insurance tariff in 1915, and subsequently tariffs for other classes of accident insurance. In 1968 the AOA had approximately 100 members, and its tariffs controlled employer's liability, engineering, motor, certain types of livestock insurances, and certain types of fidelity guarantee bonds (Carter, 1968b, p. 74). During the 1960s the motor tariff had come under growing pressure as the tariff companies lost market share to a growing number of new independent companies (Carter, 1968b, p. 93). Several of the newcomers were of dubious character and quickly failed, notably the *Fire Auto & Marine*, which had aggressively and quickly built up a large portfolio of business. Its failure in 1966 led to the prosecution and conviction for fraud of its founder and chief executive Dr Savundra, and induced the government to strengthen supervisory legislation. The collapse in 1971 of the largest of the newcomers, the *Vehicle & General*, which was a member of the BIA, affected 800,000 policyholders. The failure of BIA's members to meet the underwriting debts of the *V & G*, apart from third party liability, rather undermined the British Insurance Association's advertising campaign that, after the previous failure of non-member companies, exhorted the public to 'Get the strength of British insurance companies around you'.

The tariff companies pre-empted a reference to the Monopolies Commission by announcing that they were voluntarily abandoning all of the accident tariffs, starting with motor insurance as from 31 December 1968 and ending with engineering insurance on 31 December 1970.

The *Livestock Offices Association* was founded in 1912 and the *Engineering Offices Association* was formed in 1920 by the AOA to administer the tariffs for those classes of insurance.

Cooperative bodies

The *Association of Mutual Insurers (AMI)* was formed in September 2004 by 13 mutual insurers in the UK to focus on (i) lobbying to represent the interests of members to the FSA, the UK Treasury, the ABI, the EU and the International Association of Insurance Supervisors, and (ii) public relations.

The *Aviation Insurance Clauses Group (AICG)* was established in 2005 to draft, propose and publish recommended policy wordings and clauses in the London Market. Its members include Lloyd's Market Association Aviation Committee and the International Underwriting Association.

The *British Insurers' European Committee* was formed in the early 1950s to represent the interests of UK insurers, Lloyd's and the P & I Clubs to the EU and to the relevant UK government departments, regarding matters under discussion in the EU. It operates as part of the ABI.

The *British Insurance Association (BIA)*. An association of composite offices that was being formed to consider questions affecting the interests of insurance both at home and abroad became in 1917 the British Insurance Association to provide information and express views to government departments and other bodies, and to monitor affairs worldwide that might affect member offices. In the 1930s it extended its work as an umbrella organisation to deal with investment protection and give advice to the government.

An important part of its work from 1945 was to advise government on such matters as health and safety and a number of insurance and company law amendments.

After vigorously opposing the dual threats to nationalise industrial life insurance, and, as its history states, '...accident offices had for some time appreciated that workmen's compensation business would be lost to them when it became part of the national (health) insurance scheme' (Catchpole and Elverston, 1967, p. 44), it became active in public relations work until its functions were transferred to the *Association of British Insurers* in 1985.

The *Association of British Insurers (ABI)* was formed in 1985 from the merger of the BIA, the AOA, the FOC and the LOA so that all sections of the industry could be represented by one trade association. It acts to represent its over 400 member insurance companies (in 2007) to the Government, and to the regulatory and other authorities, within and outside the UK in order to benefit the industry collectively. Since its formation the ABI has been involved in almost all policy issues affecting the insurance company market. It operates through four main policy departments – General Insurance, Life and Pensions, Financial Regulation and Taxation, and Investment Affairs.

The *Motor Insurers Bureau* (*MIB*) was formed in 1946 following agreement with the government to provide for unsatisfied judgments in respect of third party liability for bodily injury required under the Road Traffic Act, 1930, and to make awards to victims of accidents involving untraced motorists. All insurance companies and Lloyd's syndicates writing motor business are required to be members and contribute to its funding. The scheme was extended to include property damage following the Road Traffic Act, 1988. The MIB was crucial to the UK's participation in the Green Card system for travel abroad.

Association of Friendly Societies (AFS) represents some 60 friendly societies. It was established in 1995, from the merger of various bodies representing collecting friendly societies. It provides representation on regulatory matters with official bodies and promotes the movement. In 2006 AFS members had assets of £17.5bn and a premium income of £1.4bn, collected mostly from low-income individuals who want to save and who wish to supplement NHS provision with healthcare insurance.

The *General Insurance Standards Council* (*GISC*) was a short-lived self-regulatory body set up in 2000 by organisations representing most of the general insurance business after the government announced its intention to repeal the Insurance Brokers (Registration) Act, 1977, though still supporting the principle of self-regulation for general insurance. The *GISC* replaced the *ABI*'s 1986 Code of General Insurance Practice, and it embraced all intermediaries. The Director General of Fair Trading in 2001 approved its rule requiring insurers to do business only with *GISC*-registered intermediaries who were bound by its rules, but the Competition Commission subsequently ruled against it, causing fears of loss of support for the *GISC*. After the FSA assumed responsibility for the regulation of general insurance in 2001, it took over the *GISC*'s regulatory role in 2005, when the FSA's regulation was extended to all intermediaries.

The *London International Reinsurance Market Association* (*LIRMA*) was formed in 1991 as the successor to the *Reinsurance Offices Association* which was formed in 1968 as an association of UK and foreign companies writing reinsurance business. LIRMA oversaw the opening of the London Underwriting Centre in October 1993 as an international marketplace for companies operating in the London Market. It was itself merged into the *IUA* in 1998.

The *International Underwriting Association* (*IUA*) was formed in 1998 through the merger of *LIRMA* and the *ILU*. It exists to protect and strengthen the business environment for member companies that write international and wholesale insurance and reinsurance in London. Its corporate objectives include promoting market reform and good practice, improving efficiency of doing business, advancing expertise and innovation, and influencing public policy and compliance regulations. It provides research and technical support, represents members' interests, and promotes education and training. It had in January 2002 70 ordinary members (many being branches or subsidiaries of foreign companies operating in the London Market) and 48 associate members (Leonard, 2002, p. 75). Since then continuing consolidation in the industry has reduced the numbers of ordinary members to 39 and associate members to 19 in 2008.

The *Investment and Life Assurance Group* (*ILAG*) is a representative trade body which acts as a forum for producers or distributors of life and health protection insurance and of pension and investment products. It was formed in 1972, first as the *Linked Life Assurance Group*, and its full members in 2007 comprise life and health insurance companies, unit trust groups, friendly societies and life reassurers.

The *Lloyd's Market Association* was formed in 2001 to represent the interests of Lloyd's Underwriters, Managing Agents and Members Agents. It aims to increase the flow of business into the market, to maintain capital flexibility and to reduce costs, working in partnership with the Corporation of Lloyd's and other associations.

Lloyd's Insurance Brokers Association (*LIBA*) was formed in 1910 to serve the interests of just Lloyd's brokers. It continued as an independent body until 1977 when it joined with the other brokers' associations to form the *British Insurance Brokers Association*. LIBA was renamed the *London Market Insurance Brokers Committee*, which remains an autonomous body in so far as matters relating to Lloyd's brokers are concerned.

The *Corporation of Insurance Brokers* (*CIB*) was formed in 1918 to serve the interests of insurance brokers. It continued to exist as an independent body until it was amalgamated into *BIBA* in 1977.

In the 1960s there was a large rise in the numbers of provincial brokers handling motor and other personal and small trade insurances. Some felt that the CIB did not adequately represent their interests, and proceeded to form the following three associations.

The *Association of Insurance Brokers* (*AIB*) was founded in 1948 in response to insurers reducing commission on motor insurance. Following the failure of the *Fire Auto & Marine*, which had obtained its business from small High Street brokers, *in* 1966 the AIB lobbied the government for the registration of all brokers.

The *Federation of Insurance Brokers* and the *Institute of Insurance Brokers* were founded in 1967 because of dissatisfaction with existing bodies.

The *British Insurance Brokers Association* (*BIBA*) was formed in 1977 from an amalgamation of the existing four brokers' associations. Following the enactment of the Financial Services Act, 1986, *BIBA* in 1988 extended its membership to include Independent Financial Advisers and the association altered its name to the *British Insurance and Investment Brokers Association (BIIBA)*. It was the driving force for the establishment in 1994 of the *Independent Financial Advisers Association* and in 1999 *BIIBA*'s name reverted to *BIBA*.

The *Institute of Insurance Brokers* was founded in 1987 to represent smaller brokers.

The Financial Services Act, 1986, set up a system of self-regulation for individuals or firms engaged in 'investment business', which included most classes of life assurance and individual pensions. The *Financial Intermediaries, Managers and Brokers Regulatory Association (FIMBRA)* formulated the requirements for the authorisation of, including a code of conduct for, all independent intermediaries. As from December 2001 the FSA took over its responsibilities.

The *Insurance Ombudsman Bureau (IOB)* was established by five major groups of companies in 1981 in response to media criticisms of the handling of insurance disputes and by organisations such as the Consumers' Association. Quickly many other companies, and in 1989 Lloyd's, became members. The Council of the Bureau, which included consumer representatives, appointed the Ombudsman to deal with policyholders' disputes relating to *personal insurances* arranged with authorised insurers in the UK, other than industrial life assurances. The dispute had to be referred to the chief executive of the company concerned before it could be referred to the IOB. The Ombudsman was empowered to act in relation to any dispute as counsellor, conciliator, adjudicator or arbitrator able to make awards binding on the member insurer concerned.

The *Policyholders Arbitration Service* was also established in 1981 as a rival scheme to the IOB by 28 groups of insurance companies in conjunction with the Chartered Institute of Arbitrators to deal with disputes for persons resident in the UK on insurances effected in a personal capacity under policies issued in the UK, excluding life assurance, and to make awards in accordance with the Arbitration Acts.

The *Association of Insurance and Risk Managers in Industry and Commerce (AIRMIC)*. The *Association of Insurance Managers in Industry and Commerce (AIMIC)* had been formed in 1963, and by the mid-1970s was already making its presence felt in the market, with the FOC having to concede premium discounts for the very large 'exceptional cases'. Shortly after the publication of Horrigan's booklet in 1969 (Horrigan, 1969), *AIMIC* (renamed *AIRMIC* in 1977) arranged conferences to explain to members the principles of risk management.

A separate organisation, the *National Forum for Risk Management in the Public Sector (ALARM)*, was founded in 1991 to cater for the special needs of local authorities, government departments, the emergency services, universities, and any other bodies involved in the provision of public services.

Quasi-official bodies

The *Insurance Brokers Registration Council* was formed in 1977 by the Insurance Brokers (Registration) Act, 1977, being governed by a Council consisting of brokers and government nominees. It had the responsibility of registering individuals and firms that wished to use the title 'insurance broker', 'reinsurance broker' or similar titles. Individuals and firms seeking registration had to satisfy the qualifications laid down in the Act. Members had to comply with the *IBRC*'s Code of Conduct and maintain professional indemnity insurance. It could require members to compensate policyholders who suffered loss as the result of the broker's actions. Lloyd's brokers were exempted from the provisions of the Act but had to comply with similar provisions imposed by Lloyd's.

The main weakness of the Act was that it did not control other insurance intermediaries or the use of titles such as 'insurance consultant' or 'insurance adviser'. Following the enactment of the Financial Services and Markets Act 2000, the 1977 Act was repealed, the Council was wound up and the regulation of all intermediaries passed to the Financial Services Authority.

The Financial Services Act, 1986, provided for a system of self-regulation, organised by the *Securities and Investments Board* (*SIB*), of persons and companies engaged in 'investment business', including most classes of life insurance and pensions. The following three self-regulatory organisations were established. All operated until responsibility for all financial services was passed to the *Financial Services Authority* (*FSA*) under the provisions of the Financial Services and Markets Act, 2000. Life insurance companies selling investment-type life policies and pensions were required to be members of *IMRO* and *LAUTRO*.

1. The *Life Assurance and Unit Trust Regulatory Organisation* (*LAUTRO*), established in 1988, regulated the giving of advice and the marketing of life policies, unit trusts and other collective investments.
2. The Investment Management Regulatory Organisation (IMRO).
3. The *Financial Intermediaries, Managers and Brokers Regulatory Association* (*FIMBRA*) was responsible for a code of conduct regarding the marketing of 'investments' and for authorising all persons and companies giving advice on, arranging or dealing in 'investment business' (other than tied representatives of life companies that were governed by *LAUTRO*'s code of conduct). All independent intermediaries had to be members of *FIMBRA*.

Educational bodies

The *Institute of Actuaries*

Founded in 1848, the Institute holds qualifying examinations for student members. It is also involved in actuarial research through research committees and, since 1996, the funding of applications for actuarial research. The Institute had 806 members in 1901, which increased to 11,424 by 2001, 45 per cent of whom were students. Although the profession's primary interest was in life insurance it had an interest in general insurance from the outset, but it was not until 1978 that it introduced a general insurance paper into its qualifying examinations. In 2001 78 per cent of members worked in the UK and Europe, the remaining 22 per cent were overseas residents.

The *Faculty of Actuaries*

The Faculty was founded in Scotland in 1856 as the Scottish counterpart to the Institute of Actuaries, with which it works to support the actuarial profession. It had a membership of 174 in 1901 which increased to 1,795 by 2000, including students. The merger of the two actuarial bodies was under discussion in 2008.

The *Chartered Insurance Institute*

During the last quarter of the nineteenth century local insurance institutes were formed in provincial cities, originally for senior managers (CII, 1998, p. 32), leading to the establishment of the *Chartered Insurance Institute* when in 1912 it received its Royal Charter with powers to award diplomas for part-time study.

After World War II the Institute embarked on the provision of training courses, and opened the College of Insurance. A variety of innovations were introduced in the last quarter of the century, including:

- The introduction of new syllabuses;
- The opening of the College of Insurance in 1956 to provide courses with both an educational and training content;
- The introduction of a Certificate of Proficiency in 1987 in recognition of the need to cater for staff not requiring the degree of knowledge provided by the Associateship examinations;
- The Financial Planning Certificate was introduced in 1989 leading to the establishment of the *Society of Financial Advisers* (SFA) in 1991. The SFA merged with the Life Insurance Association in 2005 to form the *Personal Finance Society*. The syllabuses and assessment methodology for the Financial Planning Certificate were accepted by the *SIB*;
- The creation of an International Division in 1991 following the extension of the Institute's activities into Eastern Europe, and later into Vietnam, though the first overseas institute had been set up in 1884 (CII, 1997, p. 16). Now there are institutes in many countries with examinations being held in over 150 countries;
- The Society of Fellows was set up in 1987 to 'ensure suitable further study and research opportunities' (CII, 1998, p. 32). In 2002 the Society was converted to the Professional Standards Board;

176   The British Insurance Industry Since 1900

- From 2002 it formed five faculties to promote education on the following subjects: insurance broking, the London Market, underwriting, claims, and life and pensions;
- Annual continuous professional development programmes for members were commenced;
- The Institute introduced a number of Chartered titles for members who attain appropriate work experience and examination passes and accept the Code of Conduct. In 2007 almost a quarter of the Institute's members were chartered title holders.

The CII explored during 2008 the possibility of merging with the Australian and New Zealand Institutes with the object of deepening its international profile. It was expected to bring 12,000 new members to the CII, bringing the total foreign membership to 25,000 (including the existing 13,000 foreign members).

During the period from 1995 to 2003 the number of applicants for the Certificate of Insurance Practice examination fluctuated between 2,074 and 3,961 (with the latter number reached in 2003), although only a proportion of these completed the course.

The CII membership was 27,051 in 1945 and the total reached 51,000 by 1964. Following a spurt of growth during the late 1980s the total reached 70,000 in 1990 and the latest figure in 2007 was 91,818 (CII Membership Statistics, 2007).

Comparable data shows that the CII membership amounted to 18.9 per cent of total UK insurance employment in 1976, 18.2 per cent in 1994 and 29.7 per cent in 2007. The CII Group (comprising the CII and PFS) continued to increase its membership and in June 2008 the total membership reached 92,900, including 24,380 PFS members, an increase of 5 per cent during the year. 13,944 of these were international members.

The *Institute of Risk Management (IRM)*

The Institute was promoted by *AIRMIC* in 1986 to provide education and a formal qualification in risk management – a Diploma in Risk Management, leading to the Fellowship of the Institute. By 2008 it had members in around 50 countries and held examinations in well over 30 countries. Besides education it seeks to promote technical and ethical good practice. The IRM works with partner organisations in developing new educational programmes and in promoting the Risk Management Standard.

14
Distribution Channels

Key to the success of an insurer is the ability to establish cost-effective distribution channels to enable it to make contact with potential policyholders for the sale of its products. This chapter deals with the confluence of several major innovations since the 1960s, all aimed at reducing distribution costs in life and non-life business, reshaping the existing distribution systems and giving individual companies a competitive advantage.

During the first half of the twentieth century both insurance companies and Lloyd's were content to employ their traditional methods of distributing their products. Companies used a combination of part-time agents, brokers and networks of branches to service the needs of policyholders and agents, while business could be placed with Lloyd's syndicates only by authorised Lloyd's brokers.

Brokers had been active in placing business with underwriters, including Lloyd's from its beginning; and in 1950 there were 229 Lloyd's brokers. By the start of the twentieth century very large broking groups were emerging partly as the result of mergers, including *C T Bowring, Leslie & Godwin, C E Heath, Willis Faber & Dumas, Sedgwick Collins* and *Stewart Wrightson*; despite the mergers the total number reached 271 in 1975, but thereafter fell to 167 by January 2007. Originally handling marine business, they had diversified to embrace other classes of insurance, thereby matching the composite structure of the major insurers in their ability to meet all of the insurance needs of their clients. Also some had formed links with American brokers, notably the relationship formed in 1898 between *Willis Faber* and *Johnson & Higgins*. Firms of brokers were established in the provinces to meet the requirements of small–medium-sized commercial clients who did not particularly wish to have to resort to the London Market to meet their needs (Post Magazine, 2000). The earliest insurance companies appointed agents, and opened branch offices to deal with both brokers and members of the public, but later companies that were content to rely on brokers for their business refrained from establishing extensive networks of branches.

Industrial life 'Home Service' assurance, developed in the nineteenth century by specialist new insurers and friendly societies to provide affordable life insurance for the working-class, operated with teams of full-time employed agents visiting the homes of policyholders weekly to collect small premiums and sell new policies. 'The man from the Pru' became not only an essential distribution system but also the public face of the industry for many people. It was, however, a very expensive method of distribution that raised insurers' expenses and made returns to policyholders far worse than those available on ordinary life policies. Therefore, by the mid-1900s agents were selling ordinary life policies to their increasingly more prosperous policyholders to the detriment of industrial business. *Prudential* in 1995 ceased to write new industrial life business, and other companies, such as *Pearl*, soon did the same, so that by 2000 only 95,000 new policies were issued compared with 3.4 million new policies in 1985.

Branch offices continued to be a key element in the distribution systems of both life and non-life insurance companies. Branches and their teams of inspectors provided companies with the means of selling direct to the public, for handling claims and for generally servicing both policyholders and their networks of part-time agents and brokers who supplied them with most of their business. Early in the twentieth century one of the attractions for the major companies of acquiring specialist insurance companies had been to secure their branch networks.

Agents were drawn from building societies, bank managers, solicitors, accountants, estate agents, garage proprietors and others in regular business contact with individuals and small traders; it was estimated that in 1967 there were approximately 160,000 part-time agents (Clayton, 1971, p. 241). Brokers generally handled the larger industrial and commercial business. That situation prevailed throughout the first half of the century; indeed until the 1960s some companies were still opening new district offices.

The growth in the 1950s and 1960s of private car ownership and the increasing demand for motor insurance stimulated the formation of large numbers of small firms of *High Street brokers* and consultants that soon controlled a substantial share of personal insurances. Lloyd's responded by allowing the formation of special motor syndicates to which non-Lloyd's brokers, having been introduced by an authorised Lloyd's broker, were given access. Many *High Street brokers* did not become members of the *Corporation of Insurance Brokers*, but in due course new associations were formed to cater for their interests, including the *Association of Insurance Brokers*, the *Federation of Insurance Brokers* and the *Institute of Insurance Brokers*. It was around that time that non-insurance organisations, such as banks and the AA, set up broking subsidiaries taking business away from the traditional broker market.

The new small firms of intermediaries placed much business with the cut-price motor insurers and new small life offices, whose failure in the mid-1960s brought demands not only from policyholders and consumer bodies but also from within the industry, including brokers, for the regulation of intermediaries. Many brokers wanted to restrict the function of insurance broking to themselves, excluding banks and affinity groups (Post Magazine, 2000). The government eventually responded with the enactment of the Insurance Brokers (Registration) Act, 1977, as a first-stage measure to control all intermediaries. However, the Act merely restricted the use of the title 'insurance or reinsurance broker', without excluding non-registered firms and individuals from selling insurance. The *Insurance Brokers Registration Council* was established as a self-regulatory body to control the authorisation of suitably qualified individuals and firms. It laid down a code of conduct, accounting and business requirements regulations, compulsory professional indemnity insurance for brokers, a complaints procedure and a grants scheme to compensate policyholders who suffered loss due to the negligence, dishonesty or fraud of a practising broker. Unfortunately the Act failed to embrace other intermediaries using titles such as 'insurance consultant' or 'insurance adviser', which, though remaining unregulated, were still granted agencies by the insurance companies. However, the Association of British Insurers addressed the issue by issuing a *General Insurance Business – Code of Practice* for all intermediaries and a *Statement of Long-term Insurance Practice* that gave insurers the task of enforcing the codes.

The 1960s brought major developments in regards to long-term assurance. New competition for established life insurers and their agents came from unit-trust companies. In 1961 the *M & G Group* formed *M & G Life Assurance*, and others such as *Save & Prosper* followed. Next to enter the market were *Abbey Life* and *Hambro Life*, which adopted the use of tied, commission-remunerated sales forces to aggressively market unit-linked products directly to the public. Other new companies followed in establishing direct sales forces, and, not being members of the *Life Offices Association* (*LOA*), they were not bound by the Association's agreement on the amount and timing of commission paid to intermediaries. The resulting loss of business for LOA member companies caused by salesmen seeking to maximise their commission income led to *Equity & Law* resigning from the LOA in 1971 following the Association's refusal to relax the agreement. By 1970 a number of life offices had responded by widening their own distribution networks by setting up their own unit trusts and creating direct commission-based sales forces. *Royal* went farther in 1974 by establishing a direct marketing subsidiary (*The Insurance Service*) and *Norwich Union* acquired a broking company (*Hill House Hammond*) that dealt mainly in personal insurances.

The Financial Services Act, 1986, forced major alterations on the life market relating to the marketing of long-term assurances. The Act required any person or firm that advises on, or deals in, investment business to be authorised as either an 'independent intermediary' (eventually known as an independent financial adviser (IFA)), or as a 'tied representative' of a company that then became responsible for the activities of the representative. The major life offices and composites, in order to secure their channels of distribution, not only began to appoint their own tied sales forces but also scrambled to expand their distribution base (i) by appointing building societies as tied agents and (ii) in some cases by buying chains of estate agencies to reach mortgage, home and other life-related classes of insurance. Life and non-life insurers also began to seek to forge links to affinity groups, including various big-brand retailers, usually arranging special schemes for members, often on special terms. It was a development that posed both a threat and an opportunity to brokers, some of whom responded by forming their own links and arranging special insurance schemes, mainly for affinity groups.

Broking firms ranged between those capable of handling all classes of business, even if on a departmental basis, to firms taking a specialised focused approach, including concentrating on life and pensions business.

Bancassurance, defined as 'the joint effort of banks and insurers to provide insurance services to the bank's customer base' (Swiss Re, 2007), had been a long-standing practice on the Continent[1] (Swiss Re, 2007). By the 1970s insurance and banking were drawing closer together in Britain too. Banks and building societies were seeking to:

- exploit their marketing advantages;
- achieve economies of scale and of scope;
- obtain the advantages of diversification;
- become players in the converging financial services industry.

Life offices saw the potential marketing advantages too because, unlike insurers, banks had frequent contact with large numbers of customers, so life offices sought to acquire access to banks' customer bases to market their products. However, the banks realised too what a valuable marketing tool they possessed. For example, Barclays Bank had already established *Barclays Life* in 1965, Lloyds had established *Black Horse Life* (formerly *Beehive Life*) in 1973, and *Commercial Union* and the *Midland Bank* formed a new joint venture life office in 1987.

The demutualisation of life offices gave banks and building societies an opportunity to acquire a life insurer, beginning with the acquisition of *Scottish Mutual* by *Abbey National plc* in 1992. Barclays, Lloyds TSB and some building societies formed their own insurance companies. The Royal Bank of Scotland built up a major insurance group and also provided the financial backing for the formation in 1997 of the broker consolidator *Towergate Underwriting* to provide insurance in niche markets. Banks also turned to marketing non-life personal insurances.

The Royal Bank of Scotland formed *Direct Line* in 1985 using the then latest developments in telecommunications and underwriting software, and the vigorous use of television advertising to market motor insurance direct to the public by telephone, so eliminating the need for intermediaries. The group, through *RBSI*, has subsequently expanded its insurance operations by the acquisition of *Churchill*, *NIG*, and *UK Insurance*, the last two giving them access through brokers to the commercial insurance market. *HBOS* was associated from the first with the on-line insurer *E-sure.com* to underwrite its motor insurance products. However, despite its being owned by a bank, it was not the policy before 2007 for *RBSI*, unlike *HBOS*, to sell its products through the bank branches (Post Supplement, 2007).

Life offices too were seeking to diversify into a wider range of financial services. For example:

- in 1972 the *Commercial Union* acquired *Mercantile Credit*;
- in 1974 the *Norwich General Trust* that had been established by *Norwich Union* bought the *Anglo-Portuguese Bank*;
- in 1988 the *Prudential* established the on-line bank *Egg*;
- in 1986 the *Legal & General* was granted deposit-taking facilities by the Bank of England; and
- in 1997 *Standard Life* formed *Standard Life Bank*.

Those were the first of many cases of life offices moving into financial products, even though in doing so they were at a competitive disadvantage against the far larger clearing banks. Although independent financial advisers have been able to retain a life market share of almost 65 per cent by successfully marketing the more complex insurance products, it is estimated that bancassurance in 2006 accounted for almost a quarter of total sales of life products, though its share of non-life insurance was much smaller at 10 per cent (Swiss Re, 2007). In 2005 *Barclays Financial Planning* ranked as the second largest IFA, and *HSBC Bank* ranked as the 18th largest (CII, 2007). *Liverpool Victoria*'s growth strategy, on the other hand, was to acquire other companies. Table 14.1 and Figure 14.1 show the increase in the percentage of new business handled by independent financial advisers and the decline in agents; included in the IFAs would be some that would fall into the category of bancassurance.

Table 14.1 Percentage sources of new long-term regular premiums

Year	Independent advisers %	Company agents %	Direct %	Other %
1989	36	62	3	
1993	28	69	3	
2000	45	48	4	3
2006	70	24		6

Source: Association of British Insurers, 2001, Table 37.

182 *The British Insurance Industry Since 1900*

(64.9%)

(3.3%)

(31.8%)

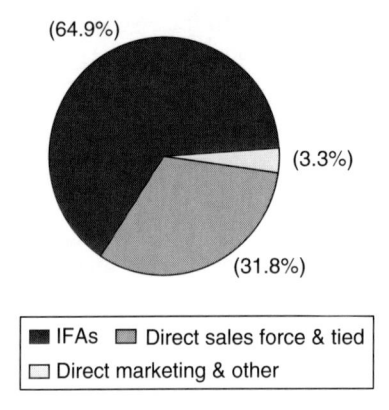

■ IFAs ▨ Direct sales force & tied
□ Direct marketing & other

Figure 14.1 Sources of new long-term premiums 2006
Source: Association of British Insurers, 2001, Table 37.

The FSA announced plans in 2002 for the depolarisation of intermediaries (FSA, 2002) to offer more choice for consumers and improve transparency around financial advice, creating three types of financial advisers: IFAs, tied agents and multi-tied agents, with IFAs having the option to charge fees to clients. The new regime came into force in 2005, leading the bancassurers to reconsider their business models. HSBC quickly signed deals with six fund providers to give its customers access to a range of funds. Barclays took advantage of the new regime to instigate a number of partnerships when launching 'Select Choice' to offer customers access to several third-party investment and protection products, sourcing the best life insurance and pensions products from across the market. Other, but not all, banks and building societies also changed their status. Thus the market for life and pensions was placed again in a state of flux, with the emphasis being placed on providing advice; advisers were required to provide full disclosure about the type of services they offered and their charges at the start of the advice process.

Brokers: the handling of the large industrial risks had for long been firmly controlled by the major national brokers. In 1987 the American *St Paul Companies* acquired *Minet Holdings*, a major Lloyd's broker. In 1980 the major national brokers were engaged in a series of mergers when the two American mega-brokers *Marsh McLellan* and *Aon* acquired leading UK Lloyd's brokers, thereby giving them access to the Lloyd's market for the placing of any business. Then in 1987 the UK's *Stewart Wrightson* merged with *Willis Faber*. The three largest global groups now include the following old-established major UK brokers:

1. *Marsh* include *C T Bowring*, and *Sedgwick Collins*;
2. *Aon* include *Hogg Robinson, Stenhouse* and *Alexander & Alexander*;
3. *Willis* include *Stewart Wrightson*.

Of the three only *Willis* is UK-owned, both *Marsh* and *Aon* being American-owned.

In 2006 another American broker, *Lockton*, acquired the Lloyd's broker *Alexander Forbes*. The mergers that occurred among brokers reduced the number of authorised Lloyd's brokers from 214 in 1995 to 167 in January 2007, and the international mega-broker groups substantially increased their share of non-motor business placed at Lloyd's. The three top groups controlled two-fifths of Lloyd's premiums in 1997 (Lloyd's, 1998, Table 10.2). In 2005 the three largest broking groups controlled one-third of the aggregate brokerage of the 50 largest UK insurance brokers; the largest five had a 49 per cent market share and the ten largest had a 67 per cent share (CII, 2007). All of the mega-brokers now compete globally in providing a wider range of services, including risk management, captive management, advice on and access to capital market products, etc. Brokers have traditionally handled the largest share of medium–large commercial insurances and still dominate the market for commercial insurance (see Figure 14.2).

Changes were occurring in the reinsurance market too. During the 1970s and early 1980s many independent reinsurance intermediaries, including *Guy Carpenter, G L Hodson & Co.* and *Golding Collins* were taken over by larger broking groups, including *Marsh, Aon, Alexander Howden* (which was later acquired by *Alexander & Alexander*) and *Stewart Wrightson* (which itself was later acquired by *Willis Faber*).

In some cases executives of firms that had been taken over left to form their own new broking companies. For example, in 1973 *Benfield, Lovick, Rees & Co.* was formed and was itself the subject of a management buyout in 1988 to form the *Benfield Group*. The old-established British reinsurance

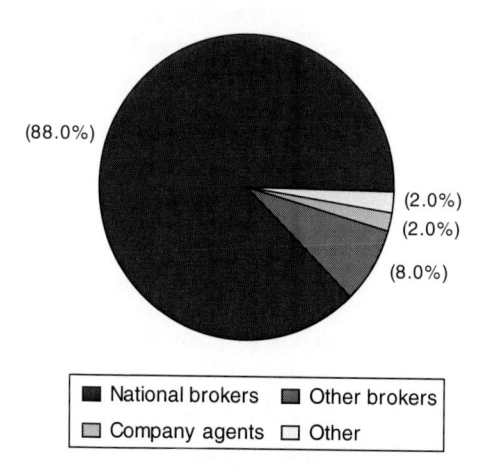

Figure 14.2 Sources of general commercial insurance premiums 2000
Source: Association of British Insurers, 2001, Table 106.

broker *Greig Fester* was acquired by the *Benfield Group* in 1997, and in 2001 it merged with *E W Blanch* to form the world's largest independent reinsurance broker. In November 2008 the *Benfield Group* merged with *Aon*.

All types of brokers and IFAs were increasingly using information technology to communicate with insurers, to improve the service offered to clients and generally increase the efficiency of their operations.

Lloyd's market

Traditionally business could be placed with Lloyd's syndicates only by authorised Lloyd's brokers, but, faced with increasing broker concentration, Lloyd's at the end of the 1990s substantially widened access to its market, giving direct access to Lloyd's underwriters to accredited and provisionally accredited Lloyd's brokers, and also to (a) approved coverholders, many of whom are overseas intermediaries, whose binding authorities have been negotiated directly with managing agents, and (b) intermediaries who satisfy para. 28 of the Underwriting Bye-Law (no. 2 of 2003) to permit acceptance by Lloyd's underwriters of personal lines business, commercial life business and commercial motor business from or through persons who are not Lloyd's brokers. With the broadening of Lloyd's distribution base, in January 2007 22 Lloyd's brokers were overseas brokers, and all brokers may apply for accreditation, initially as provisional Lloyd's brokers. The Treasury proposed in 2008 that underwriting agents should be able to accept business from any intermediary, so placing the Lloyd's market in the same situation as the company market. Lloyd's made the proposed change.

Likewise, in the company market, brokers still retain the majority share of total UK non-life commercial insurance, and as noted above IFAs still retain a majority share of the life market (see Table 14.1 and Figure 14.1).

However, the only way that regional brokers can compete globally is by being part of a network such as the *Worldwide Broker Network*.

Telephone sales

The biggest upheaval in insurers' distribution channels came with the formation of *Direct Line* in 1985 using the advances in telecommunications, sophisticated underwriting software and call centres to engage in the direct selling by telephone of personal motor insurance (later expanded to other classes of insurance, small business insurances and financial products). Thus they were able to cut expenses by eliminating the payment of commissions, thereby undermining the viability of many small brokers. Other new companies (e.g. *Churchill*) and established companies such as *Norwich Union* and *Royal Sun Alliance* likewise formed direct telephone selling operations. Some brokers also adopted telesales as a distribution system.

Affinity schemes

By the 1980s insurers were beginning to set up affinity deals with various bodies like the Automobile Association and Saga to provide special deals for their members, though in 1952 Saga set up their own insurance company in Gibraltar to cater for their 50-plus-year-old members. In 2007 the AA and Saga announced a merger. Insurers also began to enter into arrangements with motor manufacturers to offer insurance through their nationwide networks of car dealers with the sale of a new car, maybe on more favourable terms than those available on the open market. Such affinity deals improve client retention by insurers, as policyholders are more likely to stay with the insurer delivered to them by the motor manufacturer than if insurance was bought on the open market, because the customer may believe that the manufacturer will give him extra leverage if something goes wrong. However, insurers needed to invest heavily in gaining a motor manufacturer's support by providing at the dealerships their websites with quote engines. The motor manufacturers benefited from significant commission income and from other terms, such as insisting that their own brand vehicles should be used as courtesy cars. Insurers that were heavily involved in such affinity deals include *Norwich Union*, *RSA*, *the Royal Bank of Scotland*, and *Zurich*.

A variant on the affinity group was the formation of a company to serve just a certain section of the population, such as *Sheila's Wheels*, which wrote motor insurance only for women drivers.

Technological change

The rapid development in communications technology created major changes in the insurance distribution system from the mid-1990s onwards. The access of households to the internet increased from a very low figure in the early 1990s climbed to 46 per cent by 2002 and to 65 per cent by 2008.

These developments created the possibility for the creation of new insurance companies like *Esure* and *Swiftcover*, which were formed to transact business solely on-line, using television and comparison sites to advertise their services. Relying solely on the internet they not only circumvented the use of intermediaries but also had no need for call centres. The internet posed not only a threat to brokers but opportunities too with some setting up their own websites, such as *Oval On-line* catering for commercial insurances.

Aggregators

An even more influential change emerged from the late 1990s, with the creation of insurance comparison websites, also described as aggregators. These websites display the comparison of the cost and terms and conditions offered by a range of insurers for individual policyholders who are able to complete the transaction from their computer keyboard. The proposal can be completed in a few minutes on computer screens and cover arranged simultaneously upon the payment of the premium.

There has been rapid growth of these websites the first of which, *moneysupermarket.com*, was established in 1999. By 2008 there were over 30 active aggregator websites – the operation of which needs FSA approval – many of them offering a wide range of personal lines insurance products, including motor, dental, home, income protection, travel, pet, health and other products. Some sites also offer life insurance, although their share of this segment is believed to be very small. There are some sites attempting to offer business insurance to SMEs, but at the time of writing these have not progressed far.

The aggregators made a large impact on the motor market; and some estimates put the aggregators' share of motor business at 25 per cent in 2007. (Aggregators in UK general insurance 2008, Datamonitor, March 2008). The extent of use of these websites can be judged from the fact that during the first half of 2008 *moneysupermarket.com* sold 8.211 m policies. A result of these changes is that the proportion of motor business placed by brokers was down to 7 per cent by 2007.

The leading websites (including *confused.com*, *gocompare.com*, *peopleschampion.com*, *moneymarket.com* and *uswitch.com*) offer price and policy term comparisons of up to 90 insurers. Some of the national retailers are also active, including Marks & Spencer Money, Sainsbury's Finance and Tescocompare and offer a range of insurance policies including motor, home and travel covers. Some aggregators offer additional information, including comparisons of mortgages and credit cards. However, some of these offers come not from insurers but from insurance intermediaries, who have arrangements with insurance companies to accept business on the terms offered by the broker.

The use of aggregator sites is very advantageous for smaller insurers, who may not have a large enough marketing budget to advertise their policies. They make their policy terms available to the aggregator and make payment to them only when their policy is chosen (and a payment is made by the client). The aggregator sites have made a significant impact on the leading insurance companies – particularly in motor business – in terms of market share as well as in keeping premium rates low. However, insurers as well as brokers, are complaining that the use of aggregators is 'commoditising' insurance by placing the cost of premiums at the centre of the transaction.

Aggregator sites also enables insurers to target particular segments of the market e.g. those driving Honda cars, rural drivers or experienced female drivers. Having selected a group, the insurer can offer attractive terms for such groups for different aggregators. Insurers thus save a significant proportion of marketing and advertising costs.

Aggregators are not used by all insurers; *Direct Line* the market leading motor insurer is keen to distance itself from these sites, and continues to pursue its own TV and press advertising marketing campaigns. The company pointed out that comparison sites do not contain all insurers' data and claim that they are not independent and collect commissions from companies, just as brokers do. However, *Direct Line* is unwilling to test its price leadership on these sites which may become a competitive disadvantage in due course.

While policyholders benefited from wide choice and lower premiums, aggregator sites have some disadvantages from the consumer point of view. While they expect the information on these sites to be there in full, in some instances these quotes may not have a policy feature listed such as the excess level. In these instances the proposer would have to establish the full details of the policy when they click through to the insurer's website to establish the full details of the policy. However, some aggregators not only provide premium cost rating but comment on the claims services provided by the insurers, which can be of help to the consumer.

Aggregators generate their income from insurers' fees on policies sold through their site, introduction fees payable by the product provider and in some cases from advertising from insurers on the site.

So it was that by the end of the 1980s insurers possessed a range of distribution options. They had had over-blown networks of local branches and small brokers that they had needed to reduce costs. The major insurers adopted a multi-channel approach whereas others concentrated on accepting business only from intermediaries seeking to be 'broker friendly' in an attempt to persuade brokers to support them. The dynamic growth of aggregator sites, which became a leading marketing channel by the first decade of the 21st century for some of the personal lines non-life business, represented an additional challenge. Distribution had become a matter of strategic concern for insurers as they sought to balance the various distribution channels of how to achieve the cost savings offered by some channels against the problem of managing to continue to receive the support of brokers while competing against them with direct sales networks and the new telephone and internet sales, which offered consumers lower premiums than were made available to brokers.

During 1994 commissions were cut for intermediaries, and new products were launched with variable commission rates.(Post Magazine, 2000) By 2005 the proportion of people buying insurance through brokers fell from 54 per cent in 1995 to 32 per cent, while the percentage buying direct from insurers had increased to 31 per cent. Direct marketing of life insurance had achieved far less success accounting for only 7 per cent of new individual regular premium life policies, with telesales at a mere 1½ per cent (see Figure 14.1).

Insurers acquiring brokers

Some insurers controversially sought to acquire broking firms. They had to try to assure brokers and other insurers that neither would the broker be used to favour the parent company over other insurers in placing business in the market, nor would the insurer give its broker special consideration in the acceptance or rating of business compared with business emanating from other brokers. The large motor broker *Swinton* became a wholly-owned subsidiary of *Royal Sun Alliance* in the early 1990s, and in 2001 *Swinton* was acquired by the French insurer *La Mutuelle du Mans Assurance*. In 2006 *Zurich* acquired the remaining 55 per cent interest in *Endsleigh Insurance Brokers*. Then *AXA* moved in 2007 to expand and diversify its distribution base, first in the personal insurance market through the acquisition of the on-line insurer *Swiftcover*, and next it led the way for the controversial acquisition of commercial brokers by insurers, itself purchasing in 2007 four commercial brokers, including *Smart & Cook* and *Layton Blackham*, who were ranked amongst the UK's top 50 brokers. However, *AXA* was only following the example set in 1987 with the acquisition of Lloyd's broker *Minet Holdings* by the American *St Paul Companies*. Independent brokers feared that insurers would give preferential terms to their broker subsidiaries, which would lead to unfair competition, and in March 2008 the Financial Services Authority launched a discussion paper into UK commercial broking 'after admitting it was concerned about the blurred relationship between insurers and intermediaries' (Post Magazine, 2008). However, *Groupama* claimed that its purchase of brokers *Lark and Bollington* was simply to improve its distribution capability and to increase its share of the business placed with the brokers (Holt, 2008). Conversely *Norwich Union* disposed of *Hill House Hammond* in 2006, but in 2007 *Aviva* acquired a 5.1 per cent stake in broker consolidator *Jelf* and in 2008 acquired the small to medium-sized broker *Group Direct*. French company *Verlingue* established a cross-Channel link by buying the commercial broker *Alec Finch* in 2007. Also in 2007 *Norwich Union* set aside substantial funds to provide loans to brokers to prevent them from being acquired, in contrast to a 2006 scheme by *Independent Insurance* to provide its top brokers with loan facilities to take over rival intermediaries. *Ecclesiastical* purchased the equine specialists *South Essex Insurance Brokers* in 2008 to give it direct access to a top broker and an established network of sub-brokers.

Rather than forging closer links with brokers, *Prudential* in 1991 withdrew from accepting any general insurance commercial lines business from brokers.

Small brokers were leaving the market under the pressures of direct marketing competition and FSA regulatory costs. Some saw the protection of consolidation by being part of a larger group as a means of growing their business. Foremost among the consolidators was the *Towergate Underwriting*

Group formed in 1997 to provide as a 'virtual insurer' specialist insurance products in niche markets by working with a selected panel of leading insurers, including Lloyd's syndicates. The group expanded through the acquisition of brokers and in 2002 substantially expanded its operations through a merger with the consolidator *Folgate Partnership*. It had made 110 acquisitions and operated over 400 agencies by 2006 (its Annual report, 2005). Two further major acquisitions were made in 2007 with the purchase of the *Broker Network*, which had over 100 member brokers, and *Open International*, a provider of software to brokers. By 2008 it had acquired 138 brokers and it strengthened its on-line capabilities by acquiring *Insurance 4 Car Hire Agencies*, an internet-based insurance agency providing specialist products for the car rental market. It also became a strategic partner for *Countrywide* by joining its panel of insurers to offer insurance products to *Countrywide*'s 700 members. Other consolidators included *Jelf* and the *Open Group*, established in 2003 with the backing of *Caledonian Investments*, which quickly acquired both regional brokers and a Lloyd's broker.

The main changes in the London Market have been:

1. The increasing concentration of both brokers and insurers, although the increased concentration of brokers creating three dominant groups has encouraged some senior brokers to start up new, successful firms, e.g. *Benfield*. Insurer consolidation has occurred in both the Lloyd's and the company markets, which has created more highly capitalised groups capable of writing larger risks.
2. The broadening of Lloyd's distribution base. Lloyd's also during the 1990s made strenuous efforts to improve efficiency by introducing electronic accounting and claims notification and settlement systems to match the efficiency of the growing Bermuda market.

The EU Competition Commissioner issued a report in 2007 that questioned the London subscription market practice of 'horizontal cooperation' whereby underwriters openly share risks, including terms and price. Subsequently the EU officials accepted the principle of shared wordings, though leaving open the possibility that co-insurers need not necessarily follow the leading underwriter's rates, terms and conditions.

All of the above developments sharpened the already strong competitive climate and led to another cost-reducing process: the outsourcing of back-office administrative tasks and telephone response handling and invoicing. The growing profitability pressures led to a series of mergers among insurers and intermediaries who hoped that economies of scale and the ability to cull branch networks would provide some defence against the new distribution channels. The *Insurance Directory 2005* listed UK insurers as having 490 branches compared with the 2,054 branches shown for 102 of the companies listed in the 1993 *Directory*. Companies that were slow to follow major

Table 14.2 The changing shape of the UK insurance market (number of offices listed)

	2003	2005	2007
Insurance companies:			
Head offices	817	666	626
Branches	785	490	448
Total	1,602	1,156	1,074
Insurance brokers:			
Head offices	7,420	6,561	5,964
Branches	1,845	2,077	2,291
Total	9,265	8,638	8,255

Source: *Post Magazine Directory & Yearbook* (various years).

companies into direct writing distribution risked serious loss of business, the erosion of profit margins or soaring underwriting losses. Distribution channels were, however, still changing in 2000 with the numbers of branches and brokers continuing to contract (see Table 14.2).

15
The Regulation of Insurance

Regulation of insurance companies

The regulatory and legislative activity described in this chapter is characterised for most of the twentieth century by the policy of minimum intervention to encourage innovation, healthy competition, and the minimisation of the cost of the regulatory burden. It is what used to be called 'freedom with publicity'. However, in the closing decades of the century there was some departure from that guiding principle towards more regulation to underpin consumer protection.

When adverse market conditions surface, such as company failures leading to loss of cover for policyholders and others, consumer dissatisfaction, etc., two routes are available for their correction: self-regulation by market participants or statutory regulation. Though this chapter mainly deals with the latter, the parallel self-regulatory effort should be noted too. Foremost of the self-regulatory bodies is the Council of Lloyd's, though other bodies such as the *British Insurance Brokers' Association* and the *Association of British Insurers* both exercise some control over insurers and brokers, and represent the interests of the industry with the UK government and in Brussels.

Until Britain joined the European Community in 1973 the main force driving the government to regulate insurance companies, as noted above, had been the failure of companies.

Only companies transacting life assurance were regulated (under the provisions of the *Life Assurance Companies Acts, 1870, 1872*) at the beginning of the twentieth century. However, continuing failures of companies transacting non-life insurance, such as those of the *Empire Mutual Workmen's Compensation* in 1901 and the *London & County Industrial Accident* in 1902, were increasing the pressure for an extension of prudential regulation to non-life companies too. The need was recognised by the Employers' *Liability Insurance Companies Act, 1907*, before the government fully responded in 1909 by the enactment of the *Assurance Companies Act, 1909*, Mr Churchill having cited examples of company failures in introducing the Bill to

Parliament (Raynes, 1968, p. 353). The Act extended regulation beyond life assurance to include companies carrying on:

(i) fire insurance;
(ii) accident insurance (personal accident and sickness);
(iii) employers' liability insurance; and
(iv) bond investment business.

An important omission was marine insurance.

The main provisions of the Act, which did not apply to Lloyd's, closely followed those of the 1870 Act, providing for:

(i) deposits for the protection of policyholders;
(ii) the separation of funds for each class of business transacted;
(iii) the preparation of annual accounts, balance sheet, and the valuation of and report on life funds; and
(iv) winding-up, but wider powers were given to the Board of Trade to bring about the winding-up of an insurance company by the *Assurance Companies (Winding-up) Acts, 1933 and 1935*.

Every company to which the 1909 Act applied had to deposit £20,000 with the Paymaster-General, but if a company carried on more than one class of business £20,000 had to be deposited for each class, with certain exemptions for companies that had carried on a class of business before the commencement of the Act.

Although separate funds had to be maintained, it was not necessary to hold separate investments for each fund.

The Act prescribed the form of revenue accounts and balance sheet.

The *Industrial Life Assurance Act, 1923*, the *Road Traffic Act, 1930* and the *Air Navigation Act, 1935* brought industrial life assurance, motor insurance and aircraft insurance under the 1909 Act as separate classes of business.

The *Assurance Companies (Winding Up) Acts, 1933 and 1935*, strengthened the 1909 Act by giving the Board of Trade powers to intervene in cases of insolvency.

The *Industrial Assurance Act, 1923*, and the *Friendly Societies Acts, 1894 to 1924*, provided for the regulation of industrial life business, including in the 1923 Act the appointment of an Industrial Assurance Commissioner with powers to ensure that the provisions of the Act were carried out, including lodging returns with him as well as with the Board of Trade.

The shortcomings of the 1909 Act as evidenced by the failure of well over 100 companies between 1910 and 1920 led to two Departmental Committees being appointed, the first in 1924 under the chairmanship of Mr A.C. Clauson, and the second in 1936. However, new legislation strengthening prudential regulation had to wait until after World War II with the enactment of the *Assurance Companies Act, 1946*, which at last subjected marine, aviation and transport insurance to regulation, and the classes of insurance were divided into:

(a) 'long-term business' covering all life assurance and bond-investment business; and
(b) 'general business' covering all of the other classes of business to which the Act applied.

That still left various miscellaneous classes of business, such as burglary, plate glass and fidelity guarantee, outside the scope of the Act.

To obtain authorisation a company had to have a minimum paid-up capital of £50,000, and deposits (which had proved to be inadequate) were replaced by a margin of solvency; that is, its assets had to exceed its liabilities by the greater of £50,000 or for general insurance 10 per cent of the company's general premium income in its last preceding financial year.

A consolidating Act, the *Insurance Companies Act, 1958*, provided for separate revenue accounts to be prepared for each of life assurance, industrial life assurance, employers' liability insurance and bond-investment business and for receipts for each class to be carried to a separate fund.

The 1946 Act's provisions again proved to be inadequate when the late 1960s and early 1970s brought the failure in quick succession of almost 20 companies, some only recently formed by dubious characters, including:

1. a number of cut-price motor insurance companies, including *Gibraltar* (wound up 1967), *Irish American* (1967), *London & Cheshire* (1967), *Midland Northern & Scottish* (1970), *Carriage* (1970), *Automobile & General* (1971) and, most important, *Fire Auto & Marine* in 1966; and
2. a life office, *Translife*, in 1967;
3. a number of other very short-lived companies (see Table 15.1).

As noted in Chapters 5 and 12, the most spectacular failure was that of *Fire Auto & Marine* in 1966.

Those failures persuaded the government that it needed to tighten the regulation of insurance companies with the passage of Part II of the *Companies Act, 1967*, and (following the collapse of the *Vehicle and General Insurance Company* in 1971) the *Insurance Companies Amendment Act, 1973*. Then the government enacted the consolidating *Insurance Companies Act, 1974*. The 1967 Act brought all classes of insurance within its scope, strengthened the powers of the Department of Trade over the authorisation of new companies, raised the minimum paid-up share capital to £100,000, increased the solvency margin for general insurance to the minimum of £50,000 or 20 per cent of the first £2½m of its general premium income plus 10 per cent of any premium in excess thereof and, controversially at the time, restricted the persons who may be owners, directors or controllers of insurance

Table 15.1 Companies failing within 10 years of formation, 1967–74

Company	Year established	Year wound up
Bastion	1965	1974
Craven	1966	1968
Fire Auto & Marine	1963	1966
London & Home Counties	1966	1967
London & Midland	1966	1967
London & Wessex	1966	1967
Metropolitan General	1963	1971
Metropolitan & Northern Counties	1965	1967
South Yorkshire	1964	1967
Translife	1966	1967
Transport Indemnity	1964	1971

Source: *Insurance Directory* List of companies wound up (various years).

companies to being 'fit and proper persons', and gave the Department the power in granting an authorisation to impose certain restrictions. Also the Department was given powers to intervene under specified circumstances, including a company's failure to meet any of the requirements of the Acts, or if any person became a controller of a company. The Acts were consolidated in the Insurance Companies Act, 1974.

The *Insurance Companies Act, 1982*, consolidated all of the legislation and introduced new regulations. The Acts also amended UK legislation to bring it into line with the requirements of the 1973 EEC Insurance Establishment Directives, notably the solvency margin requirements distinguishing between (i) companies with a head office in the UK, (ii) companies with a head office in any other EU country, and (iii) external companies with a head office elsewhere. The 'fit and proper person' test for authorisation was extended to include underwriting agents; and the powers of the Department of Trade were extended to withdraw authorisations. (Between 1967 and 1987 the Department petitioned for the winding-up of 24 companies.) The Act incorporated the Regulations that had been issued in 1982 and 1983 requiring companies to provide more information in their annual returns regarding their reinsurance business in relation to general insurance.[1]

EEC Directives had required various changes to UK regulation and the *Insurance Companies (Third Insurance Directives) Regulations, 1994*, implemented the EEC Directives providing 'freedom of services'.

After long negotiations, in 1995 the government agreed to companies establishing equalisation reserves that qualified for tax relief in respect of specified classes of insurance business exposed to catastrophe losses (the *Insurance Companies (Reserves) Regulations, 1996*).

December 2001 heralded the start of a new regulatory regime when responsibility for the regulation of insurers was transferred to the Financial

Services Authority (FSA) under the terms of the *Financial Services and Markets Act, 2000*. The FSA adopted a principles risk-based approach to regulation and it published a document (*A New Regulator for the New Millennium*) describing its approach to meeting the following four regulatory objectives set for it in the Act:

- maintaining confidence in the investment markets;
- improving consumer awareness;
- helping to protect consumers;
- reducing financial crime.

The *FSA Handbook of Rules and Guidance* replaced the regulations under the Insurance Companies Act, 1982; it is divided into a variety of sourcebooks (that is, specialist rule books such as the *Conduct of Business Sourcebook*). A risk-based approach to capital adequacy became increasingly used for insurers, and the Capital Adequacy Standards (ICAS) were adopted by the regulators from 2005 in anticipation of the implementation of the Solvency II framework in 2010, requiring insurers and reinsurers to assess their capital needs by using robust modelling. A key feature of the FSA's system of regulation is the approved persons regime, which requires an 'approved person' holding positions of responsibility within the firm to pass the 'fit and proper' test which covers honesty, financial soundness and competence. If a firm fails to comply with all requirements, disciplinary action may be taken against senior management personally.

All firms are subject to the FSA Handbook. The FSA confirmed in 2005 that it intended to move towards a more principles-based system of regulation, which at the time of writing is still evolving.

Lloyd's

Fuller details of the regulation of the Lloyd's market can be found in Chapter 10. Suffice it to say here that Lloyd's was regulated under the terms of the Lloyd's Act, 1871, which provided for a formal organisational structure with an elected Committee. The Lloyd's Acts, 1911 and 1925, extended the Society's objects to transact other classes of business and established the Central Guarantee Fund to meet the underwriting liabilities of members. The Lloyd's Act, 1951, which repealed the 1925 Act, further extended the Society's objects and gave it the power to act as trustee for guarantees furnished by members required by the Assurance Companies Act, 1909. Following the report on self-regulation by the working party chaired by Sir Henry Fisher, the Lloyd's Act, 1982, established the Council of Lloyd's as the governing body. Lloyd's has an ongoing obligation to comply with the criteria for authorisation, and with all applicable FSA Rules. All underwriting agents must be authorised by the FSA. Finally, under the Financial Services and Markets Act, 2000, responsibility for the supervision of Lloyd's was transferred to the FSA in November 2001, though retaining the system of self-regulation.

The Council in 2003 established the Lloyd's Franchise, which governed the relationship between the Corporation and its underwriting agencies. A Franchise Board was appointed to oversee capital management and franchise performance to ensure a disciplined marketplace.

Consumer protection

The wave of consumerism that emerged during the 1970s and 1980s took alternative forms, including the formation in 1957 of *Which?*, which issued its first report on insurance, 'Insurance against Rain', in July 1960 and has since issued reports on various other aspects of insurance, including cars, household and travel insurance. However, most reforms were legislative to ensure that the legal framework was more supportive of consumers' interests. But the government also introduced less prescriptive measures that were more of an advisory or indicative nature to modify commercial practices via a more robust regime of self-regulation.

First, following the collapse of the cut-price motor insurers and of *Translife* in 1967 and of *Nation Life* in 1974, rather than further increasing the required capitalisation of insurance companies, the government in 1975 took steps to protect policyholders, mainly individuals, from the financial consequences of the failure of an insurance company.

The *Policyholders Protection Act, 1975*, established the Policyholders Protection Board with powers to impose a levy on authorised insurance companies transacting the type of insurance concerned (and in certain cases on insurance intermediaries too) to enable the Board to make payments to private policyholders in respect of contracts effected in the UK with an authorised insurer that goes into liquidation or is unable to pay its debts. In the case of life companies the Board could also seek to transfer its business to another company. Amendments were made to the Act by the Policyholders Protection Act, 1997. The *Financial Services and Markets Act, 2000*, replaced the compensation scheme from December 2001 with the *Financial Services Compensation Scheme (FSCS)*. The FSA collects any levies on behalf of the FSCS. If an insurance company fails, a claimant may receive 100 per cent of the first £2,000 of a claim and 90 per cent of the balance, with no upper limit.

Policyholders may suffer financial loss not merely due to the failure of an insurer but also because of the negligence of an intermediary in placing an insurance or in handling a claim. Therefore, the government acted in 1977 to protect consumers in such circumstances with the enactment of the *Insurance Brokers (Registration) Act, 1977*, which restricted the use of 'insurance broker' and similar titles to intermediaries registered with the *Insurance Brokers Registration Council (IBRC)*. The Council could require a registered broker to compensate policyholders who suffered loss due to the broker's actions.

When the government proposed to abolish the *IBRC* and expressed its support for self-regulation, it encouraged the industry to produce unified standards for all methods of distribution. All sections of the industry responded by setting up the *General Insurance Standards Council* (see below). The FSA took over the regulation of general insurance in 2001, and in 2005 the regulation of intermediaries, independent financial advisers, multi-tie and single-tie firms dealing with authorisation, prudential requirements on solvency, professional indemnity, etc., and the *GISC* handed over its regulatory role to the FSA in January 2005.

The *Insurance Companies (Advertisements) (Amendment) Regulations, 1983*, required that advertisements inviting people to enter into long-term insurance contracts must provide details about (a) the company, (b) the intermediary marketing the products, (c) the trustees and (d) the relationships between them.

The *Office of Fair Trading* was established by the Fair Trading Act, 1973, to provide a different method of consumer protection from the legislative route. It was given a watching brief over business practices that affect consumer interests, to encourage businesses to comply with competition and consumer law and to recommend action where required.

It has prepared several reports on insurance. Its 1985 report on household (buildings and contents) insurance, based on extensive consumer market research, recommended that, in addition to the generally used new-for-old policy terms, indemnity-based claims payments should be more widely available, which was disputed by the insurance industry. The ABI responded with the preparation of a guide on building insurance.

The OFT's 1986 report on the selling of insurance investigated the extent of the problem with buying insurance (including life, motor, personal accident and sickness and holiday insurances). It found that the highest rate of dissatisfaction was with motor insurance. Its 1988 report on motor insurance found that 28 per cent of the 9,000 policyholders interviewed could not identify their insurers (confusing them with their brokers), but found only 3 per cent dissatisfied with the sales process. However, far more were dissatisfied with the claims process, though only 6 per cent were dissatisfied with the final offer. Further reports during the 1990s dealt with the marketing of investment-linked products, extended warranties on electrical goods and on health insurance (with supplements on critical illness and permanent health insurance). The latest (October 2006) OFT report on payment protection insurance found that the marketing methods of this product were 'failing consumers'.

Complaints regarding mis-selling

The Financial Services Act, 1986, laid the foundations for the regulatory bodies, first *LAUTRO* and subsequently the Financial Services Authority (FSA) and the Financial Services Ombudsman Service (FOS), to deal with customer complaints regarding the products they had been sold. During the 1990s a number of lines of personal insurances gave rise to a plethora of complaints from consumers and from the financial press, consumer organisations and eventually from regulatory bodies regarding extended warranty, private medical insurance, payment protection, and travel insurances in the non-life sector (see Chapter 5), and with-profits endowments, critical illness and personal pensions in the life sector (see Chapter 6).

Mis-selling

A common theme running through those complaints was that of mis-selling through overzealous distribution networks remunerated by commissions. In the case of *with-profits endowments* sold to repay mortgages, falling bonus rates from the early 1990s meant that expected policy maturity values would be insufficient to repay mortgages. The FSA fined nine companies for 'procedural deficiencies resulting in mis-selling', 'defective complaints handling' and the 'mishandling of complaints', with fines totalling £5.2m.

The Treasury Select Committee found that many personal pension plans were inappropriately sold to members of good occupational pension schemes as the result of bad advice from commission-remunerated company and independent financial advisers (Treasury, 1998, vol. 1, p. xvi). The FSA again imposed large fines as well as mandating compensation costs on insurers and intermediaries of over £8.4bn.

The problem with *payment protection insurances* largely arose from the insurance being sold without any explanation of policy terms and conditions to unsuitable persons by retailers of high-value equipment or providers of consumer loans influenced by obtaining commissions that helped retailers to rebuild their margins in a highly competitive retail market. The Citizens Advice Bureau published a highly critical study of PPI products that was summed up in the title the 'Protection racket'. It claimed that 'high pressure sales practices have been used to sell inappropriate insurance to vulnerable consumers' (CAB, 2005, p. 25). Likewise the FOS's 2007–08 report said that the increase in complaints from 1,832 in 2006 to 10,852 in 2007 was largely due to inappropriate sales methods and policy exclusions not explained at the time of purchase.

An undesirable feature of PPI insurances was that prospective policyholders were not asked any questions for the purpose of determining premiums about individual borrowers' risk characteristics, which might have alerted them to key issues. The ABI were forced to respond to all of the criticisms by issuing in October 1995 a Statement of Practice dealing with the construction of policies and claims practices. The ABI Director General, Mark Boleat, in 1997 emphasised the importance of giving advice to prospective policyholders regarding the suitability of the contract for the self-employed, and on the vetting of intermediaries (Boleat, 1997, p. 5).

Continuing criticism forced the ABI to carry out research that found that 'most PPI policyholders felt that the product offered good value for money' and that '81% of those that made claims said that the process had run smoothly' (ABI, March 2001, p. 3). Yet, as noted above, the complaints kept flooding in.

Travel insurance too was the subject of criticism and many complaints. The Treasury Select Committee reported that 'there is significant evidence of consumer detriment in the travel insurance market. Consumers are at risk of being sold policies which do not meet their needs' (Treasury report, p. 1). It also expressed concern that most policies excluded cover for terrorist incidents. The Treasury's view was that 'there is increasing concern from consumer groups and sections of the industry that the market is not working as well as it could' (Treasury, p. 1). It also reiterated the view of the FOS that 'the policy terms for travel insurance remain complicated and the sales process frequently limited' (Treasury, p. 11), especially with regards to the sales of insurance bundled with other travel services by travel agents. The Financial Ombudsman's 2006 report also noted that 'there is widespread misunderstanding on the part of the consumers about the scope of the cover and the eligibility criteria'. The Treasury Committee went on to discuss the possibility of FSA regulation of the business of bundled travel insurance (Treasury, 2006–07, p. 19).

Policy terms and conditions

Frequently complaints of mis-selling involved criticisms of the scope of cover, conditions and exclusions of policies, often a 'small-print' problem for prospective policyholders. When the market was in a turmoil of frenzied competition the Consumers' Association produced a Which? report on motor insurance, which recommended that a statutory standard form of policy be produced. One commentator said in its favour that:

> it would not restrict the insurer anxious to provide wider cover; in fact extensions made available by specific endorsement would have the advantage of drawing attention to additional benefits. Conversely any restriction of cover likewise would be obvious if the approved form was used. (Carter, 1966)

However, the suggestion was resisted by the industry.

Insurers and/or distributors/agents have laid down codes of practice to avoid legislative intervention. Unfortunately it usually has taken a long time for the desired customer-friendly selling practices to become general. Hopefully, the more alert supervisory regime together with a more financially knowledgeable customer base may limit occurrences of mis-selling in the future.

Dispute resolution

As recorded in Chapter 13, insurers set up two dispute resolution services in the 1980s for personal policyholders – the *Insurance Ombudsman Bureau (IOB)* and the *Personal Insurance Arbitration Service (PIAS)*, which provided for disputes to be referred to arbitration with awards in accordance with the Arbitration Acts, being binding on both parties with only limited right of appeal.

The Ombudsman could only act after a dispute had been referred to the insurer's chief executive for a decision. The Ombudsman could act as counsellor, conciliator or arbitrator. The IOB annual reports showed that most disputes related to claims. The Ombudsman's awards were binding on members but limited to £100,000.

The *Financial Services and Markets Act, 2000*, created as from 1 December 2001 the *Financial Ombudsman Service (FOS)*, modelled on the old PIAS scheme, as the single compulsory ombudsman for 'retail' complaints about financial products and services, operating under the rules and procedures laid down by the FSA. The scope of the FOS was extended to include general insurance from January 2005. Thus the FOS became responsible for all disputes between insurers, intermediaries and private and small business and small charity policyholders, taking over the duties of the IOB and PIAS. The findings of the FOS are binding on the authorised firm, which must pay amounts awarded up to £100,000. The service is free to consumers but not to large businesses and is paid for by fees levied on firms against which a complaint is made. The FSA encouraged all insurers to subscribe to Alternative Dispute Resolution procedures for commercial lines policies and for disputes on other matters not dealt with by the FOS.

Self-regulation

The *Financial Services Act, 1986*, set up a system of self-regulation administered by a number of Self-Regulatory Organisations overseen by the *Securities and Investments Board* to regulate the activities of firms or persons that advise on, arrange deals in or manage investments, which includes some life policies. It gave persons buying such contracts the protection of the Act and its compensation scheme.

The *Insurance Companies Regulations, 1981*, required insurance companies to hand or send to each person who enters into a contract of ordinary life assurance a notice in specified form explaining the right to withdraw from the contract within ten days. The Regulations also specified that an intermediary must inform a prospective insured if (a) the company with which he proposes to place the business is not authorised in the UK, or (b) the intermediary is connected with the proposed insurance company.

The *Financial Services Act, 1986*, governed the marketing, including advertising, of investment-type life assurances. Life insurers had to become members of the *Life Assurance and Unit Trust Regulatory Organisation (LAUTRO)* in respect of their marketing activities and also, if they transacted pension fund management business, had to become members of the *Investment Management Regulatory Organisation* (*IMRO*). Independent financial intermediaries had to become members of the *Financial Intermediaries Managers and Brokers Regulatory Association* (*FIMBRA*). In December 2001 the Act was repealed by implementation of the Financial Services and Markets Act, 2000, and the self-regulatory organisations ceased to exist.

When the government proposed to abolish the Insurance Brokers Registration Council, it still expressed its support for self-regulation, and the industry responded in 2000 by establishing the *General Insurance Standards Council* (*GISC*) to regulate the conduct of general insurance business covering the sale and servicing of insurance products replacing the ABI's Code of Practice for the Selling of General Insurance. In January 2001 the *Office of Fair Trading* decided that the *GISC*'s rules did not infringe s.1 of the Competition Act, 1998. However, in the end self-regulation of general insurance intermediaries was transferred to the FSA, despite earlier government support for self-regulation.

16
Retrospect and Prospect

A century of transformation

The preceding chapters have traced the numerous massive changes undergone by the British insurance industry that have reflected the social, political and economic upheavals that occurred in Britain from the beginning of the twentieth century until the onset of the 2008 financial crisis. In 1900 the non-life insurance industry was still largely concentrated on marine and fire insurance. Liability and motor insurances were still new forms of business destined to become major sources of business. The main changes to the industry during the twentieth century can be summarised as follows, with almost every aspect of the insurance market undergoing far-reaching changes, notably:

Life insurance
- This has changed from being mainly a protection product to a savings-based product.
- Until the last quarter of the century mutual life offices controlled a large share of the UK life market. Their demutualisation was followed in many cases by their takeover by banks and other financial institutions.
- Life offices have diversified into other financial products.
- Companies, especially those writing pensions business, are now facing considerable problems arising from increasing longevity, and since the 2008 financial crisis falling investment incomes and asset values.
- The last quarter of the twentieth century witnessed the decline of the highly labour- intensive industrial life assurance.

Non-life insurance
- This was transformed to a large extent as personal insurances became a consumer product with the growth, following the purchase by households of houses, new goods and services, of motor, home, health, travel

and other new classes of insurance that have replaced fire insurance as the largest class of insurance.
- There was a similar expansion in the commercial insurance sector of new liability, aviation, credit, nuclear risks, and other products.
- The Lloyd's market has been restructured with the traditional unlimited liability. Names largely being replaced by limited liability corporate members, and the market has become concentrated on fewer managing agencies, syndicates and Lloyd's brokers.
- The international insurance and reinsurance industry has had to respond to an enormous growth in the size of individual risks and in exposures arising from natural and man-made disasters. Insured losses from natural hazard catastrophes have broken records, not only in North America but in Europe and elsewhere. While costing less than the usually large weather losses in the US, the European January 2007 windstorm Kyrill caused insured losses totalling $6 billion. Additional risk transfer capacity for catastrophe risks has been mobilised by capital market investors providing new forms of risk transfer and new financial products.

Other structural changes

The UK company market has been transformed by:

1. the entry of foreign companies that have taken a larger share of the UK domestic market, and dominate the London company market in the writing of international insurance and reinsurance;
2. the entry of banks and other financial institutions into the life and non-life markets;
3. the absorption of major brokers into international mega-groups and the growth and then takeover of provincial and specialist brokers;
4. education for both actuaries and for insurance employees generally had become well-established by the early 1900s. Since then the *Chartered Insurance Institute* has extended the scope of its activities and setup educational facilities for financial advisers.

Many of the changes evidenced considerable enterprise and innovation, but in some cases moves took companies beyond their areas of expertise, sometimes with very adverse consequences.

Information technology has:

1. improved the administration of the business and enabled companies to outsource many tasks to low-wage countries;
2. radically changed the distribution channels for personal and small trade insurances, including the emergence of the aggregators;
3. made possible developments in underwriting systems, including catastrophe modelling;

4. facilitated the transfer of risks to capital markets, as catastrophe modelling made possible the development of weather derivatives and catastrophe bonds.

Social, legal and technological changes

Most classes of non-life insurance felt the impact of technological advance. Property and transport insurances have had to provide cover for considerably larger industrial complexes, commercial properties and forms of transport.

Liability insurance has been transformed. New products and processes, combined with a growing public demand that those responsible for accidental injury and damage to the persons and property of others should compensate victims leading to legislative changes, has created a demand for insurance and escalating claims costs. The liability claims that arose from asbestosis and environmental pollution may be exceeded by the future adverse impact of new technologies, such as nanotechnology, space travel and the implementation of new laws such as the EU's 2004 Environmental Liability Directive, which imposes substantial liabilities on polluters who will be liable to:

(a) pay for any damage to protected species, natural habitats, water or land, and
(b) restore the environment without any limit to the amount of remediation costs.

Supervision

Regulation of the industry has been greatly strengthened in response to company failures, plus the transfer of the supervision of companies and intermediaries to the Financial Services Authority with its risk-based approach to supervision, and the need for the UK to adopt EU Directives.

Consumer protection

This is now a major issue, with the FSA, the Competition Commission and other bodies taking steps to deal with such issues as mis-selling of life and pension products, and the cover provided by critical illness and long-term products.

The minimum rate tariffs

By the 1970s the continuance of the long-standing fire and accident tariffs was being challenged as the result of:

1. the entry to the market of new UK and foreign companies;
2. large buyers exercising their countervailing powers; and
3. government intervention (the Monopolies Commission).

Innovation

Innovation has been a feature of the development of the industry in relation to:

- Demands mainly from commercial buyers for insurers to broaden the boundaries of insurability, including cover for newly emerging risks, such as satellites, nuclear and environmental damage, professional indemnity and other liability risks, and terrorism. As noted above, technological advance will continue to create new risks to which insurers will be expected to respond, even though the magnitude of the potential risks that may arise is imponderable at present.
- Distribution systems employing advances in information technology, including the internet.
- Administration.

Terrorism

Mounting political violence in the 1980s forced insurers to reassess the cover traditionally provided in property insurances, and led to cooperation between governments and the industry, including in the UK the formation of *Pool Re*. In America at the end of 2007 the federal government extended the backstop it provided for losses from terrorism under the 2002 Terrorism Risk Insurance Act by enacting the Terrorism Risk Insurance Program Reauthorization Act (TRIPRA). The private market for terrorism cover has grown substantially.

Political instability in many countries is a breeding ground for terrorism, and the threat of terrorists turning to the use of chemical, biological, nuclear and radioactive (CBNR) weapons presents the prospect of disasters of enormous magnitude. *Pool Re* and *GAREAT* in France (but not TRIPRA) cover acts of CBNR terrorism, but at present the private terrorism market is very limited, with very few insurers being willing to cover the risk.

Risk management

The widespread adoption of the practice of risk management fundamentally changed the way in which large firms and multinationals addressed and handled not only their insurable but also their operating and other risks too. For direct insurers it has resulted in some loss of business through firms retaining more of their own risks and by forming captive insurance companies (many in low tax overseas locations) but reinsurers have benefited from reinsurances ceded by captives. Moreover, it has created a demand for insurance against new types of risk, such as product recall, environmental liability and political risks. It has also enabled brokers to diversify into captive management and the development of capital market alternative risk transfer products.

Enterprise risk management has also become an essential management tool for insurers in managing their own operating and financing risks, with the FSA having adopted a risk-based approach to regulation.

Overseas business

The international operations of UK insurers had a mixed experience during the twentieth century. Largely due to Britain's colonial heritage, for most of the first eight decades the majority of insurance companies' UK non-life business was exceeded by overseas premium income, while after the 1990s the home market provided the largest share. Rapid growth at home and difficult conditions in many overseas markets pushed the domestic proportion of the company market from 33.8 per cent in 1961 to 77.7 per cent by 2006. Lloyd's continued to obtain the bulk of its business overseas and it reduced its home market premiums from 29 per cent of the total in 1982 to 24 per cent in 2007.

International business was disrupted by the two World Wars, and after 1950 it suffered from the spread of domestication and nationalisation of many countries' insurance industries. North America had for long been the main source of overseas insurance and reinsurance business for UK insurers, but severe losses in the US led most companies in the second half of the century to pull out from that market, although Lloyd's maintained its presence, especially in the reinsurance market.

The last 20 years of the century brought about major changes leading to the globalisation of business following the breakdown of the Soviet bloc in Eastern Europe, and the formation in 1993 of the World Trade Organisation and the General Agreement on Trade in Services (GATS), which has enabled European and American insurers to re-enter countries in Eastern Europe and especially the emerging industrial economies of India, China and South-East Asia, which had been closed to foreign insurers and reinsurers. The major UK life offices have secured large market shares of life insurance in Asia, but general business has largely focused on corporate and motor insurances.

Life business was always primarily UK-based, with foreign business accounting usually for below 30 per cent of the total premiums, and the 2006 ratio was 19 per cent, by which time expanding EU markets accounted for 43 per cent of this segment. The expansion abroad that has followed trade liberalisation, however, has necessitated foreign insurers securing effective local distribution channels and adjusting to different cultures by supplying new forms of insurance, notably Muslim-approved Takaful life and non-life insurances. The major life offices, however, greatly expanded their American business from the 1980s by acquiring local companies.

Performance of companies

Regrettably, we have been unable to produce any reliable analysis of the comparative long-term performance of companies because of mergers and the differences in accounting practice. For example, in speaking of the wide variations between companies in calculating provisions for short-term business, Sir Brian Mountain, in commenting on forms of accounting, stated in the *Eagle Star*'s 1970 report and accounts that:

> the methods employed can be so different that companies with broadly similar business and experience can report entirely dissimilar results.

There were many other discrepancies and changes in accounting practice over the years that bedevilled sound analysis of comparative performance, such as the treatment of investment earnings on insurance funds and the valuation of funds (in 1968 when the leading five composite companies first published the market values of their general fund investments the aggregate excess market values were larger than the book values), and in 1969 the *Commercial Union* led the way in introducing an equalisation reserve for classes of business exposed to catastrophe losses with the establishment of an 'Extreme Weather Reserve'.

The failure of companies

Despite the steps taken by the government since 1900 to strengthen its regulation of insurers, beginning with the Assurance Companies Act, 1909, many companies still failed during the twentieth century. There are many reasons cited as causes of insolvency, such as market forces, including intense competition, underwriting incompetence, falls in investment returns and in asset values, fraud, and supervisory failure. Research on insurance insolvencies in the USA in the 1980s identified non-recoverable reinsurance balances as the single most significant cause of failure (Best, 1999). However, a detailed study of European insolvencies by EU Insurance Supervisors (the London Working Group) showed that such factors were merely 'the tip of the iceberg' (Ashby *et al.*, 2003). It found that typically a company's failure was caused by a combination of factors with poor management at the root.

The Group found that the identified management problems mainly took four forms:

- managerial incompetence;
- an excessive risk appetite;
- a lack of integrity;
- local managers lacking autonomy.

As recorded in Chapter 6, the largest UK life company failure was that of *Equitable Life*, where the management set policies that gambled on future economic conditions; that is, they gave guaranteed annuity options, and when market interest rates fell and life expectancy was rising management was reluctant to admit the problem, although it tried some financial engineering by purchasing financial reinsurance. The supervisory authority too failed in its duties. Consequently the company was forced to cut the values of with profits policyholders' pension funds, to cease writing new business and to sell off parts of its business. Eventually the Parliamentary Ombudsman held that there had been regulatory failure and that the government should compensate policyholders (Parliamentary Ombudsman 2007).

The problems for the five London market subsidiaries of London United Investments arose from their managing agent specialising in writing US market casualty and professional indemnity business during a period of extreme unprofitability, so that the five KWELM companies in 1993 went into run-off.

Cases of losses caused by systems failure generally are not made public. However, in 1984 the *Iron Trades* reported that a senior employee had accepted without authorisation a programme of reinsurance of a size and nature never before undertaken by the company. Senior management only became aware of the commitment after the event, and had prudently made provision for substantial possible losses.

Prime examples of management lack of integrity were *Fire Auto & Marine* in 1966 and *Independent Insurance* in 2001. In both cases executives were convicted of fraud. Both companies also exhibited classical features of insurance company failures in that they had grown far faster than the market average at a time of intense competition, had failed to maintain adequate claims reserves, and exhibited defective accounting.

The takeover of a company or a portfolio of business can prove to be a costly case of managerial fraud and incompetence, as the Australian company *HIH* found after its takeover of *FAI*. The insolvency of *Chester Street Holdings Ltd* in 2001 was 'largely due to the asbestos related employer's liability claims which it acquired when it accepted the transfer of earlier claims from *Iron Trades Employers' Association*' (Youngman, 2008).

The insurance industry has a history of attracting charlatans and frauds and the government recognized that the traditional prudential requirements for regulatory supervision needed to be supplemented when, after the collapse of *Fire Auto & Marine* and *Vehicle & General*, it introduced the 'fit and proper' persons test for owners and controllers of insurance companies. Now the FSA is giving a high priority to governance, risk management and systems and controls (Tiner, 2002).

The cause of the huge losses suffered by many banks was the investing of funds in securitised US sub-prime market mortgage loans, which raises the question of whether their managements all fully understood the risks involved. As financial markets continue to develop ever more sophisticated products, the threats to the solvency of companies due to managerial incompetence must be increasing, even though we know of no UK-based insurance company insolvency to date that could be attributed to that cause.

Contribution to the UK economy

The industry's primary roles remain:

(a) the spreading of risks more widely over time and between persons and organisations by providing individuals, firms and other organisations with a means of transferring the risk of uncertain financial losses to an insurer in return for a known or determinable premium, thereby permitting the more efficient handling of risks; and
(b) as an important means of personal saving through life and pensions contracts.

However, it makes other important contributions to the UK economy, notably:

Balance of payments

Thanks to the intensive participation of British insurance institutions in international activities, Britain earns significant sums from overseas, by a variety of insurance services. These include the direct and reinsurance activities of Lloyd's and the insurance companies, insurance brokers' and investment services (mostly by life companies investing in overseas securities and earning investment income). However, while dividends are received from the overseas subsidiaries of British insurers, as well as income from the insurance and reinsurance of overseas' risks , foreign insurers active in the UK create a corresponding outflow of reinsurance and dividends.

Those earnings vary widely from year to year, due to competitive pressures, catastrophe loss experience and exchange rate fluctuations. During the past 30 years the UK insurance sector consistently earned an insurance surplus, with the largest positive figure achieved in 1995 (£7,243m) and the lowest of £450m in 1975 (see Table 16.1).

It is noteworthy that in 2007 Britain was the world's second largest insurance market, with total life and non-life premium income of $464bn, representing an 11 per cent global market share (Swiss Re, 2008). This was a steep increase from the 7 per cent share seen in 1996.

Employment

The insurance industry provides an important source of employment in the UK. No reliable statistics on employment in insurance existed until the mid-1970s, before then being included by the Ministry of Labour under the heading of 'insurance, banking and finance'. The combined employment figure for the financial sector expanded dynamically after World War II, with a 29 per cent increase between 1955 and 1965, which may give an indication of trends in the insurance industry as well. 1976 was the first

Table 16.1 Net overseas earnings of UK insurance institutions (£m)

	£m
1975	450
1980	968
1985	3,318
1990	3,165
1991	3,672
1992	3,801
1993	5,166
1994	4,197
1995	7,243
1996	5,645
1997	6,150
1998	2,851
1999	3,997
2000	3,794
2001	4,562
2002	6,566
2003	6,756
2004	4,965
2005	1,552
2006	3,525

Sources: ABI Statistics Yearbook, 2001, ONS UK Balance of Payments Yearbook.

Table 16.2 Trends in insurance employment: Great Britain insurance employment (000) (end year figures)

	Insurance and pension funding	Auxiliary to insurance and pension funding	Total
1982	227.0	66.0	293.0
1987	211.3	105.6	316.9
1990	240.3	132.2	372.5
1994	218.1	136.1	354.2
2001	221.7	135.2	356.9
2004	187.2	139.5	326.7
2007*	174.5	134.8	309.3

Note: *June.
Source: Office of National Statistics.

available figure for insurance (see Table 16.2); it put the insurance industry total at 263,000 (which excluded insurance staff employed by the public sector). A further breakdown showing a split between employment in insurance and pension funding and employment auxiliary to insurance and pension funding was provided from 1982 (where the latter heading includes intermediaries and underwriting agents and loss adjusters).

The figures in the table show a significant growth in insurance employment from the 1970s to the peak year of 1990, representing a 41.6 per cent increase during this period. While the first column recording the main segment of the industry remained larger than the auxiliary group, the total in the main heading declined by 27 per cent between 1990 and 2007. The auxiliary segment, which includes intermediaries, changed relatively little during the 17 year period since 1990 (although the precise numbers of intermediary employment are not known).

Male employment as a ratio of the total changed little from 2001 to 2007, for which we have data, at around 49 per cent. The significant difference between male and female employment patterns was that the ratio of part-time female employees increased steeply, from 18.8 per cent in 2001 to 23.3 per cent in 2007. For males the part-time ratio was much lower, at 4.4 per cent in 2001 and 3.2 per cent in 2007.

The post-1990 decline in insurance employment is difficult to reconcile with the general expansion of the insurance and pension funding industry. However, there are some well-recognised trends in recent years that all point to a smaller labour force. These include the decline and closure of the labour-intensive industrial life business, the growth of internet-based electronically executed distribution channels as well as the outsourcing of customer handling activity, such as call centres and software development, to companies outside the insurance industry or abroad. The numerous company mergers during the 1990s also may have been a contributory factor, as one of the principal incentives was the reduction of redundant layers of management and branch offices. The rate of decline in male employment in insurance since 2001 was 14 per cent and for females the drop was 13 per cent. The overall trend for the insurance industry also showed a decline as a percentage of all industries, from 1.4 per cent in 2001 to 1.2 per cent by 2007.

Climate change and natural disasters

The insurance industry is facing new challenges arising from the risk of climate change and an exposure to natural disasters of substantially increasing magnitude. In various parts of the United States windstorms, and particularly earthquakes, have the potential to cause losses in excess of $100 bn. The UK is expected to be exposed to a significant rise in inland and coastal flood risk associated with global warming. Already major expanding cities in economically emerging developing countries are highly exposed to future climatic disasters. To cater for such exposures global insurance and reinsurance capacity will need to be supplemented by alternative risk transfer and capital market investment. Insurers will need to monitor developments in climate change science and exercise risk management to control their potential future exposures.

The financial crisis fallout

The insurance industry has not been immune to the turmoil in the world's economy and the world's financial markets arising from the collapse of US sub-prime mortgages and the country's housing market, but to date the UK insurance industry has not been hit to anything near the same extent as the banks, whose financial business models and funding arrangements are fundamentally different from those of insurers. A feature of insurance is that for a time insurers can finance claims from an inflow of premiums so that they do not have the same liquidity problems as banks, though a prolonged serious recession could reduce their premium inflows. Also, unlike banks, they are not exposed to the same panic withdrawal of funds, like *Northern Rock*. Of course, because insurers invest their funds in financial assets, though they are to a large extent long-term investors, they have been exposed to falls in equity prices and corporate bond defaults, However, whereas a major Japanese life insurer, *Yamato Life*, has failed, and the world's largest insurance group, the *American International Group*, has had to be bailed out by a massive injection of funds by the American federal government, to date no UK insurance company has succumbed to the financial crisis, though some companies have reported large falls in their asset values, and so solvency margins. The earlier strengthening of the regulatory and capital regimes has better prepared insurers for dealing with the adverse market conditions, and some of the FSA's rules have been changed to give insurers more flexibility.

Life offices generally have been more badly affected by the financial crisis than general insurers. The extent of the damage caused by the decline in security values was not clear at the time of writing, but it could cause significant problems for the long-term insurance market. It is also believed that the introduction of the new Market Consistent Reporting Embedded Value financial reporting standard is likely to cause capital problems for pensions and annuity providers and for life companies.

Non-life insurers generally have not been badly damaged by the financial crisis, apart from those companies, like *AIG*, that became directly involved in providing financial guarantees. *AIG*'s problems also arose from large losses incurred on derivatives managed by its Financial Products subsidiary, which operated without adequate corporate supervision or regulation by its US and French regulators, rather than by the group's insurance operations. The main impact of the crisis can be summed up as follows:

1. A major market response to the 'credit crunch' for non-life insurance has been the withdrawal of credit insurance that protects the suppliers on credit of goods and services against bad debts. In November 2008 *Atradius* (the largest credit insurer, established in 2001 from the merger of *Gerling Credit* with *NCM Credit*) withdrew cover from a reported 20,000 companies as fears grew that an increasing number of firms would be

unable to pay their suppliers. Besides increasing premium rates, other insurers also cancelled policies.
2. However, at the same time the *Exports Credit Guarantee Department* extended the insurance it provides to business contracts of less than five years' duration.
3. Directors' and Officers' business is another class of insurance exposed to a potential large increase in claims because of shareholders' dissatisfaction with the performance of companies. Also, following the alleged $50 billion fraud by Bernard Madoff, both D and O and professional indemnity insurances could be exposed to claims from actions brought against financial institutions that invested clients' assets in Madoff's funds.
4. AIG, besides now being exposed internationally to the loss to business to competitors, has also been forced to consider the disposal of some of its overseas subsidiaries, including its UK companies.
5. The *Royal Bank of Scotland* has been forced to try to dispose of its insurance subsidiaries, including the highly successful *Direct Line* and *Churchill*, which could trigger new moves on market consolidation. The banking crisis may also dampen the appetite of other banks for being involved in insurance business.

Looking to the future

No-one in 1900 could have forecast the degree to which the insurance industry would be transformed over the next 100 years, and it is equally impossible to forecast the changes that will occur over the next century. All that is certain is that it is an invaluable service that will continue to evolve as it responds to changes in demand and to economic, social, legal and technological forces. In this section we aim to speculate about the shape of certain aspects of the market. These should not be regarded as forecasts, but merely as indications of where future threats and opportunities may emerge for the insurance industry in coming years.

Professionalism

It is widely accepted that the success of the industry in general and the London Market in particular depends upon the quality of its practitioners. The Chartered Insurance Institute has done much to enhance the insurance education and training of staff. The number of Chartered Insurance Institute members increased throughout the twentieth century, from 6,970 in 1920, to 27,051 in 1945, 70,031 in 1990 and 91,818 in 2007. Of the last figure the number of foreign members was some 13,000.

Nevertheless the *Journal of the CII* frequently carries articles committing the industry to greater professionalism. It is difficult to see what can be done to encourage employees to obtain appropriate qualifications unless all employers commit themselves to the promotion of only qualified persons.

CII membership as a proportion of total UK insurance employment continued to advance, climbing from 18.9 per cent in 1976 to 29.7 per cent by 2007. The growing number of actuarially trained people also contributes to the expansion of professionally skilled staff available to the industry, with the membership of the Institute of Actuaries rising from 770 in 1895 to 10,088 by 2000.

Aggregators and consolidators

These are the latest innovations in the ever-shifting insurance distribution system which has remained in continuing flux since the 1980s. Aggregators have provoked criticism from insurers, brokers and others who claimed that they provided insufficient information on which to decide upon a 'best-buy'. They demanded that aggregators should be subject to FSA regulation, an issue still to be decided at the time of writing. No doubt insurers and intermediaries will continue to look for new, including electronic, ways to distribute their services.

The process of broker consolidation could have been running out of steam by 2008. *Towergate*, the most successful consolidator, announced that having failed in 2007 to achieve its target organic growth it would scale back its acquisitions and focus on integration.

Demographic change

The coming decades will be challenging for the life insurance market, mainly due to the demographic changes generated by increasing life expectancy. This may make it necessary to redesign retirement products and annuity policies, to reflect the higher costs falling on them from those entering retirement. As the ability of the governments of advanced industrialised nations to maintain adequate public sector and social security retirement provisions is likely to diminish, opportunities will grow for increased personal saving and private provision, which the life insurance industry is well prepared to provide.

There may be a similar extension of demand for privately provided long-term care and health care and the associated private medical insurance, as increased longevity is likely to cause longer periods of declining health for the older generation, which the state sector may not be able to meet.

Demographic change in the form of population growth and the movement from rural to urban areas is likely to create problems for non-life insurers too. As noted above, the increase in values at risk in many areas exposed to natural catastrophes, which climate change experts warn are likely to become more severe, may exceed insurers' capacity, necessitating greater participation by governments and capital markets. Indications are that to date issues of catastrophe bonds are continuing to rise, with insurance securitisation offering capital market investors non-correlated investment opportunities.

The industry has always been proactive in loss prevention. Following the floods in England in June and July 2007 that resulted in insured losses of £150m and £1 billion respectively (*Sigma* No 1/2008), the ABI was very critical of the government's plans for building new houses and improving flood protection.

Policyholder protection

The demand for consumer protection is likely to deepen further, with regulators insisting on the protection of consumer rights. Regulators may promote improved product transparency and point of sale information and facilitate consumer redress without the need to resort to litigation. The Financial Ombudsman Service and consumer champions such as Which? are increasing their efforts to 'name and shame' firms engaged in inappropriate marketing drives. The efforts to maintain consumer loyalty by insurers may depend increasingly on 'Treating Customers Fairly' as well as providing them with effective sales and claims services.

Critics of the industry have long claimed that insurance contract law regarding disclosure is too heavily weighted in favour of insurers. It is a situation which the proposals of the Law Commission are intended to redress, including the substitution of 'reasonable insured' for that of the 'reasonable insurer' in the materiality test, and excusing innocent misrepresentation of facts (Law Commission, 2006). However, for insurers such changes are likely to exacerbate the problem of moral hazard, which will call for sensitive handling.

Insurance capacity

There is little hope for the control of the periodic over-abundance of insurance capacity and the resultant fall in premium rates as a result of increased supply. Globalisation, easier market entry conditions and the wider opening of capital markets enables the influx of capital to most markets, quickly leading to oversupply. This is already evident in the largest developing market, China, which is attracting new entrants and capital on a massive scale. These trends are likely to maintain highly competitive markets in coming years.

Bancassurance and holding companies

The financial crisis seen in 2008 may diminish the propensity of banks and financial holding companies to purchase insurance operations, since there could be problems in the promotion of insurance company products if the holding company is later forced to sell the insurer to a third party and thus interrupt its franchise. The twentieth century practices of 'Allfinanz', 'bancassurance', and 'one-stop shopping' may have to be curtailed in a new environment. By 2000 a number of banks had already disposed of their insurance interests. After its takeover of *Abbey National* the Spanish bank

Banco Santander quickly disposed of Abbey's Scottish Mutual assets, and in 2007 Prudential sold its on-line bank Egg.

Widening insurability

The twentieth century has witnessed a continual widening of the borders of insurability for nuclear, environmental liability, terrorism and other risks. This movement is likely to continue, with the application of innovative risk management techniques. As recorded in Chapter 9, traditional risk transfer products are already supplemented by new risk financing instruments and the transfer of risks into capital markets. Walter Kielholz, the CEO of the Swiss Re, has observed that:

> Boundaries between reinsurance and investment banking have blurred considerably during the past 15 years. It would be no exaggeration to state that both industries, reinsurance in particular, have changed more than in the previous 100 years.

He also pointed out that:

> reinsurers already act as the primary insurer's asset manager; it is the reinsurer who is responsible for profitably investing the premiums ceded to it. (Kielholz and Liedtke, 2001, p. 87)

In regards to personal lines insurances, new policies such as pet or holiday insurances and a host of other consumer covers are likely to be followed up in the twenty-first century with new products as new needs arise and sustain the trend towards increasing the weight of personal lines policies over commercial insurance business.

The Last Word

The British insurance industry has lived through a turbulent century with two World Wars, as well as the Great Depression of the 1930s, numerous natural and man-made disasters, and worldwide economic, political, social, legal and technological upheaval. At times these threatened the financial stability of Lloyd's and companies, but mergers and reconstructions managed to correct most of these upheavals. The industry has been enterprising, having innovated and adapted to changing conditions. It has not only survived but has grown to be a much larger, highly globalised and more important sector of the UK and world economy.

A key driver of the development of the non-life sector has been the growth of personal lines insurances, there being no substitute for insurance available to households (and small firms) that desire financial security against uncertain losses. Terrorism and technological change presenting new risks will pose further challenges to the whole (insurance and reinsurance) non-life sector.

The role of the industry in gathering personal savings has also grown massively in the shape of pension and life insurance provisions. It will have to adapt to increased longevity and volatile financial markets by continuing its innovative product development policies if it is to maintain its central position in the savings market.

Based on our analysis of the past century we have little doubt that Britain's insurance industry is capable of meeting future challenges if it maintains its adaptability and innovative skills.

Appendix 1

Principal works on pre-1900 British insurance market

Clayton G, *British Insurance*, (London: Elek Books, 1971)
Dickson P G M, *The Sun Insurance Office 1710–1960* (London: Oxford University Press, 1960)
Dinsdale W A, *History of accident insurance in Great Britain* (London: Stone & Cox Publications, 1954)
Hannah, Leslie, *Inventing retirement* (Cambridge: Cambridge University Press, 1986)
Johnston J & Murphy G W, 'The growth of life assurance in the UK since 1880' *Transactions of the Manchester Statistical Society 1956–57*
Living E, *A Century of insurance: The Commercial Union Assurance Group 1861–1961* (London: Witherby 1961)
Raynes H E, *A history of British insurance*, (London: Pitman, 2nd edn, 1964)
Supple B, *The Royal Exchange Assurance*, (Cambridge University Press, 1970)
Wright C & Fayle C E, *A history of Lloyd's 1927* (London: Macmillan, 1928)

Appendix 2

Reading list on insurance company investments

Carter R L, *Economics & Insurance*, P H Press 2nd edn, 1979, Chapter 3, p. 48

Clayton G, *British Insurance* 1971, Elek, 1971, Chapter 15, Insurance & the capital market, pp. 313–339

Clayton G & Osborn W T, *Insurance company investment – Principles & Policy* George Allen & Unwin, London, 1965

Dickinson G M, The regulation of investment policies of insurance companies within OECD in *Policy issues in Insurance*, OECD, Paris, 1993, pp. 205–254

Dickinson G M, *Determinants of insurance company asset choice*, Withdean, Brighton, 1971

Dickinson GM & Dinenis E, Investment regulations across the OECD, in *Policy issues in insurance*, 1996, OECD, Paris

Hadley B ed., 'Investment management: financial issues for the insurance industry in the nineties', *Reactions* 1992, pp. 97–129

International Association of Insurance Supervisors, *Supervisory standards on asset management for insurance companies*, IAIS, 1999, Basle

Paish F W & Schwartz G L, *Insurance funds & their investments*, King & Co, London, 1934

Policyholder Insurance Journal, 'Fund: investment policy in the British insurance industry', April 26 1962

Swiss Re, 'Direct Insurers' capital investments', *Sigma*, 5 1991

Appendix 3

Life and composite offices amalgamated 1989–2000

Date	Company acquired	Acquiring company
1989	Crown Life & Gen	Private Patients Plan
	FS Assurance	Britannia Bldg Socy
	London Life	Australian Mutual Provident (AMP)
	Pearl	AMP
	Prolific Group	Hafnia
	Property & Equity Life	Eurolife
	Sentinel Life	Century Group
1990	City of Edinburgh Life	Sentinel Life
	UK Life	Windsor Life
1992	CCL Assurance	Century Life
1993	British National Life	Lincoln National
	Life Asscn of Scotland	Britannia Life
1994	Irish Progressive Life	Prudential
	Windsor Life	Life Assce Holdings
	Scottish Equitable	AEGON
1995	Laurentian Life	Lincoln National
	Premium Life	Countrywide Assce
	Liberty Life	Lincoln National
	Provident Mutual	General Accident
1996	Royal	Sun Alliance & London
	Integral Life UK	Reliance Mutual
	Midland Life	HSBC Bank
	UTD Friendly Insce	Royal London
	Refuge	United Assce Group
1997	Scottish Amicable	Prudential
	Medical Sickness Annuity	Wesleyan
	Threadneedle Pensions	Zurich Financial Services
	Preferred Assce	Eagle Star
	Albany Life	Canada Life
	PPP Healthcare	Guardian Royal Exchange
1998	General Accident	Commercial Union
	Countrywide Assce	Countrywide
	Eagle Star	Zurich Financial Services
	Wessex Life	Domestic & Gen Life
	GAN Life	Life Assce Holdings
	Ambassador Life	Abbey Life
	London & Manchester	Friends Provident
	NPI	Australian Mutual Provident

Continued

Appendix 3 Continued

Date	Company acquired	Acquiring company
1999	Clerical Medical & Gen	Halifax
	Guardian Royal Exchange	AXA
	Bankers Life	Assurant Inc.
	Britannia Life	Britannic
	M & G Life	Prudential
	Caledonian	Royal Liver
	Scottish Widows	Lloyds TSB
	St James Place	Halifax
	United	Royal London
	Scottish Provident	Abbey National
	Scottish Life	Royal London
	Royal Pension Fund for Nurses	Liverpool Victoria
	Woolwich Life	Barclays Life
	Canterbury Life	Royal London
	Colonial Mutual Life	Credit Suisse
	Nat West Life	Royal Bank of Scotland

Appendix 4

Commercial lines premiums 1995, 2007 (£m)

	1995	2007
Employers' liability	1,914	1,656
Public and product liability	1,053	1,785
Professional indemnity	n.a.	874
Directors' and Officers'	n.a.	175
Commercial vehicle	1,781	2,725
Consequential Loss	n.a.	602
Fidelity and contract guarantee	208	150
Credit	136	246
Trade fire	1,837	3,065
Trade burglary	329	188
Engineering	242	534
Contractors' All Risks	157	164
Plate glass	13	6
Livestock	70	49
Suretyship	n.a.	76
Commercial contingency	n.a.	91
Other Fire and Accident	646	871
Total commercial lines	7,721	13,261

Note: Company market only, excluding Lloyd's & non-contributors.
Source: ABI.

Notes

1 The Industry from the End of the Victorian Era to 1914

1. *Vulcan Boiler* was established in 1859 and *British Engine* in 1878

6 Life Insurance

1. Form 40 of Prudential's 1990 annual supervisory return showed expenses of £215.3m against earned premiums of £405.7m
2. America accounted for 24 per cent of the world's total life premiums in 2007 (Swiss Re, 2008)

7 Commercial Insurances

1. It was estimated that the cost of the total claims was spread between five reinsurers and 160 retrocessionaires located in 46 countries
2. The Dutch businessman Dr Tiede Herrema was kidnapped by the IRA in 1975, and the former Italian premier Aldo Moro by the Red Brigade in 1978
3. See *Lanphier v Phipos* (1838). However, cases such as *Hedley Byrne and Co Limited v Heller and Partners Ltd* (1963), and *Midland Bank Trust Co Ltd v Hett Stubbs & Kemp* (1981) also defined the duty of care

8 Reinsurance

1. Facultative reinsurance – the reinsurance of individual risks that a reinsurer is free to accept or reject
2. Surplus treaty reinsurance is a form of proportional reinsurance under which the premiums and losses on a portfolio of risks with sums insured above the ceding company's retention are shared proportionately with the reinsurer. With a quota share the reinsurer accepts liability for a fixed share of all claims incurred by the ceding company
3. Treaty reinsurance is an agreement whereby the ceding company is bound to cede and the reinsurer is bound to accept liability for all losses arising on a portfolio of risks defined in the treaty
4. Non-proportional (or excess of loss) reinsurance is where the reinsurer accepts liability only for losses exceeding the reinsured's own retention subject to an upper limit
5. The March 1989 oil spillage from the tanker *Exxon Valdez* grounded in Prince William Sound Alaska caused devastating oil pollution

12 Competition and Mergers

1. *Prudential* first acquired a minority shareholding in *Mercantile & General Reinsurance Co.* in 1968

14 Distribution Channels

1. ASLK/CGER, a former Belgian savings bank, now part of *Fortis*, began practising bancassurance in 1889. H. Bartelds, R. van der Meer & K. Rutten 'Some reflections on bancassurance' in W. Kielholz & P. M. Liedtke, *Strategic Issues in Insurance* (New York & Oxford: Blackwell, 2001)

15 The Regulation of Insurance

1. The Insurance Companies (Accounts and Statements) (Amendment) (no. 2) Regulations, 1982, and the Insurance Companies (Accounts and Statements) (Amendment) (General Business Reinsurance) Regulations, 1983

References

Ashby, S., Sharma, P. and W. McDonnell (2003) *Lessons about Risk: Analysing the Causal Chain of Insurance Company Failure* (Nottingham: Centre for Risk & Insurance, Nottingham University Business School).
Association of British Insurers (1992) *ABI Companies* Represented Overseas (7 September).
Association of British Insurers (1993) *Insurance Statistics Year Book 1983–1993*.
Association of British Insurers (1985) *General Business Key Statistics 1950–1985*.
Association of British Insurers (2001) *Insurance Statistics Yearbook 1990–2000*.
Association of British Insurers (March 2001) *Creditor Insurance Research*, Final Report prepared for ABI by NOP Financial.
Association of British Insurers (2005) *UK Commercial Insurance Fraud Study 2005: A Summary of a Research Report Prepared by MORI for The Commercial Insurance Fraud Steering Group*.
Association of British Insurers (2007a) *General Insurance Claims Fraud*.
Association of British Insurers (2007b) *Financial Inclusion and Insurance*, ABI market studies No. 3.
Association of British Insurers (September 2008) *UK Insurance – Key Facts*.
Bacon & Woodrow (1992) Motor Insurance: Where is the Profit? (EPSOM: Bacon & Woodrow).
Bannister, J. and P. Bawcutt (1981) *Practical Risk Management* (London: Witherby).
Best, A.M. (February 1999) Special Report, *Insolvency – Will Historic Trends Return?* (Oldwick, N.J.: A M Best & Co).
Boleat, M. (1997) 'Regulation of the Creditor Insurance Industry', Speech by M. Boleat, ICB Creditor Insurance Conference, December.
Brighton, D., Saunders, G. and T. Sparkes (1991) *AIMIC to AIRMIC* (London: AIRMIC).
Business Insurance Europe, 5 November 2007.
Butler, G. and B. Butler (2000) *20th Century British Political Facts 1900–2000* (London: Macmillan).
Butt, J. (1984) 'Life Assurance in War and Depression: Standard Life Assurance and its Environment 1914–1939', in ed. Westall, O. M., *The Historian and the Business of Insurance* (Manchester: Manchester University Press).
Carter, R.L. (6 September 1962) 'A Correspondent' (R.L. Carter) 'Industrialists and Indemnity' *Post Magazine and Insurance Monitor*.
Carter, R.L. (17 February 1966) 'After "Which?"', *Policy Holder Insurance Journal*.
Carter, R.L. (22 September 1967) 'G.A. and Yorkshire: a Tariff Rethinking?', *Policy Holder Insurance Journal*.
Carter, R.L. (14 August 1965) 'The Insurance Practices of Local Authorities', *Local Government Chronicle*.
Carter, R.L. (9 August 1968a) 'Top Ten in 1967' *Policy Holder Insurance Journal*.
Carter, R.L. (1968b) *Competition in the British Fire and Accident Market*, an unpublished thesis, University of Sussex.
Carter, R.L. (10 October 1969) 'Top Ten in 1969', *Policy Holder Insurance Journal*.
Carter, R.L. (1970) 'Mergers and their Effects: Economic Aspects', *Journal of the Chartered Insurance Institute*.
Carter, R.L. (29 October 1971) 'Top Ten in 1970', *Policy Holder Insurance Journal*.

References

Carter, R.L. (24 October 1975) 'Top Ten in 1974', Stockport: *Policy Holder Insurance Journal*.
Carter, R.L. (22 October 1976) 'Top Ten in 1975: a Yearly Analysis of Performance', *Policy Holder Insurance Journal*.
Carter, R.L. (1979) *Economics and Insurance* (Stockport: PH Publishing).
Carter, R.L. (1980) *Top Ten in 1979: An Analysis* (Stockport: Policy Holder Publishing).
Carter, R.L. (1993) *Study on the Use of the Word 'Mutual' in the Insurance Industry* (Report prepared for the Life Assurance and Unit Trust Regulatory Organisation).
Carter, R.L. and G.M. Dickinson (1992) *Obstacles to the Liberalization of Trade in Insurance* (London: Harvester Wheatsheaf).
Carter, R.L. and P. Falush (July 1995) *The London Insurance Market* (London: Association of British Insurers).
Carter, R.L. and A.H. Godden (1984) *The British Insurance Industry: A Statistical Review* (Brentford: Kluwer Publishing).
Carter, R.L. and A.H. Godden (1985) *The British Insurance Industry: A Statistical Review 1984–85* (Brentford: Kluwer Publishing).
Carter, R.L., Lucas, L. and N. Ralph (2000) *Reinsurance*, 4th edn, p. 646 (London: Reactions Publishing Group).
Catchpole, W.L. and E. Elverston (1967) *BIA Fifty: 1917–1967 Fifty Years of the British Insurance Association* (Stockport: PH Press).
Working party of the Historic Records Committee of the Insurance Institute of London (1968) 'A short history of aviation insurance in the United Kingdom' *Journal of the CII*, vol. 65.
Chartered Insurance Institute (CII) (March 1997) 'In days of old', *Journal of the Chartered Insurance Institute*.
Chartered Insurance Institute (November 1998) 'promoting mutual respect' *Journal of the Chartered Insurance Institute*.
Chartered Insurance Institute (1981) *Motor Fleet Underwriting*, College of Insurance.
Chartered Insurance Institute (2007) *The Knowledgepack*, www.cii.co.uk
Citizens Advice Bureau (September 2005) *Protection racket, Evidence on cost and effectiveness of PPI*.
Clayton, G. (1971) *British Insurance* (London: Elek Books).
Cockerell, H. (21 January 1983) 'The changing insurance scene 1883–1983', *Policy Holder Insurance News*.
Competition Commission (2008) *Profitability of PPI*, Interim report.
Couchman, A. (2001) *Insurance and UK healthcare*, Informa, UK.
Crockford, G.N. (April 1982) 'The Bibliography and History of Risk Management', *The Geneva Papers on Risk and Insurance*, vol. 7.
Cummins J. David and Mary A. Weiss (2004) *Consolidation in the European Insurance Industry: Do Mergers and Acquisitions Create Value for Shareholders?* (Philadelphia: Wharton School).
Defaqto (1999) *Pet Accessories & Insurance* (Haddenham: Defaqto).
Derby, P.J. (1975) 'The Performance of Life Offices', *Journal of the Chartered Insurance Institute*.
Dickson, P.G.M. (1960) *The Sun Insurance Office 1710–1960* (London: Oxford University Press).
Dinsdale, W.A. *History of Accident Insurance in Great Britain* (London: Stone & Cox Publications, 1954).

Dover, V. (1946) 'Marine insurance through two wars', *Banker*, vol. 79.
Dugdale, P. (1983) 'Changes in Organisational Structure' a talk at the Chartered Insurance Institute Conference.
The Economist (16 September 2004) 'Insuring for the future?'.
The Economist Insurance Supplement 1970.
Essen, Y. (15 July 2008) 'Lifeline for Equitable Victims as Report Blames Government,' *Telegraph Money*.
EU Insurance Committee Working Group on Financial Reinsurance, Commission Working Document for the meeting on 5 February 1998.
Financial Ombudsman Service Annual Report 2007–08, May 2008.
Financial Services Authority (2002) Consultation paper CP121 'Reforming polarisation, making the market work for consumers'.
Financial Services Authority (July 2005) *Mortgage Endowments: Progress Report & Next Steps*.
Financial Times, 9 August 2008.
Finsinger, J., Hammond, E. and J. Tapp (1985) *Insurance: Competition or Regulation* (London: Institute for Fiscal Studies).
Franklin, P.J. and W. Caroline (1980) *The UK Life Assurance Industry* (London: Croom Helm).
Gibb, D.E.W. (1957) *Lloyd's of London* (London: Macmillan).
Global Aerospace (2008) 'Keeping pace with new technology', www.global-aero.co.uk/our_history.php
Golding, C.E. (1927) *A History of Reinsurance* (London: Sterling Offices Ltd).
Goshay, R.C. (1964) 'Captive Insurance Companies', in *Risk Management* ed. H.W. Snider (Holmwood, IL: R D Irwin Inc).
Hannah, L. (1986) *Inventing Retirement: The Development of Occupational Pensions in Britain* (Cambridge: Cambridge University Press).
Hartwig Robert, P. (5 April 2007) *Financial and Market Impact of Hurricanes on Property/Casualty Insurers*, National Hurricane Conference, New Orleans.
Hickmott, G. (1977) *Flixborough Disaster* (London: Mercantile & General Reinsurance Co.).
Hill, N. (1927) *War & Insurance* (London: Oxford University Press).
Holt, A. (February 2008) 'Consolidation: Will the Market Eat Itself', *The Journal of the Chartered Insurance Institute*.
Horrigan, W. (1969) *Risk, Risk Management & Insurance* (Brighton: Withdean Publications).
Horrigan, W. and W.A. Dinsdale (1967) 'The Theory of Risk', 'Analysis of Risk', 'Methods of Handling Risk' and 'The Work of the Risk Manager', *Post Magazine and Insurance Monitor*, 13th July, 10th August, 31st August and 12th October, 1967.
Haufler, V. (1997) *Dangerous Commerce* (New York and London: Cornell University Press).
Holmes, D. (2002) 'From the Ashes of Disaster', *World @ Risk* (London: International Underwriting Association).
Holt, A. (February 2008) 'Consolidation: Will the Market Eat Itself', *The Journal of the Chartered Insurance Institute*.
Hosking, G.L. (1947) *Salute to Service, the Prudential in the Second World War* (London: Prudential Assurance).
House of Commons Treasury Select Committee (2007) *'Are You Covered? Travel Insurance and its Regulation'*, 2006–07, HC 50.

Insurance Company Performance (2007) Centre for Risk and Insurance Studies, Nottingham University Business School, 2005.
Insurance Day (17 July 2008) London: Lloyd's of London Press.
Johnston, J. and G.W. Murphy (1957) 'The Growth of Life Assurance in the UK since 1880', *Proceedings of the Manchester Statistical Society 1956–57*.
Kielholz, W. and P. Liedtke (2001) *Financial Market Thinking Penetrates Reinsurance* (Oxford: Blackwell).
Key Note Publications (2006) *General Insurance, 2006*.
Key Note Publications (2007) *Personal lines Insurance, 2007*.
Laing & Buisson (2001) *Healthcare Market Review, 2001* (London: Laing & Buisson).
Laing & Buisson (2002) *UK Private Medical Insurance 2002* (London: Laing & Buisson).
Laing & Buisson (2003) *UK Private Medical Insurance 2003* (London: Laing & Buisson).
Laing & Buisson (2007) *UK Health & care covers 2006, 2007* (London: Laing & Buisson).
Law Commission (September 2006) *Insurance Contract Law' Issues Paper 1, Misrepresentation and Non-disclosure*.
Law Commission (2007) Consultation paper no. 182.
Lay, H.G. (1925) *Textbook of Marine Insurance History* (Post Magazine).
Leftwich, R.H. (1966) *The Price System and Resource Allocation*, Ch. 11 (New York: Holt Rinehart & Winston Inc.).
Leonard, A. (2002) 'All for one' in *World@Risk* (London: IUA).
Lloyd's of London (1984) *Statistics Relating to Lloyd's* (London: Lloyd's of London).
Lloyd's of London (1994) *Statistics Relating to Lloyd's* (London: Lloyd's of London).
Lloyd's of London (1998) *Statistics Relating to Lloyd's* (London: Lloyd's of London).
Lloyd's of London (1999) *Statistics Relating to Lloyd's* (London: Lloyd's of London).
Lloyd's of London (2001) *Statistics Relating to Lloyd's, 2000* (London: Lloyd's of London).
Lloyd's of London (2007) *Eyes on the future, Annual report 2007*.
Lloyd's of London (2008) *History & Chronology*, Key Dates Fact Sheet 1, www.lloyds.com/About_Us/History
London Market Association (2006) *Terrorism insurance – Physical Loss or Physical Damage Wording* T3 LMA3030.
Maddison, A. (1989) *The World Economy in the 20th Century*, (Paris: OECD).
Malinowski, W.R. (1971) 'European Insurance and the Third World', *Journal of World Trade Law*, Geneva, August–September 1971, and José Ripoll, 'UNCTAD and Insurance', *Journal of World Trade Law*, January–February 1974.
Marsh Risk Consulting Practice (2007) *Fit for Purpose? Benchmarking the Continuing Contribution of Captives* (London: Marsh).
Mason, E. (1946) 'Fire department in war-time', *Journal of the Chartered Insurance Institute*, vol. 43.
Mintel Financial (March 1997) *Home & Contents Insurance*.
Mitchell, B.R. (1990) *British Historical Statistics* (Cambridge: Cambridge University Press).
Mitchell, B.R. and P. Deane (1971) *Abstract of British Historical Statistics* (Cambridge: Cambridge University Press).
Monopolies Commission (1972) *Report on the Supply of Fire Insurance* (London: HMSO).

Neave, J.A.S. (5 February 1971) 'Current problems of the reinsurance market', *Policy Holder Insurance Journal*, vol. 89.
Neave, J.A.S. (1966) 'Reinsurance today; a general survey', *Journal of the Chartered Insurance Institute*, vol. 63.
Neave, J.A.S. (May 1976) 'International Reinsurance: Changing Patterns in Economic Relationship', *Policy*.
NHS Litigation Authority, http://www.nhsla/home.htm
North British & Mercantile (1946) *The War Record of the North British & Mercantile Insurance Co* (Company publication).
Noyes, A.F. (1953) 'British Insurance and the World Economy', *Journal of the Chartered Insurance Institute*.
O'Brien, C. and S. Diacon (2005) *Closed Life Funds: Causes, Consequences and Issues* (Nottingham: Centre for Risk and Insurance Studies, Nottingham University Business School).
OECD Secretariat (1983) *International Trade in Services: Insurance – Identification and Analysis of Obstacles*.
Office of Fair Trading (OFT) (1982) *Household Insurance, A Discussion Paper*.
Office of Fair Trading (OFT) (October 2006) *Report on PPI*.
Parliamentary Ombudsman (2008) *Equitable Life: A Decade of Regulatory Failure*, HC 815-V.
Phelps Brown, E.H. and J. Wiseman (1966) *A Course in Applied Economics*, 2nd edn (London: Pitman & Sons).
Pitney Bowes (2008) *The Dynamics of Defection*, London.
Plymen, J. and S. Pullan (1968) 'Insurance Profitability Past Present and Future', *Chartered Insurance Institute 1968 Conference papers*.
Policy Studies Institute, Whyley, C., McCormick, J. and Kempson, E. (1998) *Paying for a Peace of Mind*, London.
Pool Re, www.poolre.co.uk/History of Pool Re.
Post Magazine Almanac, 1918.
Post Magazine Almanac, 1935–36.
Post Magazine Directory & Yearbook, 2003.
Post Magazine Directory & Yearbook, 2005.
Post Magazine Directory & Yearbook, 2007.
Post Magazine Insurance Directory, 1939–40.
Post Magazine Insurance Directory, 1942–43.
Post Magazine Insurance Directory, 1945–46.
Post Magazine (2000) *Review of the Century*.
Post Magazine (7 January 2005) *The Insurance Directory*, 'Historical Company Changes'.
Post Magazine Supplement (27 September 2007) 'The King of Scotland', *Top 100 UK Insurers* Post Supplement.
Post Magazine (6 December 2007) 'Aggregator growth stalls'.
Post Magazine (27 March 2008).
Raynes, H.E. (1964) *A History of British Insurance* (London: Pitman, 2nd.edn, 1964; reprinted 1968).
Ross, S. (2002) 'Pulling together', *World @ Risk* (London: International Underwriting Association).
Royal Insurance Co (1965) *Annual Report & Accounts*.
Samuel, A. (9 April 2003) 'Endowments – the Complaints Deluge' *Compliance Monitor, Incisive Publication*.

Savory Milln (1968) *Insurance Share Annual*.
Sennett, W.F. (1991) 'Captive Insurance Companies – Yesterday's Solution to Tomorrow's Opportunity?' *Captive Insurance Company Review* 1979 and Captive Insurance Companies', *Handbook of Risk Management* 1991 (Hounslow: Kluwer Publishing, updated).
Sharp, C. (1986) *CII Insurance History Forum*.
Smith, Gordon D.H. (November 1915) *Insurance in Time of War* (Chartered Insurance Institute).
Standard & Poor's (2008) *Global Reinsurance Highlights* 2007 edition (London: Reactions Publishing).
Supple, B. (1970) *The Royal Exchange Assurance* (Cambridge University Press).
Sutherland, H. (July 1994) 'Whither Industrial Branch?', *Journal of the Society of Fellows*, Chartered Insurance Institute, vol. 9, Part 1.
Insurance Times (April 2008).
Swiss Reinsurance Co (1995) 'The London Market', *Sigma*, No.2/95.
Swiss Reinsurance Co (2006) 'Natural Catastrophes and Man-made Disasters 2005' *Sigma*, No.2/2006.
Swiss Re. Co (2007) 'Bancassurance: Emerging Trends, Opportunities and Challenges', *Sigma*, No.5/2007.
Swiss Reinsurance Co (2003) 'Unit-linked Life Insurance in Western Europe; Regaining momentum?', *Sigma*, No.3/2003.
Swiss Reinsurance Co (2008) 'World Insurance in 2007: Emerging Markets Lead the Way', *Sigma*, No.3/2008.
Taylor, A.J.P. (1965) *English History 1914–1945* (Oxford: Oxford University Press).
Tiner, J. (2002) *The Future Regulation of Insurance: A Progress Report* (London: Financial Services Authority).
The Treasury (March 2008) *Proposals for a Legislative Reform Order to amend Lloyd's Act, 1982*.
Treasury Committee Fourth Report 2006–07 "Are you covered?" London, Stationery Office, 2007.
Treasury Select Committee (1998) *Miss-selling of Personal Pensions*, Vol. 1 HC712-1.
Treasury Select Committee (March 2004) *Restoring Confidence in Long-term Savings: endowment mortgages* HC394.
US Department of Commerce (September 2008), *Survey of Current Business* (Washington: US Printing Office).
Ward, M.A. (1989) *Guernsey's Insurance History: an Initial Essay*, Report and Transactions of La Société Guernesiase, vol. XXII.
Westall, O.M. (October 1998) 'The Invisible Hand Strikes Back: Motor Insurance and the Erosion of Organized Competition in General Insurance, 1920–1938' *Business History*, vol. 30, no. 4.
Westall, O.M. (2006) 'Domestic distortions and the emergence of international trade in insurance', *The World Economy*.
Wikipedia (2008) 'Aviation insurance', http://en.wikipedia.org/Aviation insurance.
Wilson, Sir Arnold and H. Levy (1937) *Industrial Assurance: An Historical and Critical Study* (London: Oxford University Press).
Wright, C. and C.E. Fayle (1928) *A History of Lloyd's* (Macmillan: London).
Youngman, I. (2008) *Why Insurers Fail?*, CII Knowledge Services.

Index

Abbey Life, 66, 155, 179
accident and health, 53
accident insurance, 55
Accident Offices Association, 9, 12, 14, 21, 24, 27, 45, 151, 155, 179
Advertisements Regulations, 1983, 197
affinity schemes, 185
agents, 178
aggregators, 48, 166, 185–7, 214
AIDS, 68
AIG, 124, 213
Alliance, 12
Alternative risk transfer (ART), 120
Aon, 165, 183, 182
aquacultural insurance, 99
Associated Scottish Life Offices, 168
Association of British Insurers, 55, 67, 68, 169, 170, 179, 191, 198
Association of Friendly Societies, 171
Association of Insurance and Risk Managers In Industry & Commerce (AIRMIC), 117, 118, 173
Association of Insurance Brokers, 172, 178
Association of Mutual Insurers, 170
Assurance Companies Act, 1909, 13, 25, 62, 127, 191
Assurance Companies Act, 1946, 193
Assurance Companies (Winding-up) Acts, 25
Aviation & General, 11, 90
Aviation insurance, 11, 89
Aviation Insurance Clauses Group, 170
Aviation Insurance Offices Association, 90
Aviva, 74, 80, 81, 188
AXA, 106, 161, 166, 188
AXA Denplan, 56
AXA PPP, 54

Balance of payments, 209
bancassurance, 67, 68, 70, 156, 180, 215
Barclays Life, 70, 155, 180
Benfield, 114, 182, 183, 184
Bermuda, 101, 105, 115, 123, 130, 154
Black Horse Life, 70, 155, 180

boiler explosion, 7
bonus rates, 72
Bowring, 166, 177
Bretton Woods Agreement, 111
British & European, 10, 108, 113
British Aviation, 11, 90
British Aviation Insurance Group, 91
British Engine & Boiler, 7, 92
British General, 10
British Insurance Association, 151, 170
British Insurance Brokers Association, 172, 191
British Insurers European Committee, 170
British United Provident Association, 53, 54
brokers, 106, 165, 177, 178, 183, 184
  acquired by insurers, 188
burglary, 7

Cadbury Committee, 120
capital market products, 124
captive insurance companies, 121, 123
  offshore, 123
Car & General, 8
cars licensed, 27, 41
catastrophe bonds, 125, 214
catastrophe futures and options, 125
Catastrophe Risk Exchange, 125
catastrophe swaps, 125
Chartered Insurance Institute, 14, 118, 175, 213
China, 69, 81, 136
Churchill, 164, 181, 184
Citizens Advice Bureau, 71, 198
City University, 118
climate change, 211
closed fund consolidators, 74
closure of life funds, 74
commercial motor insurance, 86
Commercial Union, 10, 28, 43, 66, 70, 92, 136, 138, 142, 158, 180, 181
Companies Act, 1967, 45, 193
complaints, 54, 57, 59, 71, 193, 197
commercial insurances, 82
commercial motor, 86
competition, 149

232 Index

Competition Commission, 57
computer insurance, 99
consequential loss insurance, 86
consolidators, 214
construction and erection insurance, 96
consumer protection, 196, 204
Consumer Protection Act, 1987, 94, 119
Consumers Association, 71, 199
contract guarantee, 10
contract law, 11
contractors' design and construct risk, 95
Co-insurance Directive, 143
Co-operative Insurance Society, 48, 62
Cornhill Insurance, 142
corporate governance, 120
Corporation of Insurance Brokers, 86, 172, 178
credit insurance, 10, 87, 212
critical illness, 68, 197
currency fluctuation clause, 111

DAS Legal Expenses, 98
decennial liability, 96
demographic change, 214
demutualisation, 73
dental insurance, 56
derivatives, 125
Direct Line, 46, 59, 125, 152, 180, 184
directors' and officers' liability, 97, 213
dispute resolution, 112, 200
distribution
  life insurance, 68
  motor insurance, 47
domestication of insurance, 136
Dublin, 104, 115, 154
duty of disclosure, 12

Eagle Star, 91, 152, 159, 160, 161
East Coast floods, 50, 83
Ecclesiastical, 188
Emergency Protection from Forfeiture Act, 1940, 33
employers liability, 93, 94
Employers Liability Act, 1880, 9
Employers Liability (Compulsory Insurance) Act, 1969, 94
Employers' Liability Assurance, 9
Employers' Liability Insurance Companies Act, 1907, 13, 191
employment, 209
employment practices liability, 97

engineering insurance, 6, 92
Engineering Offices Association, 92
Enterprise Risk Management, 206
environmental liability insurance, 95
Environment Protection Act, 1990, 95
Equitable Life, 70, 73, 77, 207
Equitas, 129
Equity & Law, 155, 179
Estate Duty, 67
Esure, 47, 153, 181, 185
European company acquisitions, 162
European Union, 81, 140, 164, 189
Excess, 10, 113
excess of loss reinsurance, 111, 113
Export Credits Guarantee Department, 29, 88
Exxon Valdez, 113

Factories Act, 1961, 92
facultative reinsurance, 108, 133
Faculty of Actuaries, 14, 175
failure of companies, 45, 207
Federated Employers, 10
Federation of Insurance Brokers, 172, 178
Federation of Insurance Institutes, 14
fidelity guarantee, 10
financial insurance/reinsurance, 118, 123
finite risk, 124
Finance Act, 1921, 78
Finance Act, 1956, 78
Finance Act, 1970, 78
Finance Act, 1978, 78
Finance Act, 1987, 77
Finance Act, 2000, 78
financial crisis, 212
Financial Intermediaries, Managers and Brokers Regulatory Association, 71, 155, 173, 174
Financial Ombudsman Service, 55, 57, 71, 72, 197, 199, 200, 215
Financial Services Act, 1986, 68, 155, 172, 173, 174, 179, 197, 200
Financial Services & Markets Act, 2000, 128, 166, 174, 196, 201
Financial Services Authority, 57, 71, 72, 174, 182, 195, 197, 200, 204, 208
Financial Services Compensation Scheme, 196
Fine Art & General, 8
finite reinsurance, 124
Fire Auto & Marine Insurance Co, 45, 151, 159, 169, 193, 208

fire insurance, 27, 35, 83
Fire Offices Committee, 4, 5, 28, 35, 82, 84, 85, 150, 169
Fire Prevention Association, 149
fire tariffs, 83, 153
First Non-life Insurance Directive, 141
Flixborough, 86
flood insurance, 50
foreign controlled companies, 74, 75
foreign share – life, 74
fraud, 107, 208
freedom of establishment, 141, 143
freedom of services, 143
Friends Provident & Century, 152

General Accident, 12, 43, 68, 83, 92, 138, 159, 160, 163
General Agreement on Trade in Services (GATS), 81, 140
General Insurance Standards Council, 171, 197, 201
Glasgow Caledonian University, 118
Global Aerospace, 91
Goldsmiths & General, 8
Gresham Life, 136
Guardian, 8, 12, 64
Guardian Royal Exchange, 47, 86, 138, 160, 161
Guernsey, 123

Hambro Life, 66, 155, 179
Health & Safety at Work Act, 1974, 92, 119
Heath, Cuthbert, 10, 11, 107, 111
HIH, 124, 208
Hospital Cash Plans, 55
household insurance, 11, 49
household insurance penetration, 52
hurricanes, 104, 112, 113, 114, 138

Imperial Chemicals Insurance, 117, 122
Income protection, 56
Independent Financial Advisers, 156, 179
Independent Financial Advisers Association, 173
independent intermediaries, 179
index clauses – reinsurance, 114
index-linking, 51, 154
industrial all risks, 83
Industrial Assurance & Friendly Societies Act, 1948, 62
Industrial Assurance Commissioner, 62

Industrial Life Assurance Act, 1923, 62, 192
industrial life insurance, 17, 61, 178
Industrial Life Offices' Association, 14
information technology, 99, 203
innovation, 205
Institute of Actuaries, 14, 174
Institute of Insurance Brokers, 173, 178
Institute of London Underwriters, 169
Institute of Risk Management, 176
insurability, 216
Insurance Brokers (Registration) Act, 179
Insurance Brokers Registration Council, 171, 174, 201
Insurance Companies Act, 1958, 193
Insurance Companies Act, 1974, 193
Insurance Companies Act, 1982, 194
Insurance Companies Amendment Act, 1973, 46, 193
Insurance Companies Regulations, 1981, 200
Insurance Companies (Reserves) Regulations, 1994, 194
Insurance Company of North America, 83
insurance derivatives, 125
insurance fraud, 107
Insurance Intermediaries Directive, 143
Insurance Mediation Directive, 144
Insurance Ombudsman, 173
Insurance Ombudsman Bureau, 173
international business, 135
International Underwriting Association, 112, 171
internet, 167
internet liability insurance, 100
Investment & Life Assurance Group, 172
Investment Management Regulatory Organisation, 71, 156, 174, 201
Iron Trades, 9, 208
Isle of Man, 123

Kidnap and Ransom, 93

Latent Damages Act, 1986, 94
Law Accident Insurance Society, 8
Law Commission, 12, 215
Legal & General, 78, 80, 138, 139, 161, 181
legal expenses insurance, 98
liability insurance, 93, 204
liberalisation of trade, 139
Life Assurance & Unit Trust Regulatory Organisation, 71, 155, 174, 200

234 *Index*

Life Assurance Companies Acts
 1870–72, 13
Life Assurance Premium Relief, 67
life insurance, 6, 15, 25, 31, 155, 202
Life Insurance Freedom of
 Establishment Directive, 141
Life Offices Association, 155, 168, 179
Liverpool London & Globe, 5, 136
Livestock Offices Association, 170
Lloyd's
 Acts, 13, 127, 195
 brokers, 127, 130, 177, 183, 184
 Central Fund, 127
 corporate members, 127, 130
 franchise, 128, 196
 Franchise Board, 196
 growth of business, 132
 managing agents, 130
 market, 130, 184
 Names, 126, 127, 129
 Renewal & Reconstruction, 129
 syndicates, 130
 underwriting results, 113
Lloyd's Insurance Brokers
 Association, 172
Lloyd's Life, 67, 131
Lloyd's Market Association, 172
Lloyd's of London, 4, 13, 15, 22, 88, 102,
 104, 126, 195
Lloyd's Reinsurance Co. (China) Ltd, 132
LMX market, 104
Locomotives on the Highway Act, 8
London & Lancashire, 8, 25
London Assurance, 5, 7, 159
London Guarantee & Accident, 109, 113, 159
London Insurance Market Network, 131
London International Reinsurance
 Market Association, 112, 169, 171
London Market, 102, 106, 108, 113, 114,
 131, 154, 189
London Market cooperation, 131
London United Investments, 103, 112, 208
longevity, 214
long-term care, 214
loss of electronic information
 insurance, 100
loss prevention, 119

major company acquisitions, 158
M&G Group, 64, 155, 179
marine insurance, 19, 25, 34, 88, 179

Marine Insurance Act, 1906, 11
Market Reform Group, 106, 131
Married Women's Property Act, 1882, 67
Marsh McLellan, 165, 182
material fact, 12
Medical Defence Union, 99
medical malpractice, 98
Mercantile & General Reinsurance, 10, 108,
 110, 114
mergers, 157
Metropolitan Life, 6, 78
Minet Holdings, 182, 188
mis-selling, 71, 83, 153, 197, 198
Monopolies Commission, 84, 85, 153
mortgage endowments, 64, 198
Mortgage Interest Relief at Source, 67, 156
mortgage protection policies, 64
motor insurance, 8, 21, 26, 37, 43
Motor Insurance Directives, 141
Motor Insurers Bureau, 171
Motor Repair Research Centre, 46
Motor Risks Statistical Bureau, 45, 151
motor tariff, 87, 150
Motor Union, 8, 159
Munich Re, 10
mutual insurance companies, 95, 121
mutual life offices, 6, 73
mutual risk sharing, 121

Nation Life, 196
National Forum for Risk Management in
 the Public Sector, 119, 173
National Insurance (Industrial Injuries)
 Act, 1946, 9, 93
nationalisation, 62, 136
natural disasters, 211
NHS Litigation Authority, 98
non-life insurance, 202
North British & Mercantile, 5, 6, 21
Northern & Employers, 138
Norwich Union, 12, 54, 64, 70, 74, 78,
 110, 137, 153, 163, 166, 179, 181,
 184, 185, 188
Nottingham University, 118
nuclear risks insurance, 95
NW Re, 110

obstacles to trade, 135
OECD, 137
Office of Fair Trading, 50, 54, 57, 120,
 197, 201

oil crisis 1972, 66
ordinary life insurance, 6, 16, 63
overseas business, 18, 25, 80, 206
owner occupation, 50

Parliamentary Ombudsman, 73
Payment Protection Insurance, 57, 198
Pearl Group, 76, 164
pensions, 76
   individual/personal, 72, 77, 156
   occupational, 78
   s.226, 76
performance of companies, 206
permanent health insurance, 56
personal accident insurance, 6, 10, 21, 29, 56
personal lines premiums, 60
pet insurance, 59
Phoenix, 11, 65, 98, 137, 138, 159, 161
Piper Alpha, 113, 129
policyholder protection, 215
Policyholders Arbitration Service, 173
Policyholders Protection Act, 1975, 196
pollution insurance, 95
plate glass insurance, 7
Pool Re, 101, 121, 205
privacy and network insurance, 100
private medical insurance, 53
product extortion insurance, 93
products liability, 94
products recall, 94
professional indemnity insurance, 94
professionalism, 213
property insurance, 36, 82
proportional reinsurance, 111
protected cell companies, 123
Prudential, 5, 14, 63, 64, 68, 78, 80, 81, 82, 138, 160, 161, 178, 181, 188, 216
public liability insurance, 9

Railway Passengers Assurance Co., 6
Refuge, 5
regulation, 13, 24, 191
reinsurance, 10, 127
reinsurance companies, 108–9
Reinsurance Directives, 141
Reinsurance Offices Association, 112, 122, 171
Renewal and reconstruction – Lloyd's, 129
Resolution Life, 76, 163
resolution of disputes, 112

risk management, 117, 118, 205
risk transfer – by contract, 119
Road Traffic Act, 1930, 13, 26, 43
Royal Bank of Scotland, 164, 180, 185, 213
Royal Exchange, 5, 8, 18, 28, 29, 159
Royal Insurance Co., 5, 7, 23, 28, 47, 68, 80, 136, 138, 139, 155, 163, 179
Royal Sun Alliance, 70, 153, 164, 180, 184, 185, 188

Sale of Goods Act, 1893, 94
San Francisco earthquake, 5, 11, 28, 111
Save & Prosper, 64, 179
Scottish Equitable, 74
Scottish Mutual, 70, 74, 164, 180
Scottish Widows, 74, 164
Securities and Investments Board, 70, 155, 200
Sedgwick Collins, 177, 182
self insurance, 118, 121
self regulation, 200
Social Security Act, 1973, 79
Social Security Act, 1986, 77, 79
Social Security Pensions Act, 1975, 74, 76, 81
Standard Life, 16, 70, 74, 81, 181
State Cargo Insurance Office, 20
State Earnings Related Pensions (SERPS), 76, 77
State Insurance Office, 22
Stock market 1974, 66
structural changes, 203
subsidence, 50
Sun Alliance & London, 122, 138, 161, 163, 166
Supply of Goods (Implied Terms) Act, 1973, 94
Swintons, 166
switching between insurers, 48

Tanker Insurance, 117, 122
tariffs
   Employers' Liability, 93, 204
   fire, 4, 83, 150, 153
   motor, 87, 150
technological change, 185
telephone sales, 184
terminal bonuses, 64, 155
terrorism, 100–2, 114, 205
Third Life Insurance (Framework) Directive, 143

Third Non-life Insurance (Framework) Directive, 143
Towergate, 166, 180, 188, 214
trade associations, 168
trade liberalisation, 139
travel insurance, 58, 199
Treasury Select Committee, 72, 198, 199
treaty reinsurance, 108, 133
9/11 Twin towers disaster, 101, 113, 114

unauthorised trading, 93
United Kingdom Provident Institution, 33, 70
unit linked insurance, 64, 66
universal life, 68
UNCTAD, 110, 129, 136
Unfair Contract Terms Act, 1977, 120
United States, 5, 37, 80, 81, 101, 105, 136, 137

Vehicle & General Insurance Co., 46, 152, 169, 193, 208
vehicle ownership, 27, 43
Victory Reinsurance, 10, 108, 110, 113
Vulcan Boiler, 7, 92

War Damage Acts 1941 and 1943, 35
war deaths, 18, 31
War Risk Mutual Insurance Association, 19
war risks, 19, 35
Warsaw Convention, 91
war time staff shortages, 17, 21, 33, 34
Webb, Sydney, 61–2
Western Provident, 53
Willis, 177, 165, 182
with-profits endowments, 63, 64, 71
workmen's compensation, 9, 20, 24, 37
Workmen's Compensation Act, 1897, 9
Workmen's Compensation Act, 1906, 9
Workmen's Compensation Act, 1923, 24, 93
Workmen's Compensation (Coal Mines) Act, 1934, 24
World Trade Center, 101, 113, 114
World Trade Organisation, 81, 140
World War I, 15, 18
World War II, 31

Xchanging Insurance Services, 107, 131

Yorkshire Insurance, 83, 160

Zurich Financial Services, 142, 161
Zurich Insurance Co., 43, 185
Zurich Life, 68